NON SANZ DROICT.

THE
HISTORY OF
HENRIE THE
FOVRTH;

With the battell at Shrewsburie,
betweene the King and Lord
Henry Percy, surnamed
Henrie Hotspur of
the North.

With the humorous conceits of Sir
Iohn Falstalffe.

AT LONDON,
Printed by *P. S.* for *Andrew Wise*, dwelling
in Paules Churchyard, at the signe of
the Angell. 1598.

Title page of the earliest extant version of *Henry IV, Part One* (1598)

William Shakespeare

The History of Henry IV [Part One]

With New and Updated Critical Essays and a Revised Bibliography

Edited by Maynard Mack

THE SIGNET CLASSIC SHAKESPEARE
General Editor: Sylvan Barnet

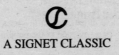

A SIGNET CLASSIC

SIGNET CLASSIC
Published by New American Library, a division of
Penguin Group (USA) Inc., 375 Hudson Street,
New York, New York 10014, U.S.A.
Penguin Books Ltd, 80 Strand,
London WC2R 0RL, England
Penguin Books Australia Ltd, 250 Camberwell Road,
Camberwell, Victoria 3124, Australia
Penguin Books Canada Ltd, 10 Alcorn Avenue,
Toronto, Ontario, Canada M4V 3B2
Penguin Books (N.Z.) Ltd, Cnr Rosedale and Airborne Roads,
Albany, Auckland 1310, New Zealand

Penguin Books Ltd, Registered Offices:
80 Strand, London WC2R 0RL, England

Published by Signet Classic, an imprint of New American Library,
a division of Penguin Group (USA) Inc. The Signet Classic edition of *The
History of Henry IV (Part One)* was first published in 1965, and an updated
edition was published in 1986.

First Signet Classic Printing (Second Revised Edition), September 1998
10 9

Library of Congress Catalog Card Number: 97-62434

Printed in the United States of America

Contents

Shakespeare: An Overview

Biographical Sketch

Between the record of his baptism in Stratford on 26 April 1564 and the record of his burial in Stratford on 25 April 1616, some forty official documents name Shakespeare, and many others name his parents, his children, and his grandchildren. Further, there are at least fifty literary references to him in the works of his contemporaries. More facts are known about William Shakespeare than about any other playwright of the period except Ben Jonson. The facts should, however, be distinguished from the legends. The latter, inevitably more engaging and better known, tell us that the Stratford boy killed a calf in high style, poached deer and rabbits, and was forced to flee to London, where he held horses outside a playhouse. These traditions are only traditions; they may be true, but no evidence supports them, and it is well to stick to the facts.

Mary Arden, the dramatist's mother, was the daughter of a substantial landowner; about 1557 she married John Shakespeare, a tanner, glove-maker, and trader in wool, grain, and other farm commodities. In 1557 John Shakespeare was a member of the council (the governing body of Stratford), in 1558 a constable of the borough, in 1561 one of the two town chamberlains, in 1565 an alderman (entitling him to the appellation of "Mr."), in 1568 high bailiff—the town's highest political office, equivalent to mayor. After 1577, for an unknown reason he drops out of local politics. What *is* known is that he had to mortgage his wife's property, and that he was involved in serious litigation.

The birthday of William Shakespeare, the third child and the eldest son of this locally prominent man, is unrecorded, but the Stratford parish register records that the infant was baptized on 26 April 1564. (It is quite possible that he was born on 23 April, but this date has probably been assigned by tradition because it is the date on which, fifty-two years later, he died, and perhaps because it is the feast day of St. George, patron saint of England.) The attendance records of the Stratford grammar school of the period are not extant, but it is reasonable to assume that the son of a prominent local official attended the free school—it had been established for the purpose of educating males precisely of his class—and received substantial training in Latin. The masters of the school from Shakespeare's seventh to fifteenth years held Oxford degrees; the Elizabethan curriculum excluded mathematics and the natural sciences but taught a good deal of Latin rhetoric, logic, and literature, including plays by Plautus, Terence, and Seneca.

On 27 November 1582 a marriage license was issued for the marriage of Shakespeare and Anne Hathaway, eight years his senior. The couple had a daughter, Susanna, in May 1583. Perhaps the marriage was necessary, but perhaps the couple had earlier engaged, in the presence of witnesses, in a formal "troth plight" which would render their children legitimate even if no further ceremony were performed. In February 1585, Anne Hathaway bore Shakespeare twins, Hamnet and Judith.

That Shakespeare was born is excellent; that he married and had children is pleasant; but that we know nothing about his departure from Stratford to London or about the beginning of his theatrical career is lamentable and must be admitted. We would gladly sacrifice details about his children's baptism for details about his earliest days in the theater. Perhaps the poaching episode is true (but it is first reported almost a century after Shakespeare's death), or perhaps he left Stratford to be a schoolmaster, as another tradition holds; perhaps he was moved (like Petruchio in *The Taming of the Shrew*) by

> Such wind as scatters young men through the world,
> To seek their fortunes farther than at home
> Where small experience grows.   (1.2.49–51)

In 1592, thanks to the cantankerousness of Robert Greene, we have our first reference, a snarling one, to Shakespeare as an actor and playwright. Greene, a graduate of St. John's College, Cambridge, had become a playwright and a pamphleteer in London, and in one of his pamphlets he warns three university-educated playwrights against an actor who has presumed to turn playwright:

> There is an upstart crow, beautified with our feathers, that with his *tiger's heart wrapped in a player's hide* supposes he is as well able to bombast out a blank verse as the best of you, and being an absolute Johannes-factotum [i.e., jack-of-all-trades] is in his own conceit the only Shake-scene in a country.

The reference to the player, as well as the allusion to Aesop's crow (who strutted in borrowed plumage, as an actor struts in fine words not his own), makes it clear that by this date Shakespeare had both acted and written. That Shakespeare is meant is indicated not only by *Shake-scene* but also by the parody of a line from one of Shakespeare's plays, *3 Henry VI*: "O, tiger's heart wrapped in a woman's hide" (1.4.137). If in 1592 Shakespeare was prominent enough to be attacked by an envious dramatist, he probably had served an apprenticeship in the theater for at least a few years.

In any case, although there are no extant references to Shakespeare between the record of the baptism of his twins in 1585 and Greene's hostile comment about "Shake-scene" in 1592, it is evident that during some of these "dark years" or "lost years" Shakespeare had acted and written. There are a number of subsequent references to him as an actor. Documents indicate that in 1598 he is a "principal comedian," in 1603 a "principal tragedian," in 1608 he is one of the "men players." (We do not have, however, any solid information about which roles he may have played; later traditions say he played Adam in *As You Like It* and the ghost in *Hamlet*, but nothing supports the assertions. Probably his role as dramatist came to supersede his role as actor.) The profession of actor was not for a gentleman, and it occasionally drew the scorn of university men like Greene who resented writing speeches for persons less educated than themselves, but it was respectable enough; players, if prosperous, were in effect members of the bourgeoisie, and there is nothing to suggest that Stratford considered William Shakespeare less than a solid citizen. When, in 1596, the Shakespeares were granted a coat of arms—i.e., the right to be considered gentlemen—the grant was made to Shakespeare's father, but probably William Shakespeare had arranged the matter on his own behalf. In subsequent transactions he is occasionally styled a gentleman.

Although in 1593 and 1594 Shakespeare published two narrative poems dedicated to the Earl of Southampton, *Venus and Adonis* and *The Rape of Lucrece*, and may well have written most or all of his sonnets in the middle nineties, Shakespeare's literary activity seems to have been almost entirely devoted to the theater. (It may be significant that the two narrative poems were written in years when the plague closed the theaters for several months.) In 1594 he was a charter member of a theatrical company called the Chamberlain's Men, which in 1603 became the royal company, the King's Men, making Shakespeare the king's playwright. Until he retired to Stratford (about 1611, apparently), he was with this remarkably stable company. From 1599 the company acted primarily at the Globe theater, in which Shakespeare held a one-tenth interest. Other Elizabethan dramatists are known to have acted, but no other is known also to have been entitled to a share of the profits.

Shakespeare's first eight published plays did not have his name on them, but this is not remarkable; the most popular play of the period, Thomas Kyd's *The Spanish Tragedy*, went through many editions without naming Kyd, and Kyd's authorship is known only because a book on the profession of acting happens to quote (and attribute to Kyd) some lines on the interest of Roman emperors in the drama. What is remarkable is that after 1598 Shakespeare's name commonly appears on printed plays—some of which are not his. Presumably his name was a drawing card, and publishers used it to attract potential buyers. Another indication of his popularity comes from Francis Meres, author of *Palladis Tamia: Wit's Treasury* (1598). In this anthology of snippets accompanied by an essay on literature, many playwrights are mentioned, but Shakespeare's name occurs more often than any other, and Shakespeare is the only play-wright whose plays are listed.

From his acting, his play writing, and his share in a playhouse, Shakespeare seems to have made considerable money. He put it to work, making substantial investments in Stratford real estate. As early as 1597 he bought New Place, the second-largest house in Stratford. His family moved in soon afterward, and the house remained in the family until a granddaughter died in 1670. When Shakespeare made his will in 1616, less than a month before he died, he sought to leave his property intact to his descendants. Of small bequests to relatives and to friends (including three actors, Richard Burbage, John Heminges, and Henry Condell), that to his wife of the second-best bed has provoked the most comment. It has sometimes been taken as a sign of an unhappy marriage (other supposed signs are the apparently hasty marriage, his wife's seniority of eight years, and his residence in London without his family). Perhaps the second-best bed was the bed the couple had slept in, the best bed being reserved for visitors. In any case, had Shakespeare not excepted it, the bed would have gone (with the rest of his household possessions) to his daughter and her husband.

On 25 April 1616 Shakespeare was buried within the chancel of the church at Stratford. An unattractive monument to his memory, placed on a wall near the grave, says that he died on 23 April. Over the grave itself are the lines, perhaps by Shakespeare, that (more than his literary fame) have kept his bones undisturbed in the crowded burial ground where old bones were often dislodged to make way for new:

> Good friend, for Jesus' sake forbear
> To dig the dust enclosed here.
> Blessed be the man that spares these stones
> And cursed be he that moves my bones.

A Note on the Anti-Stratfordians, Especially Baconians and Oxfordians

Not until 1769—more than a hundred and fifty years after Shakespeare's death—is there any record of anyone expressing doubt about Shakespeare's authorship of the plays and poems. In 1769, however, Herbert Lawrence nominated Francis Bacon (1561–1626) in *The Life and Adventures of Common Sense*. Since then, at least two dozen other nominees have been offered, including Christopher Marlowe, Sir Walter Raleigh, Queen Elizabeth I, and Edward de Vere, 17th earl of Oxford. The impulse behind all anti-Stratfordian movements is the scarcely concealed snobbish opinion that "the man from Stratford" simply could not have written the plays because he was a country fellow without a university education and without access to high society. Anyone, the argument goes, who used so many legal terms, medical terms, nautical terms, and so forth, and who showed some familiarity with classical writing, must have attended a university, and anyone who knew so much about courtly elegance and courtly deceit must himself have moved among courtiers. The plays do indeed reveal an author whose interests were exceptionally broad, but specialists in any given field—law, medicine, arms and armor, and so on—soon find that the plays do not reveal deep knowledge in specialized matters; indeed, the playwright often gets technical details wrong.

The claim on behalf of Bacon, forgotten almost as soon as it was put forth in 1769, was independently reasserted by Joseph C. Hart in 1848. In 1856 it was reaffirmed by W. H. Smith in a book, and also by Delia Bacon in an article; in 1857 Delia Bacon published a book, arguing that Francis Bacon had directed a group of intellectuals who wrote the plays.

Francis Bacon's claim has largely faded, perhaps because it was advanced with such evident craziness by Ignatius Donnelly, who in *The Great Cryptogram* (1888) claimed to break a code in the plays that proved Bacon had written not only the plays attributed to Shakespeare but also other Renaissance works, for instance the plays of Christopher Marlowe and the essays of Montaigne.

Consider the last two lines of the Epilogue in *The Tempest*:

> As you from crimes would pardoned be,
> Let your indulgence set me free.

What was Shakespeare—sorry, Francis Bacon, Baron Verulam—*really* saying in these two lines? According to Baconians, the lines are an anagram reading, "Tempest of Francis Bacon, Lord Verulam; do ye ne'er divulge me, ye words." Ingenious, and it is a pity that in the quotation the letter *a* appears only twice in the cryptogram, whereas in the deciphered message it appears three times. Oh, no problem; just alter "Verulam" to "Verul'm" and it works out very nicely.

Most people understand that with sufficient ingenuity one can torture any text and find in it what one wishes. For instance: Did Shakespeare have a hand in the King James Version of the Bible? It was nearing completion in 1610, when Shakespeare was forty-six years old. If you look at the 46th Psalm and count forward for forty-six words, you will find the word *shake*. Now if you go to the end of the psalm and count backward forty-six words, you will find the word *spear*. Clear evidence, according to some, that Shakespeare slyly left his mark in the book.

Bacon's candidacy has largely been replaced in the twentieth century by the candidacy of Edward de Vere (1550–1604), 17th earl of Oxford. The basic ideas behind the Oxford theory, advanced at greatest length by Dorothy and Charlton Ogburn in *This Star of England* (1952, rev. 1955), a book of 1297 pages, and by Charlton Ogburn in *The Mysterious William Shakespeare* (1984), a book of 892 pages, are these: (1) The man from Stratford could not possibly have had the mental equipment and the experience to have written the plays—only a courtier could have written them; (2) Oxford had the requisite background (social position, education, years at Queen Elizabeth's court); (3) Oxford did not wish his authorship to be known for two basic reasons: writing for the public theater was a vulgar pursuit, and the plays show so much courtly and royal disreputable behavior that they would have compromised Oxford's position at court. Oxfordians offer countless details to support the claim. For example, Hamlet's phrase "that ever I was born to set it right" (1.5.89) barely conceals "E. Ver, I was born to set it right," an unambiguous announcement of de Vere's authorship, according to *This Star of England* (p. 654). A second example: Consider Ben

Jonson's poem entitled "To the Memory of My Beloved Master William Shakespeare," prefixed to the first collected edition of Shakespeare's plays in 1623. According to Oxfordians, when Jonson in this poem speaks of the author of the plays as the "swan of Avon," he is alluding not to William Shakespeare, who was born and died in Stratford-on-Avon and who throughout his adult life owned property there; rather, he is alluding to Oxford, who, the Ogburns say, used "William Shakespeare" as his pen name, and whose manor at Bilton was on the Avon River. Oxfordians do not offer any evidence that Oxford took a pen name, and they do not mention that Oxford had sold the manor in 1581, forty-two years before Jonson wrote his poem. Surely a reference to the Shakespeare who was born in Stratford, who had returned to Stratford, and who had died there only seven years before Jonson wrote the poem is more plausible. And exactly why Jonson, who elsewhere also spoke of Shakespeare as a playwright, and why Heminges and Condell, who had acted with Shakespeare for about twenty years, should speak of Shakespeare as the author in their dedication in the 1623 volume of collected plays is never adequately explained by Oxfordians. Either Jonson, Heminges and Condell, and numerous others were in on the conspiracy, or they were all duped—equally unlikely alternatives. Another difficulty in the Oxford theory is that Oxford died in 1604, and some of the plays are clearly indebted to works and events later than 1604. Among the Oxfordian responses are: At his death Oxford left some plays, and in later years these were touched up by hacks, who added the material that points to later dates. *The Tempest*, almost universally regarded as one of Shakespeare's greatest plays and pretty clearly dated to 1611, does indeed date from a period after the death of Oxford, but it is a crude piece of work that should not be included in the canon of works by Oxford.

The anti-Stratfordians, in addition to assuming that the author must have been a man of rank and a university man, usually assume two conspiracies: (1) a conspiracy in Elizabethan and Jacobean times, in which a surprisingly large number of persons connected with the theater knew that the actor Shakespeare did not write the plays attributed to him but for some reason or other pretended that he did; (2) a conspiracy of today's Stratfordia s, the professors who teach Shakespeare in the colleges anc universities, who are said to have a vested interest in pres rving Shakespeare as the author of the plays they teach. In ̃act, (1) it is inconceivable that the secret of Shakespeare's ɪ ɔn-authorship could have been preserved by all of the peoplᵣ who supposedly were in on the conspiracy, and (2) academic fame awaits any scholar today who can disprove Shakespeare's authorship.

The Stratfordian case is convincing not only because hundreds or even thousands of anti-Stratford arguments—of the sort that say "ever I was born" has the secret double meaning "E. Ver, I was born"—add up to nothing at all but also because irrefutable evidence connects the man from Stratford with the London theater and with the authorship of particular plays. The anti-Stratfordians do not seem to understand that it is not enough to dismiss the Stratford case by saying that a fellow from the provinces simply couldn't have written the plays. Nor do they understand that it is not enough to dismiss all of the evidence connecting Shakespeare with the plays by asserting that it is perjured.

The Shakespeare Canon

We return to William Shakespeare. Thirty-seven plays as well as some nondramatic poems are generally held to constitute the Shakespeare canon, the body of authentic works. The exact dates of composition of most of the works are highly uncertain, but evidence of a starting point and/or of a final limiting point often provides a framework for informed guessing. For example, *Richard II* cannot be earlier than 1595, the publication date of some material to which it is indebted; *The Merchant of Venice* cannot be later than 1598, the year Francis Meres mentioned it. Sometimes arguments for a date hang on an alleged topical allusion, such as the lines about the unseasonable weather in *A Midsummer Night's Dream*, 2.1.81–117, but such an allusion, if indeed it is an allusion to an event in the real world, can be variously interpreted, and in any case there is always the possibility that a topical allusion was inserted years later, to bring the play up to date. (The issue of alterations in a text between the time that Shakespeare drafted it and the time that it was printed—alterations due to censorship or playhouse practice or Shakespeare's own second thoughts—will be discussed in "The Play Text as a Collaboration" later in this overview.) Dates are often attributed on the basis of style, and although conjectures about style usually rest on other conjectures (such as Shakespeare's development as a playwright, or the appropriateness of lines to character), sooner or later one must rely on one's literary sense. There is no documentary proof, for example, that *Othello* is not as early as *Romeo and Juliet*, but one feels that *Othello* is a later, more mature work, and because the first record of its performance is 1604, one is glad enough to set its composition at that date and not push it back into Shakespeare's early years. (*Romeo and Juliet* was first published in 1597, but evidence suggests that it was written a little earlier.) The following chronology, then, is indebted not only to facts but also to informed guesswork and sensitivity. The dates, necessarily imprecise for some works, indicate something like a scholarly consensus concerning the time of original composition. Some plays show evidence of later revision.

Plays. The first collected edition of Shakespeare, published in 1623, included thirty-six plays. These are all accepted as Shakespeare's, though for one of them, *Henry VIII*, he is thought to have had a collaborator. A thirty-seventh play, *Pericles*, published in 1609 and attributed to Shakespeare on the title page, is also widely accepted as being partly by Shakespeare even though it is not included in the 1623 volume. Still another play not in the 1623 volume, *The Two Noble Kinsmen*, was first published in 1634, with a title page attributing it to John Fletcher and Shakespeare. Probably most students of the subject now believe that Shakespeare did indeed have a hand in it. Of the remaining plays attributed at one time or another to Shakespeare, only one, *Edward III*, anonymously published in 1596, is now regarded by some scholars as a serious candidate. The prevailing opinion, however, is that this rather simpleminded play is not Shakespeare's; at most he may have revised some passages, chiefly scenes with the Countess of

Salisbury. We include *The Two Noble Kinsmen* but do not include *Edward III* in the following list.

1588–94	*The Comedy of Errors*
1588–94	*Love's Labor's Lost*
1589–91	*2 Henry VI*
1590–91	*3 Henry VI*
1589–92	*1 Henry VI*
1592–93	*Richard III*
1589–94	*Titus Andronicus*
1593–94	*The Taming of the Shrew*
1592–94	*The Two Gentlemen of Verona*
1594–96	*Romeo and Juliet*
1595	*Richard II*
1595–96	*A Midsummer Night's Dream*
1596–97	*King John*
1594–96	*The Merchant of Venice*
1596–97	*1 Henry IV*
1597	*The Merry Wives of Windsor*
1597–98	*2 Henry IV*
1598–99	*Much Ado About Nothing*
1598–99	*Henry V*
1599	*Julius Caesar*
1599–1600	*As You Like It*
1599–1600	*Twelfth Night*
1600–1601	*Hamlet*
1601–1602	*Troilus and Cressida*
1602–1604	*All's Well That Ends Well*
1603–1604	*Othello*
1604	*Measure for Measure*
1605–1606	*King Lear*
1605–1606	*Macbeth*
1606–1607	*Antony and Cleopatra*
1605–1608	*Timon of Athens*
1607–1608	*Coriolanus*
1607–1608	*Pericles*
1609–10	*Cymbeline*
1610–11	*The Winter's Tale*
1611	*The Tempest*

| 1612–13 | *Henry VIII* |
| 1613 | *The Two Noble Kinsmen* |

Poems. In 1989 Donald W. Foster published a book in which he argued that "A Funeral Elegy for Master William Peter," published in 1612, ascribed only to the initials W.S., *may* be by Shakespeare. Foster later published an article in a scholarly journal, *PMLA* 111 (1996), in which he asserted the claim more positively. The evidence begins with the initials, and includes the fact that the publisher and the printer of the elegy had published Shakespeare's *Sonnets* in 1609. But such facts add up to rather little, especially because no one has found any connection between Shakespeare and William Peter (an Oxford graduate about whom little is known, who was murdered at the age of twenty-nine). The argument is based chiefly on statistical examinations of word patterns, which are said to correlate with Shakespeare's known work. Despite such correlations, however, many readers feel that the poem does not sound like Shakespeare. True, Shakespeare has a great range of styles, but one quality that unites his work is that it is imaginative and interesting. Many readers find neither of these qualities in "A Funeral Elegy."

1592–93	*Venus and Adonis*
1593–94	*The Rape of Lucrece*
1593–1600	*Sonnets*
1600–1601	*The Phoenix and the Turtle*

Shakespeare's English

1. Spelling and Pronunciation. From the philologist's point of view, Shakespeare's English is modern English. It requires footnotes, but the inexperienced reader can comprehend substantial passages with very little help, whereas for the same reader Chaucer's Middle English is a foreign language. By the beginning of the fifteenth century the chief grammatical changes in English had taken place, and the final unaccented -*e* of Middle English had been lost (though it survives even today in spelling, as in *name*); during the fifteenth century the dialect of London, the commercial and political center, gradually displaced the provincial dialects, at least in writing; by the end of the century, printing had helped to regularize and stabilize the language, especially spelling. Elizabethan spelling may seem erratic to us (there were dozens of spellings of *Shakespeare*, and a simple word like *been* was also spelled *beene* and *bin*), but it had much in common with our spelling. Elizabethan spelling was conservative in that for the most part it reflected an older pronunciation (Middle English) rather than the sound of the language as it was then spoken, just as our spelling continues to reflect medieval pronunciation—most obviously in the now silent but formerly pronounced letters in a word such as *knight*. Elizabethan pronunciation, though not identical with ours, was much closer to ours than to that of the Middle Ages. Incidentally, though no one can be certain about what Elizabethan English sounded like, specialists tend to believe it was rather like the speech of a modern stage Irishman (*time* apparently was pronounced *toime*, *old* pronounced *awld*, *day* pronounced *die*, and *join* pronounced *jine*) and not at all like the Oxford speech that most of us think it was.

An awareness of the difference between our pronunciation and Shakespeare's is crucial in three areas—in accent, or number of syllables (many metrically regular lines may look irregular to us); in rhymes (which may not look like rhymes); and in puns (which may not look like puns). Examples will be useful. Some words that were at least on occasion stressed differently from today are *aspèct*, *còmplete*, *fòrlorn*, *revènue*, and *sepùlcher*. Words that sometimes had an additional syllable are *emp[e]ress*, *Hen[e]ry*, *mon[e]th*, and *villain* (three syllables, *vil-lay-in*). An additional syllable is often found in possessives, like *moon*'s (pronounced *moones*) and in words ending in *-tion* or *-sion*. Words that had one less syllable than they now have are *needle* (pronounced *neel*) and *violet* (pronounced *vilet*). Among rhymes now lost are *one* with *loan*, *love* with *prove*, *beast* with *jest*, *eat* with *great*. (In reading, trust your sense of metrics and your ear, more than your eye.) An example of a pun that has become obliterated by a change in pronunciation is Falstaff's reply to Prince Hal's "Come, tell us your

reason" in *1 Henry IV*: "Give you a reason on compulsion?
If reasons were as plentiful as blackberries, I would give no
man a reason upon compulsion, I" (2.4.237–40). The *ea* in
reason was pronounced rather like a long *a*, like the *ai* in
raisin, hence the comparison with blackberries.

Puns are not merely attempts to be funny; like metaphors
they often involve bringing into a meaningful relationship
areas of experience normally seen as remote. In *2 Henry IV,*
when Feeble is conscripted, he stoically says, "I care not. A
man can die but once. We owe God a death" (3.2.242–43),
punning on *debt,* which was the way *death* was pronounced.
Here an enormously significant fact of life is put into simple
commercial imagery, suggesting its commonplace quality.
Shakespeare used the same pun earlier in *1 Henry IV,* when
Prince Hal says to Falstaff, "Why, thou owest God a death,"
and Falstaff replies, " 'Tis not due yet: I would be loath
to pay him before his day. What need I be so forward with
him that calls not on me?" (5.1.126–29).

Sometimes the puns reveal a delightful playfulness;
sometimes they reveal aggressiveness, as when, replying to
Claudius's "But now, my cousin Hamlet, and my son,"
Hamlet says, "A little more than kin, and less than kind!"
(1.2.64–65). These are Hamlet's first words in the play, and
we already hear him warring verbally against Claudius.
Hamlet's "less than kind" probably means (1) Hamlet is not
of Claudius's family or nature, *kind* having the sense it still
has in our word *mankind*; (2) Hamlet is not kindly (affec-
tionately) disposed toward Claudius; (3) Claudius is not
naturally (but rather unnaturally, in a legal sense incestu-
ously) Hamlet's father. The puns evidently were not put in
as sops to the groundlings; they are an important way of
communicating a complex meaning.

2. Vocabulary. A conspicuous difficulty in reading Shakespeare is rooted in the fact that some of his words are no
longer in common use—for example, words concerned with
armor, astrology, clothing, coinage, hawking, horsemanship, law, medicine, sailing, and war. Shakespeare had a
large vocabulary—something near thirty thousand words—
but it was not so much a vocabulary of big words as a
vocabulary drawn from a wide range of life, and it is partly

his ability to call upon a great body of concrete language that gives his plays the sense of being in close contact with life. When the right word did not already exist, he made it up. Among words thought to be his coinages are *accommodation, all-knowing, amazement, bare-faced, countless, dexterously, dislocate, dwindle, fancy-free, frugal, indistinguishable, lackluster, laughable, overawe, premeditated, sea change, star-crossed*. Among those that have not survived are the verb *convive,* meaning to feast together, and *smilet,* a little smile.

Less overtly troublesome than the technical words but more treacherous are the words that seem readily intelligible to us but whose Elizabethan meanings differ from their modern ones. When Horatio describes the Ghost as an "erring spirit," he is saying not that the ghost has sinned or made an error but that it is wandering. Here is a short list of some of the most common words in Shakespeare's plays that often (but not always) have a meaning other than their most usual modern meaning:

'a	he
abuse	deceive
accident	occurrence
advertise	inform
an, and	if
annoy	harm
appeal	accuse
artificial	skillful
brave	fine, splendid
censure	opinion
cheer	(1) face (2) frame of mind
chorus	a single person who comments on the events
closet	small private room
competitor	partner
conceit	idea, imagination
cousin	kinsman
cunning	skillful
disaster	evil astrological influence
doom	judgment
entertain	receive into service

envy	malice
event	outcome
excrement	outgrowth (of hair)
fact	evil deed
fancy	(1) love (2) imagination
fell	cruel
fellow	(1) companion (2) low person (often an insulting term if addressed to someone of approximately equal rank)
fond	foolish
free	(1) innocent (2) generous
glass	mirror
hap, haply	chance, by chance
head	army
humor	(1) mood (2) bodily fluid thought to control one's psychology
imp	child
intelligence	news
kind	natural, acting according to nature
let	hinder
lewd	base
mere(ly)	utter(ly)
modern	commonplace
natural	a fool, an idiot
naughty	(1) wicked (2) worthless
next	nearest
nice	(1) trivial (2) fussy
noise	music
policy	(1) prudence (2) stratagem
presently	immediately
prevent	anticipate
proper	handsome
prove	test
quick	alive
sad	serious
saw	proverb
secure	without care, incautious
silly	innocent

sensible	capable of being perceived by the senses
shrewd	sharp
so	provided that
starve	die
still	always
success	that which follows
tall	brave
tell	count
tonight	last night
wanton	playful, careless
watch	keep awake
will	lust
wink	close both eyes
wit	mind, intelligence

All glosses, of course, are mere approximations; sometimes one of Shakespeare's words may hover between an older meaning and a modern one, and as we have seen, his words often have multiple meanings.

3. Grammar. A few matters of grammar may be surveyed, though it should be noted at the outset that Shakespeare sometimes made up his own grammar. As E.A. Abbott says in *A Shakespearian Grammar,* "Almost any part of speech can be used as any other part of speech": a noun as a verb ("he childed as I fathered"); a verb as a noun ("She hath made compare"); or an adverb as an adjective ("a seldom pleasure"). There are hundreds, perhaps thousands, of such instances in the plays, many of which at first glance would not seem at all irregular and would trouble only a pedant. Here are a few broad matters.

Nouns: The Elizabethans thought the *-s* genitive ending for nouns (as in *man's*) derived from *his*; thus the line " 'gainst the count his galleys I did some service," for "the count's galleys."

Adjectives: By Shakespeare's time adjectives had lost the endings that once indicated gender, number, and case. About the only difference between Shakespeare's adjectives and ours is the use of the now redundant *more* or *most* with the comparative ("some more fitter place") or superlative

("This was the most unkindest cut of all"). Like double comparatives and double superlatives, double negatives were acceptable; Mercutio "will not budge for no man's pleasure."

Pronouns: The greatest change was in pronouns. In Middle English *thou, thy,* and *thee* were used among familiars and in speaking to children and inferiors; *ye, your,* and *you* were used in speaking to superiors (servants to masters, nobles to the king) or to equals with whom the speaker was not familiar. Increasingly the "polite" forms were used in all direct address, regardless of rank, and the accusative *you* displaced the nominative *ye.* Shakespeare sometimes uses *ye* instead of *you,* but even in Shakespeare's day *ye* was archaic, and it occurs mostly in rhetorical appeals.

Thou, thy, and *thee* were not completely displaced, however, and Shakespeare occasionally makes significant use of them, sometimes to connote familiarity or intimacy and sometimes to connote contempt. In *Twelfth Night* Sir Toby advises Sir Andrew to insult Cesario by addressing him as *thou:* "If thou thou'st him some thrice, it shall not be amiss" (3.2.46–47). In *Othello* when Brabantio is addressing an unidentified voice in the dark he says, "What are you?" (1.1.91), but when the voice identifies itself as the foolish suitor Roderigo, Brabantio uses the contemptuous form, saying, "I have charged thee not to haunt about my doors" (93). He uses this form for a while, but later in the scene, when he comes to regard Roderigo as an ally, he shifts back to the polite *you,* beginning in line 163, "What said she to you?" and on to the end of the scene. For reasons not yet satisfactorily explained, Elizabethans used *thou* in addresses to God—"O God, thy arm was here," the king says in *Henry V* (4.8.108)—and to supernatural characters such as ghosts and witches. A subtle variation occurs in *Hamlet.* When Hamlet first talks with the Ghost in 1.5, he uses *thou,* but when he sees the Ghost in his mother's room, in 3.4, he uses *you,* presumably because he is now convinced that the Ghost is not a counterfeit but is his father.

Perhaps the most unusual use of pronouns, from our point of view, is the neuter singular. In place of our *its, his* was often used, as in "How far that little candle throws *his* beams." But the use of a masculine pronoun for a neuter noun came to seem unnatural, and so *it* was used for the possessive as well as the nominative: "The hedge-sparrow fed the cuckoo so long / That it had it head bit off by it young." In the late sixteenth century the possessive form *its* developed, apparently by analogy with the *-s* ending used to indicate a genitive noun, as in *book*'s, but *its* was not yet common usage in Shakespeare's day. He seems to have used *its* only ten times, mostly in his later plays. Other usages, such as "you have seen Cassio and she together" or the substitution of *who* for *whom,* cause little problem even when noticed.

Verbs, Adverbs, and Prepositions: Verbs cause almost no difficulty: The third person singular present form commonly ends in *-s,* as in modern English (e.g., "He blesses"), but sometimes in *-eth* (Portia explains to Shylock that mercy "blesseth him that gives and him that takes"). Broadly speaking, the *-eth* ending was old-fashioned or dignified or "literary" rather than colloquial, except for the words *doth, hath,* and *saith.* The *-eth* ending (regularly used in the King James Bible, 1611) is very rare in Shakespeare's dramatic prose, though not surprisingly it occurs twice in the rather formal prose summary of the narrative poem *Lucrece.* Sometimes a plural subject, especially if it has collective force, takes a verb ending in *-s,* as in "My old bones aches." Some of our strong or irregular preterites (such as *broke*) have a different form in Shakespeare (*brake*); some verbs that now have a weak or regular preterite (such as *helped*) in Shakespeare have a strong or irregular preterite (*holp*). Some adverbs that today end in *-ly* were not inflected: "grievous sick," "wondrous strange." Finally, prepositions often are not the ones we expect: "We are such stuff as dreams are made on," "I have a king here to my flatterer."

Again, none of the differences (except meanings that have substantially changed or been lost) will cause much difficulty. But it must be confessed that for some elliptical passages there is no widespread agreement on meaning. Wise editors resist saying more than they know, and when they are uncertain they add a question mark to their gloss.

Shakespeare's Theater

In Shakespeare's infancy, Elizabethan actors performed wherever they could—in great halls, at court, in the courtyards of inns. These venues implied not only different audiences but also different playing conditions. The innyards must have made rather unsatisfactory theaters: on some days they were unavailable because carters bringing goods to London used them as depots; when available, they had to be rented from the innkeeper. In 1567, presumably to avoid such difficulties, and also to avoid regulation by the Common Council of London, which was not well disposed toward theatricals, one John Brayne, brother-in-law of the carpenter turned actor James Burbage, built the Red Lion in an eastern suburb of London. We know nothing about its shape or its capacity; we can say only that it may have been the first building in Europe constructed for the purpose of giving plays since the end of antiquity, a thousand years earlier. Even after the building of the Red Lion theatrical activity continued in London in makeshift circumstances, in marketplaces and inns, and always uneasily. In 1574 the Common Council required that plays and playing places in London be licensed because

> sundry great disorders and inconveniences have been found to ensue to this city by the inordinate haunting of great multitudes of people, specially youth, to plays, interludes, and shows, namely occasion of frays and quarrels, evil practices of incontinency in great inns having chambers and secret places adjoining to their open stages and galleries.

The Common Council ordered that innkeepers who wished licenses to hold performance put up a bond and make contributions to the poor.

The requirement that plays and innyard theaters be licensed, along with the other drawbacks of playing at inns and presumably along with the success of the Red Lion, led James Burbage to rent a plot of land northeast of the city walls, on property outside the jurisdiction of the city. Here he built England's second playhouse, called simply the Theatre. About all that is known of its construction is that it was wood. It soon had imitators, the most famous being the Globe (1599), essentially an amphitheater built across the Thames (again outside the city's jurisdiction), constructed with timbers of the Theatre, which had been dismantled when Burbage's lease ran out.

Admission to the theater was one penny, which allowed spectators to stand at the sides and front of the stage that jutted into the yard. An additional penny bought a seat in a covered part of the theater, and a third penny bought a more comfortable seat and a better location. It is notoriously difficult to translate prices into today's money, since some things that are inexpensive today would have been expensive in the past and vice versa—a pipeful of tobacco (imported, of course) cost a lot of money, about three pennies, and an orange (also imported) cost two or three times what a chicken cost—but perhaps we can get some idea of the low cost of the penny admission when we realize that a penny could also buy a pot of ale. An unskilled laborer made about five or sixpence a day, an artisan about twelve pence a day, and the hired actors (as opposed to the sharers in the company, such as Shakespeare) made about ten pence a performance. A printed play cost five or sixpence. Of course a visit to the theater (like a visit to a baseball game today) usually cost more than the admission since the spectator probably would also buy food and drink. Still, the low entrance fee meant that the theater was available to all except the very poorest people, rather as movies and most athletic events are today. Evidence indicates that the audience ranged from apprentices who somehow managed to scrape together the minimum entrance fee and to escape from their masters for a few hours, to prosperous members of the middle class and aristocrats who paid the additional fee for admission to the galleries. The exact proportion of men to women cannot be determined, but women of all classes certainly were present. Theaters were open every afternoon but Sundays for much of the year, except in times of plague, when they were closed because of fear of infection. By the way, no evidence suggests the presence of toilet facilities. Presumably the patrons relieved themselves by making a quick trip to the fields surrounding the playhouses.

There are four important sources of information about the

structure of Elizabethan public playhouses—drawings, a contract, recent excavations, and stage directions in the plays. Of drawings, only the so-called de Witt drawing (c. 1596) of the Swan—really his friend Aernout van Buchell's copy of Johannes de Witt's drawing—is of much significance. The drawing, the only extant representation of the interior of an Elizabethan theater, shows an amphitheater of three tiers, with a stage jutting from a wall into the yard or

Johannes de Witt, a Continental visitor to London, made a drawing of the Swan theater in about the year 1596. The original drawing is lost; this is Aernout van Buchell's copy of it.

center of the building. The tiers are roofed, and part of the stage is covered by a roof that projects from the rear and is supported at its front on two posts, but the groundlings, who paid a penny to stand in front of the stage or at its sides, were exposed to the sky. (Performances in such a playhouse were held only in the daytime; artificial illumination was not used.) At the rear of the stage are two massive doors; above the stage is a gallery.

The second major source of information, the contract for the Fortune (built in 1600), specifies that although the Globe (built in 1599) is to be the model, the Fortune is to be square, eighty feet outside and fifty-five inside. The stage is to be forty-three feet broad, and is to extend into the middle of the yard, i.e., it is twenty-seven and a half feet deep.

The third source of information, the 1989 excavations of the Rose (built in 1587), indicate that the Rose was fourteen-sided, about seventy-two feet in diameter with an inner yard almost fifty feet in diameter. The stage at the Rose was about sixteen feet deep, thirty-seven feet wide at the rear, and twenty-seven feet wide downstage. The relatively small dimensions and the tapering stage, in contrast to the rectangular stage in the Swan drawing, surprised theater historians and have made them more cautious in generalizing about the Elizabethan theater. Excavations at the Globe have not yielded much information, though some historians believe that the fragmentary evidence suggests a larger theater, perhaps one hundred feet in diameter.

From the fourth chief source, stage directions in the plays, one learns that entrance to the stage was by the doors at the rear (*"Enter one citizen at one door, and another at the other"*). A curtain hanging across the doorway—or a curtain hanging between the two doorways—could provide a place where a character could conceal himself, as Polonius does, when he wishes to overhear the conversation between Hamlet and Gertrude. Similarly, withdrawing a curtain from the doorway could "discover" (reveal) a character or two. Such discovery scenes are very rare in Elizabethan drama, but a good example occurs in *The Tempest* (5.1.171), where a stage direction tells us, *"Here Prospero discovers Ferdinand and Miranda playing at chess."* There was also some sort of playing space "aloft" or "above" to represent, for instance, the top of a city's walls or a room above the street. Doubtless each theater had its own peculiarities, but perhaps we can talk about a "typical" Elizabethan theater if we realize that no theater need exactly fit the description, just as no mother is the average mother with 2.7 children.

This hypothetical theater is wooden, round, or polygonal (in *Henry V* Shakespeare calls it a "wooden *O*") capable of holding some eight hundred spectators who stood in the yard around the projecting elevated stage—these spectators were the "groundlings"—and some fifteen hundred additional spectators who sat in the three roofed galleries. The stage, protected by a "shadow" or "heavens" or roof, is entered from two doors; behind the doors is the "tiring house" (attiring house, i.e., dressing room), and above the stage is some sort of gallery that may sometimes hold spectators but can be used (for example) as the bedroom from which Romeo—according to a stage direction in one text—"goeth down." Some evidence suggests that a throne can be lowered onto the platform stage, perhaps from the "shadow"; certainly characters can descend from the stage through a trap or traps into the cellar or "hell." Sometimes this space beneath the stage accommodates a sound-effects man or musician (in *Antony and Cleopatra* "*music of the hautboys* [oboes] *is under the stage*") or an actor (in *Hamlet* the "*Ghost cries under the stage*"). Most characters simply walk on and off through the doors, but because there is no curtain in front of the platform, corpses will have to be carried off (Hamlet obligingly clears the stage of Polonius's corpse, when he says, "I'll lug the guts into the neighbor room"). Other characters may have fallen at the rear, where a curtain on a doorway could be drawn to conceal them.

Such may have been the "public theater," so called because its inexpensive admission made it available to a wide range of the populace. Another kind of theater has been called the "private theater" because its much greater admission charge (sixpence versus the penny for general admission at the public theater) limited its audience to the wealthy or the prodigal. The private theater was basically a large room, entirely roofed and therefore artificially illuminated, with a stage at one end. The theaters thus were distinct in two ways: One was essentially an amphitheater that catered to the general public; the other was a hall that catered to the wealthy. In 1576 a hall theater was established in Blackfriars, a Dominican priory in London that had been suppressed in 1538 and confiscated by the Crown and thus was not under the city's jurisdiction. All the actors in this Blackfriars theater were boys about eight to thirteen years old (in the public theaters similar boys played female parts; a boy Lady Macbeth played to a man Macbeth). Near the end of this section on Shakespeare's theater we will talk at some length about possible implications in this convention of using boys to play female roles, but for the moment we should say that it doubtless accounts for the relative lack of female roles in Elizabethan drama. Thus, in *A Midsummer Night's Dream*, out of twenty-one named roles, only four are female; in *Hamlet*, out of twenty-four, only two (Gertrude and Ophelia) are female. Many of Shakespeare's characters have fathers but no mothers—for instance, King Lear's daughters. We need not bring in Freud to explain the disparity; a dramatic company had only a few boys in it.

To return to the private theaters, in some of which all of the performers were children—the "eyrie of . . . little eyases" (nest of unfledged hawks—2.2.347–48) which Rosencrantz mentions when he and Guildenstern talk with Hamlet. The theater in Blackfriars had a precarious existence, and ceased operations in 1584. In 1596 James Burbage, who had already made theatrical history by building the Theatre, began to construct a second Blackfriars theater. He died in 1597, and for several years this second Blackfriars theater was used by a troupe of boys, but in 1608 two of Burbage's sons and five other actors (including Shakespeare) became joint operators of the theater, using it in the winter when the open-air Globe was unsuitable. Perhaps such a smaller theater, roofed, artificially illuminated, and with a tradition of a wealthy audience, exerted an influence in Shakespeare's late plays.

Performances in the private theaters may well have had intermissions during which music was played, but in the public theaters the action was probably uninterrupted, flowing from scene to scene almost without a break. Actors would enter, speak, exit, and others would immediately enter and establish (if necessary) the new locale by a few properties and by words and gestures. To indicate that the scene took place at night, a player or two would carry a torch. Here are some samples of Shakespeare establishing the scene:

This is Illyria, lady.   (*Twelfth Night,* 1.2.2)

Well, this is the Forest of Arden.   (*As You Like It,* 2.4.14)

This castle has a pleasant seat; the air
Nimbly and sweetly recommends itself
Unto our gentle senses.   (*Macbeth,* 1.6.1–3)

The west yet glimmers with some streaks of day.
                                        (*Macbeth,* 3.3.5)

Sometimes a speech will go far beyond evoking the minimal setting of place and time, and will, so to speak, evoke the social world in which the characters move. For instance, early in the first scene of *The Merchant of Venice* Salerio suggests an explanation for Antonio's melancholy. (In the following passage, *pageants* are decorated wagons, floats, and *cursy* is the verb "to curtsy," or "to bow.")

Your mind is tossing on the ocean,
There where your argosies with portly sail—
Like signiors and rich burghers on the flood,
Or as it were the pageants of the sea—
Do overpeer the petty traffickers
That cursy to them, do them reverence,
As they fly by them with their woven wings.   (1.1.8–14)

Late in the nineteenth century, when Henry Irving produced the play with elaborate illusionistic sets, the first scene showed a ship moored in the harbor, with fruit vendors and dock laborers, in an effort to evoke the bustling and exotic life of Venice. But Shakespeare's words give us this exotic, rich world of commerce in his highly descriptive language when Salerio speaks of "argosies with portly sail" that fly with "woven wings"; equally important, through Salerio Shakespeare conveys a sense of the orderly, hierarchical

society in which the lesser ships, "the petty traffickers,"
curtsy and thereby "do . . . reverence" to their superiors, the
merchant prince's ships, which are "Like signiors and rich
burghers."

On the other hand, it is a mistake to think that except for
verbal pictures the Elizabethan stage was bare. Although
Shakespeare's Chorus in *Henry V* calls the stage an
"unworthy scaffold" (Prologue 1.10) and urges the spectators to "eke out our performance with your mind" (Prologue
3.35), there was considerable spectacle. The last act of *Macbeth,* for instance, has five stage directions calling for *"drum
and colors,"* and another sort of appeal to the eye is indicated by the stage direction *"Enter Macduff, with Macbeth's
head."* Some scenery and properties may have been substantial; doubtless a throne was used, but the pillars supporting the roof would have served for the trees on which
Orlando pins his poems in *As You Like It.*

Having talked about the public theater—"this wooden
O"—at some length, we should mention again that Shakespeare's plays were performed also in other locales. Alvin
Kernan, in *Shakespeare, the King's Playwright: Theater in
the Stuart Court 1603–1613* (1995) points out that "several
of [Shakespeare's] plays contain brief theatrical performances, set always in a court or some noble house. When
Shakespeare portrayed a theater, he did not, except for the
choruses in *Henry V,* imagine a public theater" (p. 195).
(Examples include episodes in *The Taming of the Shrew, A
Midsummer Night's Dream, Hamlet,* and *The Tempest.*)

A Note on the Use of Boy Actors in Female Roles

Until fairly recently, scholars were content to mention
that the convention existed; they sometimes also mentioned
that it continued the medieval practice of using males in
female roles, and that other theaters, notably in ancient
Greece and in China and Japan, also used males in female
roles. (In classical Noh drama in Japan, males still play the
female roles.) Prudery may have been at the root of the academic failure to talk much about the use of boy actors, or
maybe there really is not much more to say than that it was
a convention of a male-centered culture (Stephen Green-

blatt's view, in *Shakespearean Negotiations* [1988]). Further, the very nature of a convention is that it is not thought about: Hamlet is a Dane and Julius Caesar is a Roman, but in Shakespeare's plays they speak English, and we in the audience never give this odd fact a thought. Similarly, a character may speak in the presence of others and we understand, again without thinking about it, that he or she is not heard by the figures on the stage (the aside); a character alone on the stage may speak (the soliloquy), and we do not take the character to be unhinged; in a realistic (box) set, the fourth wall, which allows us to see what is going on, is miraculously missing. The no-nonsense view, then, is that the boy actor was an accepted convention, accepted unthinkingly—just as today we know that Kenneth Branagh is not Hamlet, Al Pacino is not Richard II, and Denzel Washington is not the Prince of Aragon. In this view, the audience takes the performer for the role, and that is that; such is the argument we now make for race-free casting, in which African-Americans and Asians can play roles of persons who lived in medieval Denmark and ancient Rome. But gender perhaps is different, at least today. It is a matter of abundant academic study: The Elizabethan theater is now sometimes called a transvestite theater, and we hear much about cross-dressing.

Shakespeare himself in a very few passages calls attention to the use of boys in female roles. At the end of *As You Like It* the boy who played Rosalind addresses the audience, and says, "O men, . . . if I were a woman, I would kiss as many of you as had beards that pleased me." But this is in the Epilogue; the plot is over, and the actor is stepping out of the play and into the audience's everyday world. A second reference to the practice of boys playing female roles occurs in *Antony and Cleopatra*, when Cleopatra imagines that she and Antony will be the subject of crude plays, her role being performed by a boy:

> The quick comedians
> Extemporally will stage us, and present
> Our Alexandrian revels: Antony
> Shall be brought drunken forth, and I shall see
> Some squeaking Cleopatra boy my greatness.   (5.2.216–20)

In a few other passages, Shakespeare is more indirect. For instance, in *Twelfth Night* Viola, played of course by a boy, disguises herself as a young man and seeks service in the house of a lord. She enlists the help of a Captain, and (by way of explaining away her voice and her beardlessness) says,

> I'll serve this duke
> Thou shalt present me as an eunuch to him.   (1.2.55–56)

In *Hamlet*, when the players arrive in 2.2, Hamlet jokes with the boy who plays a female role. The boy has grown since Hamlet last saw him: "By'r Lady, your ladyship is nearer to heaven than when I saw you last by the altitude of a chopine" (a lady's thick-soled shoe). He goes on: "Pray God your voice . . . be not cracked" (434–38).

Exactly how sexual, how erotic, this material was and is, is now much disputed. Again, the use of boys may have been unnoticed, or rather not thought about—an unexamined convention—by most or all spectators most of the time, perhaps *all* of the time, except when Shakespeare calls the convention to the attention of the audience, as in the passages just quoted. Still, an occasional bit seems to invite erotic thoughts. The clearest example is the name that Rosalind takes in *As You Like It*, Ganymede—the beautiful youth whom Zeus abducted. Did boys dressed to play female roles carry homoerotic appeal for straight men (Lisa Jardine's view, in *Still Harping on Daughters* [1983]), or for gay men, or for some or all women in the audience? Further, when the boy actor played a woman who (for the purposes of the plot) disguised herself as a male, as Rosalind, Viola, and Portia do—so we get a boy playing a woman playing a man—what sort of appeal was generated, and for what sort of spectator?

Some scholars have argued that the convention empowered women by letting female characters display a freedom unavailable in Renaissance patriarchal society; the convention, it is said, undermined rigid gender distinctions. In this view, the convention (along with plots in which female characters for a while disguised themselves as young men) allowed Shakespeare to say what some modern gender critics say: Gender is a constructed role rather than a biological given, something we make, rather than a fixed binary opposition of male and female (see Juliet Dusinberre, in *Shakespeare and the Nature of Women* [1975]). On the other hand, some scholars have maintained that the male disguise assumed by some female characters serves only to reaffirm traditional social distinctions since female characters who don male garb (notably Portia in *The Merchant of Venice* and Rosalind in *As You Like It*) return to their female garb and at least implicitly (these critics say) reaffirm the status quo. (For this last view, see Clara Claiborne Park, in an essay in *The Woman's Part*, ed. Carolyn Ruth Swift Lenz et al. [1980].) Perhaps no one answer is right for all plays; in *As You Like It* cross-dressing empowers Rosalind, but in *Twelfth Night* cross-dressing comically traps Viola.

Shakespeare's Dramatic Language: Costumes, Gestures and Silences; Prose and Poetry

Because Shakespeare was a dramatist, not merely a poet, he worked not only with language but also with costume, sound effects, gestures, and even silences. We have already discussed some kinds of spectacle in the preceding section, and now we will begin with other aspects of visual language; a theater, after all, is literally a "place for seeing." Consider the opening stage direction in *The Tempest*, the first play in the first published collection of Shakespeare's plays: *"A tempestuous noise of thunder and Lightning heard: Enter a Ship-master, and a Boteswain."*

Costumes: What did that shipmaster and that boatswain wear? Doubtless they wore something that identified them as men of the sea. Not much is known about the costumes that Elizabethan actors wore, but at least three points are clear: (1) many of the costumes were splendid versions of contemporary Elizabethan dress; (2) some attempts were made to approximate the dress of certain occupations and of antique or exotic characters such as Romans, Turks, and Jews; (3) some costumes indicated that the wearer was supernatural. Evidence for elaborate Elizabethan clothing can be found in the plays themselves and in contemporary comments about the "sumptuous" players who wore the discarded clothing of noblemen, as well as in account books that itemize such things as "a scarlet cloak with two broad gold laces, with gold buttons down the sides."

The attempts at approximation of the dress of certain occupations and nationalities also can be documented from the plays themselves, and it derives additional confirmation from a drawing of the first scene of Shakespeare's *Titus Andronicus*—the only extant Elizabethan picture of an identifiable episode in a play. (See pp. xxxviii–xxxix.) The drawing, probably done in 1594 or 1595, shows Queen Tamora pleading for mercy. She wears a somewhat medieval-looking robe and a crown; Titus wears a toga and a wreath, but two soldiers behind him wear costumes fairly close to Elizabethan dress. We do not know, however, if the drawing represents an actual stage production in the public theater, or perhaps a private production, or maybe only a reader's visualization of an episode. Further, there is some conflicting evidence: In *Julius Caesar* a reference is made to Caesar's doublet (a close-fitting jacket), which, if taken literally, suggests that even the protagonist did not wear Roman clothing; and certainly the lesser characters, who are said to wear hats, did not wear Roman garb.

It should be mentioned, too, that even ordinary clothing can be symbolic: Hamlet's "inky cloak," for example, sets him apart from the brightly dressed members of Claudius's court and symbolizes his mourning; the fresh clothes that are put on King Lear partly symbolize his return to sanity. Consider, too, the removal of disguises near the end of some plays. For instance, Rosalind in *As You Like It* and Portia and Nerissa in *The Merchant of Venice* remove their male attire, thus again becoming fully themselves.

Gestures and Silences: Gestures are an important part of a dramatist's language. King Lear kneels before his daughter Cordelia for a benediction (4.7.57–59), an act of humility that contrasts with his earlier speeches banishing her and that contrasts also with a comparable gesture, his ironic

kneeling before Regan (2.4.153–55). Northumberland's
failure to kneel before King Richard II (3.3.71–72) speaks
volumes. As for silences, consider a moment in *Coriolanus*:
Before the protagonist yields to his mother's entreaties
(5.3.182), there is this stage direction: *"Holds her by the
hand, silent."* Another example of "speech in dumbness"
occurs in *Macbeth*, when Macduff learns that his wife and
children have been murdered. He is silent at first, as Malcolm's speech indicates: "What, man! Ne'er pull your hat
upon your brows. Give sorrow words" (4.3.208–09). (For
a discussion of such moments, see Philip C. McGuire's
Speechless Dialect: Shakespeare's Open Silences [1985].)

Of course when we think of Shakespeare's work, we think
primarily of his language, both the poetry and the prose.

Prose: Although two of his plays (*Richard II* and *King John*)
have no prose at all, about half the others have at least one
quarter of the dialogue in prose, and some have notably
more: *1 Henry IV* and *2 Henry IV*, about half; *As You Like It*

and *Twelfth Night*, a little more than half; *Much Ado About Nothing*, more than three quarters; and *The Merry Wives of Windsor*, a little more than five sixths. We should remember that despite Molière's joke about M. Jourdain, who was amazed to learn that he spoke prose, most of us do not speak prose. Rather, we normally utter repetitive, shapeless, and often ungrammatical torrents; prose is something very different—a sort of literary imitation of speech at its most coherent.

Today we may think of prose as "natural" for drama; or even if we think that poetry is appropriate for high tragedy we may still think that prose is the right medium for comedy. Greek, Roman, and early English comedies, however, were written in verse. In fact, prose was not generally considered a literary medium in England until the late fifteenth century; Chaucer tells even his bawdy stories in verse. By the end of the 1580s, however, prose had established itself on the English comic stage. In tragedy, Marlowe made some use of prose, not simply in the speeches of clownish servants but even in the speech of a tragic hero, Doctor Faustus. Still, before Shakespeare, prose normally was used in the theater only for special circumstances: (1) letters and proclamations, to set them off from the poetic dialogue; (2) mad characters, to indicate that normal thinking has become disordered; and (3) low comedy, or speeches uttered by clowns even when they are not being comic. Shakespeare made use of these conventions, but he also went far beyond them. Sometimes he begins a scene in prose and then shifts into verse as the emotion is heightened; or conversely, he may shift from verse to prose when a speaker is lowering the emotional level, as when Brutus speaks in the Forum.

Shakespeare's prose usually is not prosaic. Hamlet's prose includes not only small talk with Rosencrantz and Guildenstern but also princely reflections on "What a piece of work is a man" (2.2.312). In conversation with Ophelia, he shifts from light talk in verse to a passionate prose denunciation of women (3.1.103), though the shift to prose here is perhaps also intended to suggest the possibility of madness. (Consult Brian Vickers, *The Artistry of Shakespeare's Prose* [1968].)

Poetry: Drama in rhyme in England goes back to the Middle Ages, but by Shakespeare's day rhyme no longer dominated poetic drama; a finer medium, blank verse (strictly speaking, unrhymed lines of ten syllables, with the stress on every second syllable) had been adopted. But before looking at unrhymed poetry, a few things should be said about the chief uses of rhyme in Shakespeare's plays. (1) A couplet (a pair of rhyming lines) is sometimes used to convey emotional heightening at the end of a blank verse speech; (2) characters sometimes speak a couplet as they leave the stage, suggesting closure; (3) except in the latest plays, scenes fairly often conclude with a couplet, and sometimes, as in *Richard II*, 2.1.145–46, the entrance of a new character within a scene is preceded by a couplet, which wraps up the earlier portion of that scene; (4) speeches of two characters occasionally are linked by rhyme, most notably in *Romeo and Juliet*, 1.5.95–108, where the lovers speak a sonnet between them; elsewhere a taunting reply occasionally rhymes with the previous speaker's last line; (5) speeches with sententious or gnomic remarks are sometimes in rhyme, as in the duke's speech in *Othello* (1.3.199–206); (6) speeches of sardonic mockery are sometimes in rhyme—for example, Iago's speech on women in *Othello* (2.1.146–58)—and they sometimes conclude with an emphatic couplet, as in Bolingbroke's speech on comforting words in *Richard II* (1.3.301–2); (7) some characters are associated with rhyme, such as the fairies in *A Midsummer Night's Dream*; (8) in the early plays, especially *The Comedy of Errors* and *The Taming of the Shrew*, comic scenes that in later plays would be in prose are in jingling rhymes; (9) prologues, choruses, plays-within-the-play, inscriptions, vows, epilogues, and so on are often in rhyme, and the songs in the plays are rhymed.

Neither prose nor rhyme immediately comes to mind when we first think of Shakespeare's medium: It is blank verse, unrhymed iambic pentameter. (In a mechanically exact line there are five iambic feet. An iambic foot consists of two syllables, the second accented, as in *away*; five feet make a pentameter line. Thus, a strict line of iambic pentameter contains ten syllables, the even syllables being stressed more heavily than the odd syllables. Fortunately, Shakespeare usually varies the line somewhat.) The first speech in *A Midsummer Night's Dream*, spoken by Duke Theseus to his betrothed, is an example of blank verse:

> Now, fair Hippolyta, our nuptial hour
> Draws on apace. Four happy days bring in
> Another moon; but, O, methinks, how slow
> This old moon wanes! She lingers my desires,
> Like to a stepdame, or a dowager,
> Long withering out a young man's revenue.   (1.1.1–6)

As this passage shows, Shakespeare's blank verse is not mechanically unvarying. Though the predominant foot is the iamb (as in *apace* or *desires*), there are numerous variations. In the first line the stress can be placed on "fair," as the regular metrical pattern suggests, but it is likely that "Now" gets almost as much emphasis; probably in the second line "Draws" is more heavily emphasized than "on," giving us a trochee (a stressed syllable followed by an unstressed one); and in the fourth line each word in the phrase "This old moon wanes" is probably stressed fairly heavily, conveying by two spondees (two feet, each of two stresses) the oppressive tedium that Theseus feels.

In Shakespeare's early plays much of the blank verse is end-stopped (that is, it has a heavy pause at the end of each line), but he later developed the ability to write iambic pentameter verse paragraphs (rather than lines) that give the illusion of speech. His chief techniques are (1) enjambing, i.e., running the thought beyond the single line, as in the first three lines of the speech just quoted; (2) occasionally replacing an iamb with another foot; (3) varying the position of the chief pause (the caesura) within a line; (4) adding an occasional unstressed syllable at the end of a line, traditionally called a feminine ending; (5) and beginning or ending a speech with a half line.

Shakespeare's mature blank verse has much of the rhythmic flexibility of his prose; both the language, though richly figurative and sometimes dense, and the syntax seem natural. It is also often highly appropriate to a particular character. Consider, for instance, this speech from *Hamlet*, in which Claudius, King of Denmark ("the Dane"), speaks to Laertes:

> And now, Laertes, what's the news with you?
> You told us of some suit. What is't, Laertes?
> You cannot speak of reason to the Dane
> And lose your voice. What wouldst thou beg, Laertes,
> That shall not be my offer, not thy asking?   (1.2.42–46)

Notice the short sentences and the repetition of the name "Laertes," to whom the speech is addressed. Notice, too, the shift from the royal "us" in the second line to the more intimate "my" in the last line, and from "you" in the first three lines to the more intimate "thou" and "thy" in the last two lines. Claudius knows how to ingratiate himself with Laertes.

For a second example of the flexibility of Shakespeare's blank verse, consider a passage from *Macbeth*. Distressed by the doctor's inability to cure Lady Macbeth and by the imminent battle, Macbeth addresses some of his remarks to the doctor and others to the servant who is arming him. The entire speech, with its pauses, interruptions, and irresolution (in "Pull't off, I say," Macbeth orders the servant to remove the armor that the servant has been putting on him), catches Macbeth's disintegration. (In the first line, *physic* means "medicine," and in the fourth and fifth lines, *cast the water* means "analyze the urine.")

> Throw physic to the dogs, I'll none of it.
> Come, put mine armor on. Give me my staff.
> Seyton, send out.—Doctor, the thanes fly from me.—
> Come, sir, dispatch. If thou couldst, doctor, cast
> The water of my land, find her disease
> And purge it to a sound and pristine health,
> I would applaud thee to the very echo,
> That should applaud again.—Pull't off, I say.—
> What rhubarb, senna, or what purgative drug,
> Would scour these English hence? Hear'st thou of them?
>
> (5.3.47–56)

Blank verse, then, can be much more than unrhymed iambic pentameter, and even within a single play Shakespeare's blank verse often consists of several styles, depending on the speaker and on the speaker's emotion at the moment.

The Play Text as a Collaboration

Shakespeare's fellow dramatist Ben Jonson reported that the actors said of Shakespeare, "In his writing, whatsoever he penned, he never blotted out line," i.e., never crossed out material and revised his work while composing. None of Shakespeare's plays survives in manuscript (with the possible exception of a scene in *Sir Thomas More*), so we cannot fully evaluate the comment, but in a few instances the published work clearly shows that he revised his manuscript. Consider the following passage (shown here in facsimile) from the best early text of *Romeo and Juliet*, the Second Quarto (1599):

Ro. Would I were sleepe and peace so sweet to rest
The grey eyde morne smiles on the frowning night,
Checkring the Easterne Clouds with streaks of light,
And darknesse fleckted like a drunkard reeles,
From forth daies pathway, made by *Tytans* wheeles.
Hence will I to my ghostly Friers close cell,
His helpe to craue, and my deare hap to tell.

Exit.

Enter Frier alone with a basket.   (night,
Fri. The grey-eyed morne smiles on the frowning
Checking the Easterne clowdes with streaks of light:
And fleckeld darknesse like a drunkard reeles,
From forth daies path, and *Titans* burning wheeles:
Now ere the sun aduance his burning eie,

Romeo rather elaborately tells us that the sun at dawn is
dispelling the night (morning is smiling, the eastern clouds
are checked with light, and the sun's chariot—Titan's
wheels—advances), and he will seek out his spiritual father,
the Friar. He exits and, oddly, the Friar enters and says pretty
much the same thing about the sun. Both speakers say that
"the gray-eyed morn smiles on the frowning night," but there
are small differences, perhaps having more to do with the
business of printing the book than with the author's
composition: For Romeo's "checkring," "fleckted," and
"pathway," we get the Friar's "checking," "fleckeld," and
"path." (Notice, by the way, the inconsistency in Elizabethan
spelling: Romeo's "clouds" become the Friar's "clowdes.")

Both versions must have been in the printer's copy, and it
seems safe to assume that both were in Shakespeare's manuscript. He must have written one version—let's say he first
wrote Romeo's closing lines for this scene—and then he
decided, no, it's better to give this lyrical passage to the
Friar, as the opening of a new scene, but neglected to delete
the first version. Editors must make a choice, and they may
feel that the reasonable thing to do is to print the text as
Shakespeare intended it. But how can we know what he
intended? Almost all modern editors delete the lines from

Romeo's speech, and retain the Friar's lines. They don't do this because they know Shakespeare's intention, however. They give the lines to the Friar because the first published version (1597) of *Romeo and Juliet* gives only the Friar's version, and this text (though in many ways inferior to the 1599 text) is thought to derive from the memory of some actors, that is, it is thought to represent a performance, not just a script. Maybe during the course of rehearsals Shakespeare—an actor as well as an author—unilaterally decided that the Friar should speak the lines; if so (remember that we don't know this to be a fact) his final intention was to give the speech to the Friar. Maybe, however, the actors talked it over and settled on the Friar, with or without Shakespeare's approval. On the other hand, despite the 1597 version, one might argue (if only weakly) on behalf of giving the lines to Romeo rather than to the Friar, thus: (1) Romeo's comment on the coming of the daylight emphasizes his separation from Juliet, and (2) the figurative language seems more appropriate to Romeo than to the Friar. Having said this, in the Signet edition we have decided in this instance to draw on the evidence provided by earlier text and to give the lines to the Friar, on the grounds that since Q1 reflects a production, in the theater (at least on one occasion) the lines were spoken by the Friar.

A playwright sold a script to a theatrical company. The script thus belonged to the company, not the author, and author and company alike must have regarded this script not as a literary work but as the basis for a play that the actors would create on the stage. We speak of Shakespeare as the author of the plays, but readers should bear in mind that the texts they read, even when derived from a single text, such as the First Folio (1623), are inevitably the collaborative work not simply of Shakespeare with his company—doubtless during rehearsals the actors would suggest alterations—but also with other forces of the age. One force was governmental censorship. In 1606 parliament passed "an Act to restrain abuses of players," prohibiting the utterance of oaths and the name of God. So where the earliest text of *Othello* gives us "By heaven" (3.3.106), the first Folio gives "Alas," presumably reflecting the compliance of stage practice with the law. Similarly, the 1623 version of *King Lear* omits the oath "Fut" (probably from "By God's foot") at 1.2.142, again presumably reflecting the line as it was spoken on the stage. Editors who seek to give the reader the play that Shakespeare initially conceived—the "authentic" play conceived by the solitary Shakespeare— probably will restore the missing oaths and references to God. Other editors, who see the play as a collaborative work, a construction made not only by Shakespeare but also by actors and compositors and even government censors, may claim that what counts is the play as it was actually performed. Such editors regard the censored text as legitimate, since it is the play that was (presumably) finally put on. A performed text, they argue, has more historical reality than a text produced by an editor who has sought to get at what Shakespeare initially wrote. In this view, the text of a play is rather like the script of a film; the script is not the film, and the play text is not the performed play. Even if we want to talk about the play that Shakespeare "intended," we will find ourselves talking about a script that he handed over to a company with the intention that it be implemented by actors. The "intended" play is the one that the actors—we might almost say "society"—would help to construct.

Further, it is now widely held that a play is also the work of readers and spectators, who do not simply receive meaning, but who create it when they respond to the play. This idea is fully in accord with contemporary post-structuralist critical thinking, notably Roland Barthes's "The Death of the Author," in *Image-Music-Text* (1977) and Michel Foucault's "What Is an Author?," in *The Foucault Reader* (1984). The gist of the idea is that an author is not an isolated genius; rather, authors are subject to the politics and other social structures of their age. A dramatist especially is a worker in a collaborative project, working most obviously with actors—parts may be written for particular actors—but working also with the audience. Consider the words of Samuel Johnson, written to be spoken by the actor David Garrick at the opening of a theater in 1747:

> The stage but echoes back the public voice;
> The drama's laws, the drama's patrons give,
> For we that live to please, must please to live.

The audience—the public taste as understood by the playwright—helps to determine what the play is. Moreover, even members of the public who are not part of the playwright's immediate audience may exert an influence through censorship. We have already glanced at governmental censorship, but there are also other kinds. Take one of Shakespeare's most beloved characters, Falstaff, who appears in three of Shakespeare's plays, the two parts of *Henry IV* and *The Merry Wives of Windsor*. He appears with this name in the earliest printed version of the first of these plays, *1 Henry IV*, but we know that Shakespeare originally called him (after an historical figure) Sir John Oldcastle. Oldcastle appears in Shakespeare's source (partly reprinted in the Signet edition of *1 Henry IV*), and a trace of the name survives in Shakespeare's play, 1.2.43–44, where Prince Hal punningly addresses Falstaff as "my old lad of the castle." But for some reason—perhaps because the family of the historical Oldcastle complained—Shakespeare had to change the name. In short, the play as we have it was (at least in this detail) subject to some sort of censorship. If we think that a text should present what we take to be the author's intention, we probably will want to replace *Falstaff* with *Oldcastle*. But if we recognize that a play is a collaboration, we may welcome the change, even if it was forced on Shakespeare. Somehow *Falstaff*, with its hint of *false-staff*, i.e., inadequate prop, seems just right for this fat knight who, to our delight, entertains the young prince with untruths. We can go as far as saying that, at least so far as a play is concerned, an insistence on the author's original intention (even if we could know it) can sometimes impoverish the text.

The tiny example of Falstaff's name illustrates the point that the text we read is inevitably only a version—something in effect produced by the collaboration of the playwright with his actors, audiences, compositors, and editors—of a fluid text that Shakespeare once wrote, just as the *Hamlet* that we see on the screen starring Kenneth Branagh is not the *Hamlet* that Shakespeare saw in an open-air playhouse starring Richard Burbage. *Hamlet* itself, as we shall note in a moment, also exists in several versions. It is not surprising that there is now much talk about the *instability* of Shakespeare's texts.

Because he was not only a playwright but was also an actor and a shareholder in a theatrical company, Shakespeare probably was much involved with the translation of the play from a manuscript to a stage production. He may or may not have done some rewriting during rehearsals, and he may or may not have been happy with cuts that were made. Some plays, notably *Hamlet* and *King Lear*, are so long that it is most unlikely that the texts we read were acted in their entirety. Further, for both of these plays we have more than one early text that demands consideration. In *Hamlet*, the Second Quarto (1604) includes some two hundred lines not found in the Folio (1623). Among the passages missing from the Folio are two of Hamlet's reflective speeches, the "dram of evil" speech (1.4.13–38) and "How all occasions do inform against me" (4.4.32–66). Since the Folio has more numerous and often fuller stage directions, it certainly looks as though in the Folio we get a theatrical version of the play, a text whose cuts were probably made—this is only a hunch, of course—not because Shakespeare was changing his conception of Hamlet but because the playhouse demanded a modified play. (The problem is complicated, since the Folio not only cuts some of the Quarto but adds some material. Various explanations have been offered.)

Or take an example from *King Lear*. In the First and Second Quarto (1608, 1619), the final speech of the play is given to Albany, Lear's surviving son-in-law, but in the First Folio version (1623), the speech is given to Edgar. The Quarto version is in accord with tradition—usually the highest-ranking character in a tragedy speaks the final words. Why does the Folio give the speech to Edgar? One possible answer is this: The Folio version omits some of Albany's speeches in earlier scenes, so perhaps it was decided (by Shakespeare? by the players?) not to give the final lines to so pale a character. In fact, the discrepancies are so many between the two texts, that some scholars argue we do not simply have texts showing different theatrical productions. Rather, these scholars say, Shakespeare substantially revised the play, and we really have two versions of *King Lear* (and of *Othello* also, say some)—two different plays—not simply two texts, each of which is in some ways imperfect.

In this view, the 1608 version of *Lear* may derive from Shakespeare's manuscript, and the 1623 version may derive from his later revision. The Quartos have almost three hundred lines not in the Folio, and the Folio has about a hundred lines not in the Quartos. It used to be held that all the texts were imperfect in various ways and from various causes—some passages in the Quartos were thought to have been set from a manuscript that was not entirely legible, other passages were thought to have been set by a compositor who was new to setting plays, and still other passages were thought to have been provided by an actor who misremembered some of the lines. This traditional view held that an editor must draw on the Quartos and the Folio in order to get Shakespeare's "real" play. The new argument holds (although not without considerable strain) that we have two authentic plays, Shakespeare's early version (in the Quarto) and Shakespeare's—or his theatrical company's—revised version (in the Folio). Not only theatrical demands but also Shakespeare's own artistic sense, it is argued, called for extensive revisions. Even the titles vary: Q1 is called *True Chronicle Historie of the life and death of King Lear and his three Daughters*, whereas the Folio text is called *The Tragedie of King Lear*. To combine the two texts in order to produce what the editor thinks is the play that Shakespeare intended to write is, according to this view, to produce a text that is false to the history of the play. If the new view is correct, and we do have texts of two distinct versions of *Lear* rather than two imperfect versions of one play, it supports in a textual way the poststructuralist view that we cannot possibly have an unmediated vision of (in this case) a play by Shakespeare; we can only recognize a plurality of visions.

Editing Texts

Though eighteen of his plays were published during his lifetime, Shakespeare seems never to have supervised their publication. There is nothing unusual here; when a playwright sold a play to a theatrical company he surrendered his ownership to it. Normally a company would not publish the play, because to publish it meant to allow competitors to acquire the piece. Some plays did get published: Apparently hard-up actors sometimes pieced together a play for a publisher; sometimes a company in need of money sold a play; and sometimes a company allowed publication of a play that no longer drew audiences. That Shakespeare did not concern himself with publication is not remarkable; of his contemporaries, only Ben Jonson carefully supervised the publication of his own plays.

In 1623, seven years after Shakespeare's death, John Heminges and Henry Condell (two senior members of Shakespeare's company, who had worked with him for about twenty years) collected his plays—published and unpublished—into a large volume, of a kind called a folio. (A folio is a volume consisting of large sheets that have been folded once, each sheet thus making two leaves, or four pages. The size of the page of course depends on the size of the sheet—a folio can range in height from twelve to sixteen inches, and in width from eight to eleven; the pages in the 1623 edition of Shakespeare, commonly called the First Folio, are approximately thirteen inches tall and eight inches wide.) The eighteen plays published during Shakespeare's lifetime had been issued one play per volume in small formats called quartos. (Each sheet in a quarto has been folded twice, making four leaves, or eight pages, each page being about nine inches tall and seven inches wide, roughly the size of a large paperback.)

Heminges and Condell suggest in an address "To the great variety of readers" that the republished plays are presented in better form than in the quartos:

Before you were abused with diverse stolen and surreptitious copies, maimed and deformed by the frauds and stealths of injurious impostors that exposed them; even those, are now offered to your view cured and perfect of their limbs, and all the rest absolute in their numbers, as he [i.e., Shakespeare] conceived them.

There is a good deal of truth to this statement, but some of the quarto versions are better than others; some are in fact preferable to the Folio text.

Whoever was assigned to prepare the texts for publication

in the first Folio seems to have taken the job seriously and yet not to have performed it with uniform care. The sources of the texts seem to have been, in general, good unpublished copies or the best published copies. The first play in the collection, *The Tempest*, is divided into acts and scenes, has unusually full stage directions and descriptions of spectacle, and concludes with a list of the characters, but the editor was not able (or willing) to present all of the succeeding texts so fully dressed. Later texts occasionally show signs of carelessness: in one scene of *Much Ado About Nothing* the names of actors, instead of characters, appear as speech prefixes, as they had in the Quarto, which the Folio reprints; proofreading throughout the Folio is spotty and apparently was done without reference to the printer's copy; the pagination of *Hamlet* jumps from 156 to 257. Further, the proofreading was done while the presses continued to print, so that each play in each volume contains a mix of corrected and uncorrected pages.

Modern editors of Shakespeare must first select their copy; no problem if the play exists only in the Folio, but a considerable problem if the relationship between a Quarto and the Folio—or an early Quarto and a later one—is unclear. In the case of *Romeo and Juliet*, the First Quarto (Q1), published in 1597, is vastly inferior to the Second (Q2), published in 1599. The basis of Q1 apparently is a version put together from memory by some actors. Not surprisingly, it garbles many passages and is much shorter than Q2. On the other hand, occasionally Q1 makes better sense than Q2. For instance, near the end of the play, when the parents have assembled and learned of the deaths of Romeo and Juliet, in Q2 the Prince says (5.3.208–9),

> Come, *Montague;* for thou art early vp
> To see thy sonne and heire, now earling downe.

The last three words of this speech surely do not make sense, and many editors turn to Q1, which instead of "now earling downe" has "more early downe." Some modern editors take only "early" from Q1, and print "now early down"; others take "more early," and print "more early down." Further, Q1 (though, again, quite clearly a garbled and abbreviated text) includes some stage directions that are not found in Q2, and today many editors who base their text on Q2 are glad to add these stage directions, because the directions help to give us a sense of what the play looked like on Shakespeare's stage. Thus, in 4.3.58, after Juliet drinks the potion, Q1 gives us this stage direction, not in Q2: *"She falls upon her bed within the curtains."*

In short, an editor's decisions do not end with the choice of a single copy text. First of all, editors must reckon with Elizabethan spelling. If they are not producing a facsimile, they probably modernize the spelling, but ought they to preserve the old forms of words that apparently were pronounced quite unlike their modern forms—*lanthorn, alablaster*? If they preserve these forms are they really preserving Shakespeare's forms or perhaps those of a compositor in the printing house? What is one to do when one finds *lanthorn* and *lantern* in adjacent lines? (The editors of this series in general, but not invariably, assume that words should be spelled in their modern form, unless, for instance, a rhyme is involved.) Elizabethan punctuation, too, presents problems. For example, in the First Folio, the only text for the play, Macbeth rejects his wife's idea that he can wash the blood from his hand (2.2.60–62):

> No: this my Hand will rather
> The multitudinous Seas incarnardine,
> Making the Greene one, Red.

Obviously an editor will remove the superfluous capitals, and will probably alter the spelling to "incarnadine," but what about the comma before "Red"? If we retain the comma, Macbeth is calling the sea "the green one." If we drop the comma, Macbeth is saying that his bloody hand will make the sea ("the Green") *uniformly* red.

An editor will sometimes have to change more than spelling and punctuation. Macbeth says to his wife (1.7.46–47):

> I dare do all that may become a man,
> Who dares no more, is none.

For two centuries editors have agreed that the second line is unsatisfactory, and have emended "no" to "do": "Who dares do more is none." But when in the same play (4.2.21–22) Ross says that fearful persons

> Floate vpon a wilde and violent Sea
> Each way, and moue,

need we emend the passage? On the assumption that the compositor misread the manuscript, some editors emend "each way, and move" to "and move each way"; others emend "move" to "none" (i.e., "Each way and none"). Other editors, however, let the passage stand as in the original. The editors of the Signet Classic Shakespeare have restrained themselves from making abundant emendations. In their minds they hear Samuel Johnson on the dangers of emendation: "I have adopted the Roman sentiment, that it is more honorable to save a citizen than to kill an enemy." Some departures (in addition to spelling, punctuation, and lineation) from the copy text have of course been made, but the original readings are listed in a note following the play, so that readers can evaluate the changes for themselves.

Following tradition, the editors of the Signet Classic Shakespeare have prefaced each play with a list of characters, and throughout the play have regularized the names of the speakers. Thus, in our text of *Romeo and Juliet*, all speeches by Juliet's mother are prefixed "Lady Capulet," although the 1599 Quarto of the play, which provides our copy text, uses at various points seven speech tags for this one character: *Capu. Wi.* (i.e., Capulet's wife), *Ca. Wi., Wi., Wife, Old La.* (i.e., Old Lady), *La.,* and *Mo.* (i.e., Mother). Similarly, in *All's Well That Ends Well*, the character whom we regularly call "Countess" is in the Folio (the copy text) variously identified as *Mother, Countess, Old Countess, Lady,* and *Old Lady.* Admittedly there is some loss in regularizing, since the various prefixes may give us a hint of the way Shakespeare (or a scribe who copied Shakespeare's manuscript) was thinking of the character in a particular scene—for instance, as a mother, or as an old lady. But too much can be made of these differing prefixes, since the social relationships implied are *not* always relevant to the given scene.

We have also added line numbers and in many cases act and scene divisions as well as indications of locale at the beginning of scenes. The Folio divided most of the plays into acts and some into scenes. Early eighteenth-century editors increased the divisions. These divisions, which provide a convenient way of referring to passages in the plays, have been retained, but when not in the text chosen as the basis for the Signet Classic text they are enclosed within square brackets, [ ], to indicate that they are editorial additions. Similarly, though no play of Shakespeare's was equipped with indications of the locale at the heads of scene divisions, locales have here been added in square brackets for the convenience of readers, who lack the information that costumes, properties, gestures, and scenery afford to spectators. Spectators can tell at a glance they are in the throne room, but without an editorial indication the reader may be puzzled for a while. It should be mentioned, incidentally, that there are a few authentic stage directions—perhaps Shakespeare's, perhaps a prompter's—that suggest locales, such as *"Enter Brutus in his orchard,"* and *"They go up into the Senate house."* It is hoped that the bracketed additions in the Signet text will provide readers with the sort of help provided by these two authentic directions, but it is equally hoped that the reader will remember that the stage was not loaded with scenery.

Shakespeare on the Stage

Each volume in the Signet Classic Shakespeare includes a brief stage (and sometimes film) history of the play. When we read about earlier productions, we are likely to find them eccentric, obviously wrongheaded—for instance, Nahum Tate's version of *King Lear*, with a happy ending, which held the stage for about a century and a half, from the late seventeenth century until the end of the first quarter of the nineteenth. We see engravings of David Garrick, the greatest actor of the eighteenth century, in eighteenth-century garb as King Lear, and we smile, thinking how absurd the production must have been. If we are more thoughtful, we say, with the English novelist L. P. Hartley, "The past is a foreign country: they do things differently there." But if the eighteenth-century staging is a foreign country, what of the plays of the late sixteenth and seventeenth centuries? A foreign language, a foreign theater, a foreign audience.

Probably all viewers of Shakespeare's plays, beginning with Shakespeare himself, at times have been unhappy with the plays on the stage. Consider three comments about production that we find in the plays themselves, which suggest Shakespeare's concerns. The Chorus in *Henry V* complains that the heroic story cannot possibly be adequately staged:

> But pardon, gentles all,
> The flat unraisèd spirits that hath dared
> On this unworthy scaffold to bring forth
> So great an object. Can this cockpit hold
> The vasty fields of France? Or may we cram
> Within this wooden *O* the very casques
> That did affright the air at Agincourt?
> . . . .
> Piece out our imperfections with your thoughts.
>
> (Prologue 1.8–14,23)

Second, here are a few sentences (which may or may not represent Shakespeare's own views) from Hamlet's longish lecture to the players:

> Speak the speech, I pray you, as I pronounced it to you, trippingly on the tongue. But if you mouth it, as many of our players do, I had as lief the town crier spoke my lines. . . . O, it offends me to the soul to hear a robustious periwig-pated fellow tear a passion to tatters, to very rags, to split the ears of the groundlings. . . . And let those that play your clowns speak no more than is set down for them, for there be of them that will themselves laugh, to set on some quantity of barren spectators to laugh too, though in the meantime some necessary question of the play be then to be considered. That's villainous and shows a most pitiful ambition in the fool that uses it. (3.2.1–47)

Finally, we can quote again from the passage cited earlier in
this introduction, concerning the boy actors who played the
female roles. Cleopatra imagines with horror a theatrical
version of her activities with Antony:

> The quick comedians
> Extemporally will stage us, and present
> Our Alexandrian revels: Antony
> Shall be brought drunken forth, and I shall see
> Some squeaking Cleopatra boy my greatness
> I' th' posture of a whore.   (5.2.216–21)

It is impossible to know how much weight to put on such
passages—perhaps Shakespeare was just being modest
about his theater's abilities—but it is easy enough to think
that he was unhappy with some aspects of Elizabethan production. Probably no production can fully satisfy a playwright, and for that matter, few productions can fully satisfy
us; we regret this or that cut, this or that way of costuming
the play, this or that bit of business.

One's first thought may be this: Why don't they just do
"authentic" Shakespeare, "straight" Shakespeare, the play
as Shakespeare wrote it? But as we read the plays—words
written to be performed—it sometimes becomes clear that
we do not know *how* to perform them. For instance, in
Antony and Cleopatra Antony, the Roman general who has
succumbed to Cleopatra and to Egyptian ways, says, "The
nobleness of life / Is to do thus" (1.1.36–37). But what is
"thus"? Does Antony at this point embrace Cleopatra? Does
he embrace and kiss her? (There are, by the way, very few
scenes of kissing on Shakespeare's stage, possibly because
boys played the female roles.) Or does he make a sweeping
gesture, indicating the Egyptian way of life?

This is not an isolated example; the plays are filled with
lines that call for gestures, but we are not sure what the gestures should be. *Interpretation* is inevitable. Consider a passage in *Hamlet*. In 3.1, Polonius persuades his daughter,
Ophelia, to talk to Hamlet while Polonius and Claudius
eavesdrop. The two men conceal themselves, and Hamlet
encounters Ophelia. At 3.1.131 Hamlet suddenly says to her,
"Where's your father?" Why does Hamlet, apparently out of

nowhere—they have not been talking about Polonius—ask this question? Is this an example of the "antic disposition" (fantastic behavior) that Hamlet earlier (1.5.172) had told Horatio and others—including us—he would display? That is, is the question about the whereabouts of her father a seemingly irrational one, like his earlier question (3.1.103) to Ophelia, "Ha, ha! Are you honest?" Or, on the other hand, has Hamlet (as in many productions) suddenly glimpsed Polonius's foot protruding from beneath a drapery at the rear? That is, does Hamlet ask the question because he has suddenly seen something suspicious and now is testing Ophelia? (By the way, in productions that do give Hamlet a physical cue, it is almost always Polonius rather than Claudius who provides the clue. This itself is an act of interpretation on the part of the director.) Or (a third possibility) does Hamlet get a clue from Ophelia, who inadvertently betrays the spies by nervously glancing at their place of hiding? This is the interpretation used in the BBC television version, where Ophelia glances in fear toward the hiding place just after Hamlet says "Why wouldst thou be a breeder of sinners?" (121–22). Hamlet, realizing that he is being observed, glances here and there *before* he asks "Where's your father?" The question thus is a climax to what he has been doing while speaking the preceding lines. Or (a fourth interpretation) does Hamlet suddenly, without the aid of any clue whatsoever, intuitively (insightfully, mysteriously, wonderfully) sense that someone is spying? Directors must decide, of course—and so must readers.

Recall, too, the preceding discussion of the texts of the plays, which argued that the texts—though they seem to be before us in permanent black on white—are unstable. The Signet text of *Hamlet*, which draws on the Second Quarto (1604) and the First Folio (1623) is considerably longer than any version staged in Shakespeare's time. Our version, even_ if spoken very briskly and played without any intermission, would take close to four hours, far beyond "the two hours' traffic of our stage" mentioned in the Prologue to *Romeo and Juliet*. (There are a few contemporary references to the duration of a play, but none mentions more than three hours.) Of Shakespeare's plays, only *The Comedy of Errors*, *Macbeth*, and *The Tempest* can be done in less than three hours without cutting. And even if we take a play that exists only in a short text, *Macbeth*, we cannot claim that we are experiencing the very play that Shakespeare conceived, partly because some of the Witches' songs almost surely are non-Shakespearean additions, and partly because we are not willing to watch the play performed without an intermission and with boys in the female roles.

Further, as the earlier discussion of costumes mentioned, the plays apparently were given chiefly in contemporary, that is, in Elizabethan dress. If today we give them in the costumes that Shakespeare probably saw, the plays seem not contemporary but curiously dated. Yet if we use our own dress, we find lines of dialogue that are at odds with what we see; we may feel that the language, so clearly not our own, is inappropriate coming out of people in today's dress. A common solution, incidentally, has been to set the plays in the nineteenth century, on the grounds that this attractively distances the plays (gives them a degree of foreignness, allowing for interesting costumes) and yet doesn't put them into a museum world of Elizabethan England.

Inevitably our productions are adaptations, *our* adaptations, and inevitably they will look dated, not in a century but in twenty years, or perhaps even in a decade. Still, we cannot escape from our own conceptions. As the director Peter Brook has said, in *The Empty Space* (1968):

> It is not only the hair-styles, costumes and make-ups that look dated. All the different elements of staging—the shorthands of behavior that stand for emotions; gestures, gesticulations and tones of voice—are all fluctuating on an invisible stock exchange all the time. . . . A living theatre that thinks it can stand aloof from anything as trivial as fashion will wilt. (p. 16)

As Brook indicates, it is through today's hairstyles, costumes, makeup, gestures, gesticulations, tones of voice—this includes our *conception* of earlier hairstyles, costumes, and so forth if we stage the play in a period other than our own—that we inevitably stage the plays.

It is a truism that every age invents its own Shakespeare, just as, for instance, every age has invented its own classical world. Our view of ancient Greece, a slave-holding society in which even free Athenian women were severely circumscribed, does not much resemble the Victorians' view of ancient Greece as a glorious democracy, just as, perhaps, our view of Victorianism itself does not much resemble theirs. We cannot claim that the Shakespeare on our stage is the true Shakespeare, but in our stage productions we find a Shakespeare that speaks to us, a Shakespeare that our ancestors doubtless did not know but one that seems to us to be the true Shakespeare—at least for a while.

Our age is remarkable for the wide variety of kinds of staging that it uses for Shakespeare, but one development deserves special mention. This is the now common practice of race-blind or color-blind or nontraditional casting, which allows persons who are not white to play in Shakespeare. Previously blacks performing in Shakespeare were limited to a mere three roles, Othello, Aaron (in *Titus Andronicus*), and the Prince of Morocco (in *The Merchant of Venice*), and there were no roles at all for Asians. Indeed, African-Americans rarely could play even one of these three roles, since they were not welcome in white companies. Ira Aldridge (c.1806–1867), a black actor of undoubted talent, was forced to make his living by performing Shakespeare in England and in Europe, where he could play not only Othello but also—in whiteface—other tragic roles such as King Lear. Paul Robeson (1898–1976) made theatrical history when he played Othello in London in 1930, and there was some talk about bringing the production to the United States, but there was more talk about whether American audiences would tolerate the sight of a black man—a real black man, not a white man in blackface—kissing and then killing a white woman. The idea was tried out in summer stock in 1942, the reviews were enthusiastic, and in the following year Robeson opened on Broadway in a production that ran an astounding 296 performances. An occasional all-black company sometimes performed Shakespeare's plays, but otherwise blacks (and other minority members) were in effect shut out from performing Shakespeare. Only since about 1970 has it been common for nonwhites to play major roles along with whites. Thus, in a 1996–97 production of *Antony and Cleopatra*, a white Cleopatra, Vanessa Redgrave, played opposite a black Antony, David Harewood.

Multiracial casting is now especially common at the New York Shakespeare Festival, founded in 1954 by Joseph Papp, and in England, where even siblings such as Claudio and Isabella in *Measure for Measure* or Lear's three daughters may be of different races. Probably most viewers today soon stop worrying about the lack of realism, and move beyond the color of the performers' skin to the quality of the performance.

Nontraditional casting is not only a matter of color or race; it includes sex. In the past, occasionally a distinguished woman of the theater has taken on a male role—Sarah Bernhardt (1844–1923) as Hamlet is perhaps the most famous example—but such performances were widely regarded as eccentric. Although today there have been some performances involving cross-dressing (a drag *As You Like It* staged by the National Theatre in England in 1966 and in the United States in 1974 has achieved considerable fame in the annals of stage history), what is more interesting is the casting of women in roles that traditionally are male but that need not be. Thus, a 1993–94 English production of *Henry V* used a woman—*not* cross-dressed—in the role of the governor of Harfleur. According to Peter Holland, who reviewed the production in *Shakespeare Survey* 48 (1995), "having a female Governor of Harfleur feminized the city and provided a direct response to the horrendous threat of rape and murder that Henry had offered, his language and her body in direct connection and opposition" (p. 210). Ten years from now the device may not play so effectively, but today it speaks to us. Shakespeare, born in the Elizabethan Age, has been dead nearly four hundred years, yet he is, as Ben Jonson said, "not of an age but for all time." We must understand, however, that he is "for all time" precisely because each age finds in his abundance something for itself and something of itself.

And here we come back to two issues discussed earlier in this introduction—the instability of the text and, curiously, the Bacon/Oxford heresy concerning the authorship of the plays. *Of course* Shakespeare wrote the plays, and we should daily fall on our knees to thank him for them—and yet there is something to the idea that he is not their only author. Every editor, every director and actor, and every reader to some degree shapes them, too, for when we edit, direct, act, or read, we inevitably become Shakespeare's collaborator and re-create the plays. The plays, one might say, are so cunningly contrived that they guide our responses, tell us how we ought to feel, and make a mark on us, but (for better or for worse) we also make a mark on them.

—SYLVAN BARNET
Tufts University

Introduction

I

Readers who come to *Henry IV* [*Part One*] from *Richard II* (and they are well advised who do so) find themselves in a changed world. The new king's second word is "shaken"—"So shaken as we are, so wan with care" (1.1.1). His realm's peace, "frighted," pants to catch her breath. The English earth, invoked in vain by Richard in the earlier play for aid against Henry's invading power (3.2.4ff), like a perverted mother has been sucking "her own children's blood." Englishmen have met Englishmen "in the . . . furious close of civil butchery." The "edge" of war's knife has cut his master.

Though the new king assigns these troubles to the past, we are speedily assured they will not stay there. Present news is equally bloody. In the West, a thousand of Mortimer's men have been "butchered," and afterward mutilated. In the North, ten thousand Scottish corpses were seen by Sir Walter Blunt "balked in their own blood." Throughout the play we shall hear continually of this sort of thing: of "guns and drums and wounds" (1.3.55) and "many a good tall fellow" destroyed (61); of "bloody noses and cracked crowns" (2.3.93); wearing "a garment all of blood" (3.2.135); noblemen offered up "hot and bleeding" to "the fire-eyed maid of smoky war" (4.1.113–14); ragamuffins tossed dead into a pit—"Tut, tut, good enough to toss; food for powder. . . ." (4.2.66–67)—or consigned, maimed, to the town's end, "to beg during life" (5.3.38). Richard returned from wars in Ireland in the earlier play, and the present king, then Henry Hereford, known as Bolingbroke, invaded England; but we never heard of doings like these. This is

indeed a changed world: the world of outrage that is antici-
pated in the next-to-last scene of *Richard II* by the brutal
murder of the King and, earlier, in the deposition scene
(4.1.121–49), by the warning of the Bishop of Carlisle:

> What subject can give sentence on his king?
> And who sits here that is not Richard's subject? . . .
> My Lord of Hereford here, whom you call king,
> Is a foul traitor to proud Hereford's king;
> And if you crown him, let me prophesy
> The blood of English shall manure the ground,
> And future ages groan for this foul act;
> Peace shall go sleep with Turks and infidels,
> And, in this seat of peace, tumultuous wars
> Shall kin with kin, and kind with kind, confound;
> Disorder, horror, fear, and mutiny
> Shall here inhabit, and this land be called
> The field of Golgotha and dead men's skulls.
> O, if you raise this house against this house,
> It will the woefullest division prove
> That ever fell upon this cursèd earth!
> Prevent it, resist it, let it not be so,
> Lest child, child's children, cry against you woe.

The violence predicted by Carlisle takes over immediately in *1 Henry IV*, as we have seen. But the bishop's enunciation of what is sometimes called "the Tudor myth"—the
thesis that an ever-watchful Providence brings retribution
on peoples who displace their lawful sovereigns, and, spe-
cifically, that England's sufferings between the murder of
Richard in 1399 and the accession of the first Tudor mon-
arch in 1485 were a divinely appointed punishment for the
assault on Richard—the enunciation of this doctrine better
suits Shakespeare's earlier treatment of these disorders in
the Henry VI plays and *Richard III* than the Henry IV plays.
The world that produces Henry is changed in this respect,
too. The old scheme of celestial superintendence hangs
loosely over it, to be glanced at in moments of introspec-
tion and anxiety; but to all dramatic intents and purposes,
Henry's world, like Henry himself, is secular. One reason

may be that Shakespeare saw in secularism the necessary condition of a usurper's success. A more compelling reason, doubtless, is that his attention had increasingly shifted from the interpretive moral and theological scheme with which his sources provided him toward the complexities and crosscurrents of human beings as they act and react on one another: in Yeats's words, toward "the fury and the mire of human veins."

The best anticipation of the mood of our play, from this point of view, is Richard's own warning, addressed to the man whose betrayal of him enabled Henry to seize the throne:

> Northumberland, thou ladder wherewithal
> The mounting Bolingbroke ascends my throne,
> The time shall not be many hours of age
> More than it is, ere foul sin, gathering head,
> Shall break into corruption. Thou shalt think,
> Though he divide the realm and give thee half,
> It is too little, helping him to all;
> He shall think that thou which knowest the way
> To plant unrightful kings, wilt know again,
> Being ne'er so little urged another way,
> To pluck him headlong from the usurped throne.
> The love of wicked men converts to fear,
> That fear to hate, and hate turns one or both
> To worthy danger and deservèd death.   (5.1.55–68)

These lines pay tribute to the overall theological scheme ("foul sin, gathering head"), but this fact should not blind us to the principles of *realpolitik* which they put forward as the mode of action that will govern in the hearts of Henry and his associates.

The irony of the new king's position, we soon learn, springs from these principles. As a successful usurper with the blood of a predecessor on his conscience, he is himself a principle of the disorder on which, as Shakespeare's Macbeth will learn at length, no lasting order can be built. Lawlessness springs up about him as if like Jason he had sown the dragon's teeth. It comes not only in the form of the

Percys' rebellion and the behavior of his son, but in the knavery of Falstaff and the murky atmosphere of the inn at Rochester (to some extent an image of England), where all order is in decay and no man trusts another. All these are reflections cast by Henry in the mirror of the body politic. If there are highwaymen on the public road and other highwaymen at Glendower's plotting to snatch the Crown, these circumstances cannot be separated from the circumstance that one who has acted like a highwayman is king.

Thus the Tudor theme of the harsh wages of usurpation by no means vanishes from the play. Minimizing it as doctrine, Shakespeare makes it part of the poetic and dramatic texture, while he qualifies and complicates it by presenting to us in Henry a capable and even admirable king—one who, though never granted the security and peace he longs for, maintains his crown by a combination of strength, sagacity, severity, and lenience, and passes it on to an eventually deserving son. The ambivalence of his position is brought out by continual questioning of his title. The rebels question it on many occasions verbally (1.3.10ff, 143ff; 4.3.52ff; 5.1.30ff) and, subsequently, by force of arms. The King himself seems to cast a doubt on it when he dresses others "in his coats" to confuse the enemy at Shrewsbury, as if royalty were a costume or blazon to be laid on at will. When Falstaff "acts" the King in the tavern, this doubt assumes a compelling visual shape, as does a further doubt whether "that father ruffian," as Hal calls Falstaff when he himself assumes the King's part, is more a ruffian in some respects than the deposer and murderer of Richard. Meantime, in the language of the play, this subject is teased at incessantly: we hear of the "Grace" that Hal will or will not have when he is king; of the "*true*¹ prince" knowable by instinct; of the "heir *apparent*"¹—with a lurking pun in the second term; of false or cracked coins (bearing the King's image) to be passed current; of "nobles" appreciated to "royals"; and of many forms of "counterfeiting." Perhaps the ambiguities surrounding Henry's claim are expressed most succinctly in two remarks made by the Scottish Doug-

---

¹The italics are, of course, the editor's.

las during the battle. Douglas is engaged in killing all who wear the King's coats as fast as he can find them. "I fear thou art another counterfeit," he says as he sees Henry approach in the same garb. "And yet, in faith, thou bearest thee like a king." The first sentence suggests the emptiness of Henry's title in that he is not the rightful king; the second suggests the justness of his title in that he is a man who knows how to rule. We notice, however, that the King's life is saved neither by the stratagem of the coats nor by kingly "bearing," but by the chivalry of his son.

II

The *First Part of Henry IV* was published in 1598; it was probably written and acted in 1596–97. There are some topical allusions in the play to these years, notably the Second Carrier's reference to the high cost of oats that killed Robin Ostler (2.1.12). Topical in a more important sense, during the whole of the 1590's, was the play's general subject matter. Though contemporary concern about succession to the throne need not (though it may) have influenced Shakespeare's choice of materials for his English histories, it inevitably gave them an extra dimension. Elizabeth was now in her sixties, and there was no assured heir, only a multiplicity of candidates, including her sometimes favorite, the Earl of Essex. Many recalled anxiously the chaos in times past when the center of power in the monarchical system had ceased to be sharply defined and clearly visible. This had occurred to an extent after Henry VIII's death, and earlier after Henry V's, and still earlier after the murder of Richard II.

If Shakespeare was at all influenced by these anxieties, his rendering of them is on the whole buoyant and optimistic in his second English tetralogy and especially so in *1 Henry IV*. True, the England seen in this play and its immediate successor is far from reassuring. It has even been described as

. . . an England, on the one side, of bawdy house and thieves'-kitchen, of waylaid merchants, badgered and bewildered Justices, and a peasantry wretched, betrayed, and recruited for the wars; an England, on the other side, of the chivalrous wolf pack of

Hotspur and Douglas, and of state-sponsored treachery in the person of Prince John—the whole presided over by a sick King, hagridden by conscience, dreaming of a Crusade to the Holy Land as M. Remorse [i.e., Falstaff] thinks of slimming and repentance.[2]

But this is only half the picture. Beside it, for the first Henry IV play, we must place the warmth, wit, and high spirits of the tavern scenes, the impetuous charm of Hotspur, the amusing domesticities of Kate and Glendower's daughter, the touching loyalty of Francis, the affections that (along with sponging) bind Falstaff to Hal, and Hal's own magnanimity and self-command. For both the first and second plays, we must weigh heavily into the account the character of the story told. This, the greatest of monarchical success stories in English popular history, traces the evolution of an engaging scapegrace into one of the most admired of English kings. Chicanery and appetite in the first play, apathy and corruption in the second, form an effective theatrical background against which the oncoming sunbright majesty of the future Henry V may shine more brightly—as we are assured precisely that it will do on our first meeting with him (1.2).

When Shakespeare turned to this subject in 1596–97, he found in his historical sources, mainly Holinshed's *Chronicles*, two dominant motifs. One was the moral and theological interpretation of the troubles attending Henry IV's reign in consequence of his usurpation. This we have already discussed. The other was the legend of the madcap youth of Henry's son and heir—a legend already exploited in an anonymous play of which we have today only a debased and possibly abbreviated text: *The Famous Victories of Henry the Fifth*. The *Famous Victories* contributes to *1 Henry IV* the germ of the robbery incident (though the Prince's involvement in a thieving episode is found in the chronicles as well); the germ of the tavern high jinks and parodying of authority; the germ of the expectation of Hal's reign as a golden age of rascals; and the germ of the reconciliation

---

[2]Danby, J. F., *Shakespeare's Doctrine of Nature: A Study of King Lear* (London: Faber and Faber, 1949), pp. 97–98.

scene between the Prince and his father. The extent to which these hints are fleshed out and transfigured by Shakespeare's imagination may be seen in the character of Mistress Quickly. Her entire original in the *Famous Victories* is a sentence spoken by the Prince, favoring a rendezvous at "the old tavern in Eastcheap" because "there is a pretty wench that can talk well."

From the *Famous Victories* come also the names Gad's Hill (for the arranger of the robbery), Ned (our Ned Poins), and Jockey Oldcastle. The last was Shakespeare's name for Falstaff when the play was first performed, as references throughout the early seventeenth century show; Hal's addressing him as "my old lad of the castle" in the play as we have it (1.2.43–44) is a survival from this. By the time the play was printed, the name had been altered to Falstaff for reasons that can now only be guessed at. Possibly there had been a protest by Oldcastle's descendants, one of whom was Lord Chamberlain during part of 1596–97. How the historical Oldcastle (d.1417), a man of character who was made High Sheriff of Herefordshire and eventually Lord Cobham, came to be metamorphosed into the roisterer of the *Famous Victories* is also an unsolved mystery, though no more mysterious than the dramatic imagination that exalted this dull stage roisterer, lacking eloquence, wit, mendacity, thirst, and fat, into the Falstaff we know.

On Holinshed and minor sources like Samuel Daniel's epic *The First Four Books of the Civil Wars between the Two Houses of Lancaster and York* [1595], Shakespeare based his treatment of the Percy rebellion, recasting the materials to give them an inner coherence. The Hotspur of history, for example, was twenty-three years older than Hal and two years older than the King himself, who at the date of the battle of Shrewsbury was only thirty-seven, his eldest son being then sixteen, and Prince John thirteen. Shakespeare followed the lead of Daniel and made Hotspur a youth, in order to establish dramatic rivalry between him and Hal. He then aged Henry rapidly so that by the time of the battle the King can speak of crushing his "old limbs in ungentle steel" and be the more appropriately rescued (this episode is also derived from Daniel) by his vigorous heir.

For the same dramatic purpose, he assigned to Hal the triumph over Hotspur—though the inspiration for this may have come from misreading an ambiguous sentence in Holinshed. The reconciliation of Prince and King, touched on in the chronicles and dramatized briefly in the *Famous Victories* as occurring in Henry's latter years, he moved forward to a position before Shrewsbury, in order to enhance the human drama of father and son and further sharpen our anticipation of Hal's meeting with Hotspur. Hotspur's blunt uncourtly humor, the conception of Glendower as scholar and poet fired by a Celtic imagination, the entertaining clash of temperament and mood that this makes possible at Glendower's house, not only between Welshman and Englishman, but between romantic lovers and seasoned man and wife—all this again is Shakespeare's invention. His transformation of Holinshed, like his transformation of the *Famous Victories*, may best be indicated by a specific example. All of Hotspur's deliciously impetuous speech about the popinjay lord who came to Holmedon to demand his prisoners, not to mention the wonderfully ebullient scene in which it occurs, has behind it in Holinshed only seventeen words: "the King demanded of the Earl and his son such Scottish prisoners as were taken at Homeldon. . . ."

Hal's triumphant journey from tippling in taverns to glory on the field of battle derives from one other "source," more influential than any yet mentioned here. This is the *psychomachia* of the morality plays—that is, the struggle of virtues and vices for possession of a man's soul, a theme acted again and again in the plays of the early sixteenth century, which the drama of Marlowe and Shakespeare superseded. In these plays, youthful virtue is beset by temptations and misleaders but customarily sees the true light at last and is saved. In the same general manner, Prince Hal "has to choose, Morality-fashion, between Sloth or Vanity, to which he is drawn by his bad companions, and Chivalry, to which he is drawn by his father and brothers. And he chooses Chivalry."[3]

---

[3]Tillyard, E. M. W. *Shakespeare's History Plays* (London: Chatto and Windus, 1944), p. 265.

III

The play that Shakespeare built from these miscellaneous materials is simple in its large outlines. It brings before us three contrasting environments at once, each with a commanding personality. The court is Henry's domain; the tavern is Falstaff's; the feudal countryside is Hotspur's. What essentially takes place during the first three acts is the progress of Hal, the one unattached player, from Falstaff's environment to Henry's. Hal then returns in the last scene of Act 3 to mobilize the tavern world for war, after which Falstaff's environment dissolves. We then have two environments, both military and political in nature, one of them dominated by Hotspur, the other (beginning with Act 4) increasingly by Hal. Falstaff, now in his turn the unattached man, makes appropriate comments on each.

Within this simple framework, Shakespeare accomplishes an articulation of complementary images, crossreferences, and ironic contrasts that is without parallel in the history of English stage comedy. The highway robbery comments on the Percys' plot and also on the King's usurpation, as we saw a few moments ago. Gadshill, boasting of the quality of his confederates (2.1), anticipates Hotspur's misplaced confidence in the fidelity of his fellow rebels (2.3). Falstaff bawling for his horse (2.2) has satirical affinities with Hotspur chattering to the same purpose (2.3). Hal describes Hotspur talking to his wife (2.4) as if he had been an eavesdropper in the scene preceding, and points our attention to a tavern monomania in Francis which is perhaps reminiscent of Hotspur's monomania for "palisadoes, frontiers, parapets." Hotspur describes a presumed but perhaps wholly imaginary fight between Glendower and Mortimer in epic terms (1.3); Falstaff does the same for a definitely imaginary contest with eleven men in buckram (2.4). Falstaff keeps telling us he is about to reform; Hal actually does so. Hal's interview with his father (3.2) is broadened and deepened for us in advance by the burlesque of it (2.4) and by the failure of Hotspur to achieve a similar self-discipline (3.1). Glendower and Hotspur mirror each other in egoism, contrast vividly in the pedantic refinements of the one, the countrified heartiness of the other. Falstaff's remarks on honor, as everyone knows, complement those we have heard earlier from Hotspur; the comic account of Falstaff's conscripted derelicts corrects and supplements the description of Hal's army by a general who loves parades (4.1.97ff) and the anticipation of destroying it by a general who loves carnage (113ff); Falstaff's cynical "They'll fill a pit as well as better" hangs over the ensuing battle, enveloping especially those who are to fill a pit simply because the King has dressed them in his coats; etc. This list of cross-references could be extended almost indefinitely.

Only through such qualifying optics as these does Shakespeare allow us to view the simple Morality "choice" described by Professor Tillyard. Hotspur is one term in that choice—at first glance, a wholly negative term. He misjudges Henry, seeing only the King's duplicity. He misjudges Hal, seeing only the truant, overlooking Hal's sagacity and versatility. Magnanimity is also beyond his reach. His manners are rude, not courtly. His reaction to Glendower is both impolitic and provincial. Yet the play shows us there is much to be said on behalf of this misguided and hotheaded young man. In many respects, he is set apart from, and above, the company he keeps. In being free of scheming policy, he is differentiated from his uncle Worcester and the King. In fighting (for a time) the nation's battles, he has in the past surpassed Hal. He can be counted on when needed and is thereby distinguished from Glendower, Mortimer, and his father. His valor in battle is total. In this he is unlike Douglas, who makes a fine display of fearlessness but in the pinch flees. And he is naively frank-hearted. Hotspur, Worcester knows, would be moved to meet what seems the King's generous offer of amnesty with equal generosity, and the battle would probably not be fought.

Falstaff, the other term of the choice, is similarly complex. First of all, he is endowed by Shakespeare with a comic imagination that enables him (as Antony will later be enabled by the imagination of Cleopatra) to show his back above the element he lives in. His shattering of official clichés and stained-glass attitudes throughout the play is a measure of his penetration as well as, sometimes, his irre-

sponsibility: "Why, Hal, 'tis my vocation, Hal. 'Tis no sin
for a man to labor in his vocation" (1.2.108–09); "A plague
of sighing and grief, it blows a man up like a bladder"
(2.4.332–33); "Thou knowest in the state of innocency
Adam fell, and what should poor Jack Falstaff do in the
days of villainy? Thou seest I have more flesh than another
man, and therefore more frailty" (3.3.169–73); "Rebellion
lay in his way, and he found it" (5.1.28). These show the
same gift of comic insight that enables him to multiply images of himself as a shotten herring or a poulterer's hare, to
raise the stock role of *miles gloriosus*, or braggart soldier,
into the most rapturous flight of mendacity the comic stage
has ever seen (2.4), and to fling into the tense silence before
the robbery one of those searching questions about the nature of man and his societies that a wide-eyed child will
sometimes propound: "Zounds, will they not rob *us*?"
(2.2.64). (In *2 Henry IV*, appealing to "law of nature" to account for the way of a pike with a dace, he will make this
Hobbist question a proposition.)

Falstaff is also set apart by his genuine affections, his joy
in his friends: "Gallants, lads, boys, hearts of gold, all the titles of good fellowship come to you!" (2.4.278–80). He is
even set apart by a certain kind of honesty. He will lie to
others inexhaustibly, but that life is sweeter to him than
honor, sack than killing, money in the pocket more gratify-
ing than a fine squad of soldiers, he never seeks to hide from
himself. Yet it would be folly to ignore that his honesty
makes him no less a rascal, his affection no less a parasite,
his perspicacity about some matters no less willful-blind
about the rest. Falstaff is much more than—but he also is—
a glutton, drunkard, liar, coward, and thief.

Hotspur and Falstaff are extremes, and we see the gulf
that separates them when Hotspur goes down fighting while
Falstaff plays dead to save his skin. But extremes (so runs
the familiar saying) meet, and we see them meet when Falstaff, having taken Hotspur's body on his back, assures Hal
he is "not a double man." The phrase reminds us that he
and Hotspur are in some respects outsized versions of the
same thing. Both are chivalric figures, Falstaff being, however backslidden, a knight; both exemplify ways in which

chivalry may go to seed. "A hare-brained Hotspur, governed by a spleen," as his uncle Worcester describes him (5.2.19), can sacrifice to spleen a true knight's fealty and stain the honor he so prizes by making it the ground his egoism walks on. As for Falstaff, that "huge bombard of sack," that "roast Manningtree ox with the pudding in his belly": in his knight's bosom, "there's no room for faith, truth, nor honesty; . . . it is all filled up with guts and midriff."

Falstaff and Hotspur help us see that Hal's course is a mean between extremes. King Henry helps us see that Hal's mean is not a path of least resistance but a creative will that points toward a new kind of world. A master of appearances, as his description of his behavior in King Richard's time informs us (3.2), Henry is at the same time their victim. If he seriously imagines that he would ever actually go on that Crusade whose "dear expedience" occupies his council at the opening of the play (1.1), he is obviously self-deceived; if he does not intend to go, it is a calculated charade. The sketches of Hotspur and his son which he draws for us in the same scene are unmistakably sincere; but we soon discover they are wrong—mere stereotypes of martial prowess and libertinism. Henry does not really understand either his son or Hotspur. When he holds up Hotspur for a model in the reconciliation scene (3.2), when he exhibits his delusion that what he was to King Richard, Hotspur is now to Hal, when he speaks of Hal's "barren pleasures" to us who have just seen the tavern bulge with an energy and feeling never to be matched at Henry's court, we understand how far he has become prisoner of a royalism that is less imaginative than his son's. And when the battle comes, we understand more clearly against this background the meaning of the contrasts there: the King "hath many marching in his coats" (5.3.25), the Prince offers to decide the issue by taking the danger on himself alone; the King, thinking in political terms, sends his enemies to execution and within these terms is perfectly right to do so; the Prince thinks in larger terms and spares Douglas, not for political reasons (though doubtless he is aware of these), but because, as in his praise of Hotspur, he can cherish "high deeds/Even in the bosom of our adversaries" (5.5.30–31). Even Falstaff at his most ignominious, wounding Hotspur's corpse and claiming credit for having killed him, the Prince can bring himself to excuse; he will gild his lie "with the happiest terms I have" (5.4.156).

Thus by the play's end, Hal casts an inclusive shadow. He has met the claims of Hotspur's world, of Falstaff's, and of Henry's, without narrowing himself to any one. He has practiced mercy as well as justice, politics as well as friendship, shown himself capable of mockery as well as reverence, detachment as well as commitment, and brought into a practicable balance court, field, and tavern. He is on the way to becoming the luminous figure toward whom, In *Henry V,* Welshman, Irishman, Scot, and Englishman will alike be drawn. In this figure, combining valor, courtliness, hard sense, and humor in an ideal image of the potentialities of the English character, Shakespeare seems to have discerned grounds for that optimism about the future of his country which permeates his historical vision in the plays from *Richard II* to *Henry V.*

—MAYNARD MACK
Yale University

The History of Henry IV
[PART ONE]

[Dramatis Personae

King Henry the Fourth
Henry, Prince of Wales   } the King's sons
Prince John of Lancaster
Earl of Westmoreland
Sir Walter Blunt
Thomas Percy, Earl of Worcester
Henry Percy, Earl of Northumberland
Henry Percy ("Hotspur"), his son
Edmund Mortimer, Earl of March
Richard Scroop, Archbishop of York
Archibald, Earl of Douglas
Owen Glendower
Sir Richard Vernon
Sir John Falstaff
Sir Michael, a friend of the Archbishop of York
Poins
Gadshill
Peto
Bardolph
Francis, a waiter
Lady Percy, Hotspur's wife and Mortimer's sister
Lady Mortimer, Glendower's daughter and Mortimer's
    wife
Mistress Quickly, hostess of the tavern
Sheriff, Vintner, Chamberlain, two Carriers, Ostler, Mes-
    sengers, Travelers, Attendants

Scene: England and Wales]

The History of Henry IV

[PART ONE]

[ACT 1

Scene 1. *London. The palace.*]

*Enter the King, Lord John of Lancaster, Earl of
Westmoreland, [Sir Walter Blunt,] with others.*

King. So shaken as we are, so wan with care,
Find we a time for frighted peace to pant°¹
And breathe short-winded accents of new broils
To be commenced in stronds° afar remote.
No more the thirsty entrance of this soil   5
Shall daub her lips with her own children's blood,
No more shall trenching° war channel her fields,
Nor bruise her flow'rets with the armèd hoofs
Of hostile paces. Those opposèd eyes
Which, like the meteors° of a troubled heaven,   10
All of one nature, of one substance bred,°
Did lately meet in the intestine° shock
And furious close° of civil butchery,
Shall now in mutual well-beseeming° ranks
March all one way and be no more opposed   15
Against acquaintance, kindred, and allies.

¹The degree sign (°) indicates a footnote, which is keyed to the text by
line number. Text references are printed in **boldface** type; the annotation
follows in roman type.
1.1.2 **pant** catch (her) breath   4 **stronds** shores   7 **trenching** (1) cutting (2) encroaching   10 **meteors** atmospheric disturbances   11 **All . . .
bred** i.e., because believed to originate from vapors   12 **intestine** internal   13 **close** grappling   14 **mutual well-beseeming** interdependent
well-ordered

The edge of war, like an ill-sheathèd knife,
No more shall cut his master. Therefore, friends,
As far as to the sepulcher of Christ°—
20   Whose soldier now, under whose blessèd cross
We are impressèd and engaged° to fight—
Forthwith a power° of English shall we levy,
Whose arms were molded in their mother's womb
To chase these pagans in those holy fields
25   Over whose acres walked those blessèd feet
Which fourteen hundred years ago were nailed
For our advantage on the bitter cross.
But this our purpose now is twelvemonth old,
And bootless° 'tis to tell you we will go.
30   Therefor we meet not now.° Then let me hear
Of you, my gentle cousin° Westmoreland,
What yesternight our council did decree
In forwarding this dear expedience.°

Westmoreland. My liege, this haste was hot in question°
35   And many limits of the charge° set down
But yesternight; when all athwart° there came
A post° from Wales, loaden with heavy news,
Whose worst was that the noble Mortimer,
Leading the men of Herefordshire to fight
40   Against the irregular and wild° Glendower,
Was by the rude hands of that Welshman taken,
A thousand of his people butcherèd;
Upon whose dead corpse there was such misuse,
Such beastly shameless transformation
45   By those Welshwomen done, as may not be
Without much shame retold or spoken of.°

19 **As ... Christ** i.e., to Jerusalem   21 **impressèd and engaged** conscripted and pledged (i.e., by Henry's vow after the murder of Richard:
cf. *Richard II,* 5.6.45–50)   22 **power** army   29 **bootless** useless
30 **Therefor ... now** that is not the reason we now meet   31 **gentle
cousin** noble kinsman   33 **dear expedience** urgent enterprise   34 **hot
in question** undergoing hot discussion   35 **limits of the charge** appor-
tionings of tasks and costs   36 **athwart** crosswise, i.e., interfering
37 **post** messenger   40 **irregular and wild** i.e., as border-raider and
guerrilla   43–46 **such ... spoken of** (the phrasing in Holinshed, Shakespeare's source, suggests that the dead English were castrated)

King. It seems then that the tidings of this broil
  Brake off our business for the Holy Land.

Westmoreland. This, matched with other, did, my
    gracious lord;
  For more uneven° and unwelcome news   50
  Came from the north, and thus it did import:
  On Holy-rood Day° the gallant Hotspur there,
  Young Harry Percy, and brave Archibald,
  That ever-valiant and approvèd Scot,
  At Holmedon° met, where they did spend   55
  A sad and bloody hour;
  As by discharge of their artillery
  And shape of likelihood° the news was told;
  For he that brought them,° in the very heat
  And pride of their contention° did take horse,   60
  Uncertain of the issue° any way.

King. Here is a dear, a true industrious° friend,
  Sir Walter Blunt, new lighted from his horse,
  Stained with the variation of each soil
  Betwixt that Holmedon and this seat° of ours,   65
  And he hath brought us smooth and welcome news.
  The Earl of Douglas is discomfited;
  Ten thousand bold Scots, two and twenty knights,
  Balked° in their own blood did Sir Walter see
  On Holmedon's plains. Of prisoners, Hotspur took   70
  Mordake, Earl of Fife and eldest son
  To beaten Douglas, and the Earl of Athol,
  Of Murray, Angus, and Menteith.
  And is not this an honorable spoil?
  A gallant prize? Ha, cousin, is it not?   75

Westmoreland. In faith it is. A conquest for a prince
    to boast of.

---

50 **uneven** cf. "smooth," line 66   52 **Holy-rood Day** September 14
55 **Holmedon** Humbleton in Northumberland   58 **shape of likelihood**
probability   59 **them** i.e., the news   59–60 **heat . . . contention** peak of
battle   61 **issue** outcome   62 **true industrious** loyally zealous   65 **seat**
dwelling, i.e., the palace   69 **Balked** (1) heaped (2) thwarted

King. Yea, there thou mak'st me sad, and mak'st me
    sin
    In envy that my Lord Northumberland
    Should be the father to so blest a son:
80   A son who is the theme of honor's tongue,
    Amongst a grove the very straightest plant;
    Who is sweet fortune's minion° and her pride;
    Whilst I, by looking on the praise of him,
    See riot and dishonor stain the brow
85   Of my young Harry. O that it could be proved
    That some night-tripping fairy° had exchanged
    In cradle clothes our children where they lay,
    And called mine Percy, his Plantagenet!°
    Then would I have his Harry, and he mine.
90   But let him from my thoughts. What think you, coz,°
    Of this young Percy's pride? The prisoners
    Which he in this adventure hath surprised°
    To his own use he keeps, and sends me word
    I shall have none but Mordake, Earl of Fife.

Westmoreland. This is his uncle's teaching, this is
95   Worcester,
    Malevolent to you in all aspects,°
    Which makes him prune° himself and bristle up
    The crest of youth against your dignity.

King. But I have sent for him to answer this;
100   And for this cause awhile we must neglect
    Our holy purpose to Jerusalem.
    Cousin, on Wednesday next our council we
    Will hold at Windsor, so inform the lords:
    But come yourself with speed to us again,
105   For more is to be said and to be done
    Than out of anger can be utterèd.°

Westmoreland. I will, my liege.   *Exeunt.*

82 **minion** darling 86 **fairy** (fairies were thought sometimes to steal a
beautiful infant, leaving an ugly "changeling" in its place) 88 **Plantag-
enet** family name of Henry IV 90 **coz** kinsman (short for "cousin")
92 **surprised** taken 96 **Malevolent . . . aspects** (an astrological expression comparing Worcester to a planet whose influence obstructs Henry's
designs) 97 **prune** preen his feathers for action (like a hawk) 106 **ut-
terèd** transacted in public

[Scene 2. *London. The Prince's lodging.*]

Enter Prince of Wales and Sir John Falstaff.

Falstaff. Now, Hal, what time of day is it, lad?

Prince. Thou art so fat-witted with drinking of old
sack,° and unbuttoning thee after supper, and sleeping upon benches after noon, that thou hast forgotten to demand that truly which thou wouldest   5
truly know. What a devil hast thou to do with the
time of the day? Unless hours were cups of sack,
and minutes capons, and clocks the tongues of
bawds, and dials° the signs of leaping houses,° and
the blessed sun himself a fair hot wench in flame-   10
colored taffeta, I see no reason why thou shouldst
be so superfluous to° demand the time of the day.

Falstaff. Indeed you come near me° now, Hal; for we
that take purses go by° the moon and the seven
stars,° and not by Phoebus,° he, that wand'ring   15
knight so fair.° And I prithee, sweet wag, when thou
art a king, as, God save thy Grace°—Majesty I
should say, for grace thou wilt have none—

Prince. What, none?

1.2.3 **sack** Spanish white wine   9 **dials** sundials   9 **leaping houses** broth-
els   12 **so superfluous to** so irrelevant as to   13 **near me** i.e., close to
understanding me (as if Hal were shooting at a mark)   14 **go by** (1) walk
under (2) tell time by (3) regulate our lives by   14–15 **seven stars** con-
stellation Pleiades   15 **Phoebus** the sun   15–16 **he ... fair** (Falstaff
possibly quotes here, or sings, a line of a lost ballad; the sun was readily
thought of as an eternal wanderer or "knight-errant")   17 **Grace** (Falstaff puns on "your Grace"—a title which Hal as king will exchange for
"your Majesty"—and spiritual grace and, in lines 20–21, on grace before
eating)

20   *Falstaff.* No, by my troth; not so much as will serve to
be prologue to an egg and butter.

Prince. Well, how then? Come, roundly, roundly.°

Falstaff. Marry,° then, sweet wag, when thou art king,
let not us that are squires of the night's body be
25   called thieves of the day's beauty.° Let us be
Diana's° foresters, gentlemen of the shade, minions°
of the moon; and let men say we be men of good
government,° being governed, as the sea is, by our
noble and chaste mistress the moon, under whose
30   countenance we steal.

Prince. Thou sayest well, and it holds well° too; for
the fortune of us that are the moon's men doth ebb
and flow like the sea, being governed as the sea is
by the moon. As for proof now: a purse of gold
35   most resolutely snatched on Monday night and most
dissolutely spent on Tuesday morning; got with
swearing "Lay by," and spent with crying "Bring
in";° now in as low an ebb as the foot of the ladder,°
and by and by in as high a flow as the ridge of the
40   gallows.

Falstaff. By the Lord, thou say'st true, lad—and is not
my hostess of the tavern a most sweet wench?

---

22 **roundly** i.e., get to the point (but possibly with a glance at Falstaff's
girth)   23 **Marry** (a mild oath, from "By the Virgin Mary")   24–25
squires . . . beauty (Falstaff's puns on "night/knight"—knights were often
attended by body-squires—and probably on "body/beauty/booty." The
"day's beauty" in one of its senses here is the sun and balances "the night's
body," which in one sense is the moon)   26 **Diana** goddess of the moon
and the hunt (by identifying the hunt with hunting for "booty"—and
"beauty"—Falstaff presents himself and his crew as Diana's companion
foresters, her titled "Gentlemen of the Shade," her "minions," who
"steal"—i.e., [1] move silently [2] take purses under her "countenance"—
i.e., under [1] her face [2] her protection)   26 **minions** servants and favorites   27–28 **of good government** (1) well-behaved (2) ruled by a good
ruler   31 **it holds well** it's a good comparison   37–38 **Lay by . . . Bring
in** (the highwayman's commands: the first to his victims, the second to the
waiter in the tavern where he spends his gains)   38 **ladder** (leading up to
the gallows)

Prince. As the honey of Hybla,° my old lad of the castle°—and is not a buff jerkin° a most sweet robe of durance?   45

Falstaff. How now, how now, mad wag? What, in thy quips and thy quiddities?° What a plague have I to do with a buff jerkin?

Prince. Why, what a pox° have I to do with my hostess of the tavern?   50

Falstaff. Well, thou hast called her to a reckoning° many a time and oft.

Prince. Did I ever call for thee to pay thy part?

Falstaff. No; I'll give thee thy due, thou hast paid all there.   55

Prince. Yea, and elsewhere, so far as my coin would stretch; and where it would not, I have used my credit.

Falstaff. Yea, and so used it that, were it not here apparent that thou art heir apparent—But I prithee,   60 sweet wag, shall there be gallows standing in England when thou art king? And resolution thus fubbed° as it is with the rusty curb of old father Antic° the law? Do not thou, when thou art king, hang a thief.

Prince. No; thou shalt.   65

Falstaff. Shall I? O rare! By the Lord, I'll be a brave° judge.

---

43 **Hybla** Sicilian source of fine honey   43–44 **old lad of the castle** rowdy (with pun on "Oldcastle," Falstaff's original name, and probably on "The Castle," a well-known London brothel)   44 **buff jerkin** tan (leather) jacket (a "robe of durance" because both durable and suggesting imprisonment [durance] because worn by the sheriff's officers) 46–47 **What ... quiddities** "So you're in a witty mood, are you?" 49 **pox** (the Prince turns Falstaff's "plague" into a disease more characteristic of tavern hostesses)   51 **called her to a reckoning** (1) called her to a showdown (2) asked her for the bill (3) In the context of **pox** (49), **pay** (53), **paid** (54), **stretch** (57), **called ... reckoning** may carry a sexual innuendo   62 **resolution thus fubbed** courage (i.e., in the highwayman) thus cheated of its reward   63 **old father Antic** i.e., "that old screwball"   66 **brave** (1) excellent (2) handsomely decked out

Prince. Thou judgest false already. I mean, thou shalt
have the hanging of the thieves and so become a rare
70   hangman.

Falstaff. Well, Hal, well; and in some sort it jumps
with my humor° as well as waiting in the court, I
can tell you.

Prince. For obtaining of suits?°

75   *Falstaff.* Yea, for obtaining of suits, whereof the hangman hath no lean wardrobe. 'Sblood,° I am as
melancholy as a gib-cat° or a lugged° bear.

Prince. Or an old lion, or a lover's lute.

Falstaff. Yea, or the drone° of a Lincolnshire bagpipe.

80   *Prince.* What sayest thou to a hare,° or the melancholy
of Moorditch?°

Falstaff. Thou hast the most unsavory similes, and art
indeed the most comparative,° rascalliest, sweet
young prince. But, Hal, I prithee trouble me no
85   more with vanity.° I would to God thou and I knew
where a commodity° of good names were to be
bought. An old lord of the council rated° me the
other day in the street about you, sir, but I marked
him not; and yet he talked very wisely, but I re-
90   garded him not; and yet he talked wisely, and in the
street too.

71–72 **jumps with my humor** agrees with my frame of mind   74 **suits**
petitions for court favor (but Falstaff takes it in the sense of the victim's
garments, which were forfeit to the executioner)   76 **'Sblood** by God's
(i.e., Christ's) blood   77 **gib-cat** tomcat   77 **lugged** i.e., tied to a stake
and baited by dogs, as entertainment   79 **drone** single note of a bagpipe's bass pipe   80 **hare** (proverbially melancholy)   81 **Moorditch**
foul London drainage ditch   83 **comparative** full of (insulting) comparisons   85 **vanity** i.e., worldly considerations (Falstaff here takes up
one of his favorite humorous roles, assuming for the next several lines
the sanctimonious attitudes and vocabulary of Elizabethan Puritanism)
86 **commodity** supply   87 **rated** scolded

Prince. Thou didst well, for wisdom cries out in the streets, and no man regards it.°

Falstaff. O, thou hast damnable iteration,° and art indeed able to corrupt a saint. Thou hast done much 95 harm upon me, Hal—God forgive thee for it! Before I knew thee, Hal, I knew nothing; and now am I, if a man should speak truly, little better than one of the wicked.° I must give over this life, and I will give it over! By the Lord, and° I do not, I 100 am a villain! I'll be damned for never a king's son in Christendom.

Prince. Where shall we take a purse tomorrow, Jack?

Falstaff. Zounds,° where thou wilt, lad! I'll make one. An° I do not, call me villain and baffle° me. 105

Prince. I see a good amendment of life in thee—from praying to purse-taking.

Falstaff. Why, Hal, 'tis my vocation,° Hal. 'Tis no sin for a man to labor in his vocation.

Enter Poins.

Poins! Now shall we know if Gadshill have set a 110 match.° O, if men were to be saved by merit,° what hole in hell were hot enough for him? This is the most omnipotent villain that ever cried "Stand!" to a true° man.

92–93 **Thou . . . it** (Hal quotes Proverbs 1:20–24: "Wisdom crieth without, and putteth forth her voice in the streets . . . saying . . . 'I have stretched out my hand, and no man regarded' ")   94 **damnable iteration** i.e., a sinful way of repeating and (mis)applying holy texts   99 **the wicked** (Puritan idiom for those who were not Puritans; cf. "saint" in 95, which glances at the Puritans' way of referring collectively to themselves)   100 **and** if   104 **Zounds** by God's (i.e., Christ's) wounds   105 **An** if   105 **baffle** hang upside down (a punishment allotted perjured knights)   108 **vocation** calling (with reference to the Puritan stress on a man's being "called" by God to his work)   110–11 **set a match** arranged a robbery   111 **merit** i.e., good works (in Puritan doctrine wholly insufficient for salvation)   114 **true** honest

115 *Prince.* Good morrow, Ned.

Poins. Good morrow, sweet Hal. What says Monsieur
    Remorse? What says Sir John Sack and Sugar?°
    Jack, how agrees the devil and thee about thy soul,
    that thou soldest him on Good Friday last° for a cup
120 of Madeira and a cold capon's leg?

Prince. Sir John stands to his word, the devil shall
    have his bargain; for he was never yet a breaker of
    proverbs. He will give the devil his due.

Poins. Then art thou damned for keeping thy word
125 with the devil.

Prince. Else he had been damned for cozening° the
    devil.

Poins. But, my lads, my lads, tomorrow morning, by
    four o'clock early, at Gad's Hill!° There are pil-
130 grims going to Canterbury with rich offerings,° and
    traders riding to London with fat purses. I have
    vizards° for you all; you have horses for yourselves.
    Gadshill lies tonight in Rochester. I have bespoke
    supper tomorrow night in Eastcheap.° We may do
135 it as secure as sleep. If you will go, I will stuff your
    purses full of crowns; if you will not, tarry at home
    and be hanged!

Falstaff. Hear ye, Yedward:° if I tarry at home and
    go not, I'll hang you for going.

140 *Poins.* You will, chops?°

Falstaff. Hal, wilt thou make one?

Prince. Who, I rob? I a thief? Not I, by my faith.

Falstaff. There's neither honesty, manhood, nor good

117 **Sack and Sugar** (sack sweetened with sugar was particularly the
drink of the elderly, but there may be a pun, in this context, on sackcloth,
symbol of penance)   119 **soldest . . . last** i.e., by breaking a strict fast
day   126 **cozening** cheating   129 **Gad's Hill** (a place notorious for
holdups on the road from Rochester to London)   130 **offerings** i.e., for
the shrine of St. Thomas à Becket   132 **vizards** masks   134 **Eastcheap**
London street and district   138 **Yedward** (dialect form of Edward)
140 **chops** "fat-face"

fellowship in thee, nor thou cam'st not of the blood
royal° if thou darest not stand for° ten shillings.   *145*

Prince. Well then, once in my days I'll be a madcap.

Falstaff. Why, that's well said.

Prince. Well, come what will, I'll tarry at home.

Falstaff. By the Lord, I'll be a traitor then, when thou
art king.   *150*

Prince. I care not.

Poins. Sir John, I prithee, leave the Prince and me
alone. I will lay him down such reasons for this
adventure that he shall go.

Falstaff. Well, God give thee the spirit of persuasion   *155*
and him the ears of profiting, that what thou speak-
est may move° and what he hears may be believed,
that the true prince may (for recreation sake) prove
a false thief; for the poor abuses of the time want
countenance.° Farewell; you shall find me in East-   *160*
cheap.

Prince. Farewell, the° latter spring! Farewell, All-
hallown summer!°   [*Exit Falstaff.*]

Poins. Now, my good sweet honey lord, ride with us
tomorrow. I have a jest to execute that I cannot   *165*
manage alone. Falstaff, Bardolph, Peto, and Gadshill
shall rob those men that we have already waylaid;°
yourself and I will not be there; and when they have
the booty, if you and I do not rob them, cut this
head off from my shoulders.   *170*

Prince. How shall we part with them in setting forth?

---

145 **royal** (pun on "royal," a ten-shilling coin)   145 **stand for** (1) pass
for (as a coin) (2) contest for (in a robbery)   155–57 **God . . . move**
(mimicry again of the Puritans, who claimed to act only when the spirit
moved in them)   159–60 **want countenance** lack protection (royal and
aristocratic)   162 **the** (sometimes used in the sixteenth century for
"thou" and "you")   162–63 **All-hallown summer** (Hal compares Falstaff's youthfulness in old age to the belated summer that occurs around
All Hallows day)   167 **waylaid** set our trap for

Poins. Why, we will set forth before or after them and
appoint them a place of meeting, wherein it is at our
pleasure to fail; and then will they adventure upon
175   the exploit themselves, which they shall have no
sooner achieved, but we'll set upon them.

Prince. Yea, but 'tis like that they will know us by our
horses, by our habits,° and by every other appointment,° to be ourselves.

180   *Poins.* Tut! Our horses they shall not see—I'll tie them
in the wood; our vizards we will change after we
leave them; and, sirrah,° I have cases of buckram
for the nonce,° to immask our noted outward garments.

185   *Prince.* Yea, but I doubt° they will be too hard for us.

Poins. Well, for two of them, I know them to be as
true-bred cowards as ever turned back; and for the
third, if he fight longer than he sees reason, I'll
forswear arms. The virtue of this jest will be the
190   incomprehensible° lies that this same fat rogue will
tell us when we meet at supper: how thirty, at least,
he fought with; what wards,° what blows, what ex-
tremities he endured; and in the reproof° of this
lives the jest.

195   *Prince.* Well, I'll go with thee. Provide us all things
necessary and meet me ·tomorrow night° in Eastcheap. There I'll sup. Farewell.

Poins. Farewell, my lord.   *Exit.*

Prince. I know you all, and will awhile uphold
200   The unyoked humor° of your idleness.

178 **habits** dress   178–79 **appointment** piece of equipment   182 **sirrah** (term of address showing great familiarity)   182–83 **cases . . .
nonce** outer coverings of coarse linen for the purpose   185 **doubt** fear
190 **incomprehensible** unlimited   192 **wards** strategies of defense (in
swordsmanship)   193 **reproof** disproof   196 **tomorrow night** (they
will meet for the robbery tomorrow morning, but Hal is thinking ahead
to the jest on Falstaff that night)   200 **unyoked humor** undisciplined
inclinations

Yet herein will I imitate the sun,°
Who doth permit the base contagious° clouds
To smother up his beauty from the world,
That, when he please again to be himself,
Being wanted,° he may be more wond'red at   205
By breaking through the foul and ugly mists
Of vapors that did seem to strangle him.
If all the year were playing holidays,
To sport would be as tedious as to work;
But when they seldom come, they wished-for come,   210
And nothing pleaseth but rare accidents.°
So when this loose behavior I throw off
And pay the debt I never promisèd,
By how much better than my word I am,
By so much shall I falsify men's hopes;°   215
And, like bright metal on a sullen° ground,
My reformation, glitt'ring o'er my fault,
Shall show more goodly and attract more eyes
Than that which hath no foil° to set it off.
I'll so offend to make offense a skill,   220
Redeeming time° when men think least I will.   *Exit.*

201 **sun** (royalty's traditional symbol) 202 **contagious** (clouds were
thought to breed pestilence) 205 **wanted** lacked, missed 211 **rare accidents** unexpected or uncommon events 215 **hopes** expectations
216 **sullen** dull 219 **foil** contrasting background 221 **Redeeming
time** making amends (Hal alludes to Ephesians 5:7ff, which bears in a
general way on much that has been said in this scene: "Be not ye therefore partakers with them, for ye were sometimes darkness, but now are ye
light in the Lord: walk as children of light. . . . See then that ye walk cir-
cumspectly, not as fools, but as wise. Redeeming the time, because the
days are evil).

[Scene 3. *Windsor. The council chamber.*]

Enter the King, Northumberland, Worcester,
Hotspur, Sir Walter Blunt, with others.

King. My blood hath been too cold and temperate,
    Unapt to stir at these indignities,
    And you have found me,° for accordingly
    You tread upon my patience; but be sure
5   I will from henceforth rather be myself,°
    Mighty and to be feared, than my condition,°
    Which hath been smooth as oil, soft as young down,
    And therefore lost that title of respect
    Which the proud soul ne'er pays but to the proud.

Worcester. Our house, my sovereign liege, little de-
10   serves
    The scourge of greatness to be used on it—
    And that same greatness too which our own hands
    Have holp° to make so portly.°

Northumberland.   My lord—

King. Worcester, get thee gone, for I do see
15   Danger and disobedience in thine eye.
    O, sir, your presence is too bold and peremptory,
    And majesty might never yet endure
    The moody frontier° of a servant brow.
    You have good leave to leave us: when we need
20   Your use and counsel, we shall send for you.
                          Exit Worcester.
    You were about to speak.

1.3.3 **found me** found me out   5 **myself** i.e., what I am as king   6 **my condition** i.e., what I am by nature   13 **holp** helped   13 **portly** stately   18 **frontier** rampart (as if Worcester were an enemy fortress)

Northumberland   Yea, my good lord.
  Those prisoners in your Highness' name demanded
  Which Harry Percy here at Holmedon took,
  Were, as he says, not with such strength denied
  As is deliverèd to your Majesty.   25
  Either envy,° therefore, or misprision°
  Is guilty of this fault, and not my son.

Hotspur. My liege, I did deny no prisoners.
  But I remember, when the fight was done,
  When I was dry with rage and extreme toil,   30
  Breathless and faint, leaning upon my sword,
  Came there a certain lord, neat and trimly dressed,
  Fresh as a bridegroom, and his chin new reaped°
  Showed like a stubble land at harvest home.
  He was perfumèd like a milliner,   35
  And 'twixt his finger and his thumb he held
  A pouncet box,° which ever and anon
  He gave his nose, and took 't away again;
  Who° therewith angry, when it next came there,
  Took it in snuff;° and still he smiled and talked;   40
  And as the soldiers bore dead bodies by,
  He called them untaught knaves, unmannerly,
  To bring a slovenly unhandsome corse°
  Betwixt the wind and his nobility.
  With many holiday and lady° terms   45
  He questioned° me, amongst the rest demanded
  My prisoners in your Majesty's behalf.
  I then, all smarting with my wounds being cold,
  To be so pest'red with a popingay,°
  Out of my grief° and my impatience   50
  Answered neglectingly, I know not what—
  He should, or he should not; for he made me mad
  To see him shine so brisk, and smell so sweet,

---

26 **envy** malice   26 **misprision** misapprehension   33 **reaped** i.e., with
the closely clipped beard of a man of fashion   37 **pouncet box** perfume
box   39 **Who** i.e., his nose   40 **Took it in snuff** (proverbial, meaning
"took offense," but here with pun on "snuffing" the perfume)   43 **corse**
corpse   45 **holiday and lady** fastidious and effeminate   46 **questioned**
talked to   49 **popingay** parrot (here, one who is gaudy in dress and chat-
ters emptily)   50 **grief** pain

        And talk so like a waiting gentlewoman
        Of guns and drums and wounds—God save the
55   mark!°—
        And telling me the sovereignest° thing on earth
        Was parmacity° for an inward bruise,
        And that it was great pity, so it was,
        This villainous saltpeter should be digged
60   Out of the bowels of the harmless earth,
        Which many a good tall° fellow had destroyed
        So cowardly, and but for these vile guns,
        He would himself have been a soldier.
        This bald unjointed chat of his, my lord,
65   I answered indirectly,° as I said,
        And I beseech you, let not his report
        Come current° for an accusation
        Betwixt my love and your high Majesty.

Blunt. The circumstance considerèd, good my lord,
70   Whate'er Lord Harry Percy then had said
        To such a person, and in such a place,
        At such a time, with all the rest retold,
        May reasonably die, and never rise
        To do him wrong,° or any way impeach
75   What then he said, so° he unsay it now.

King. Why, yet he doth deny his prisoners,
        But with proviso and exception,
        That we at our own charge shall ransom straight
        His brother-in-law, the foolish Mortimer;
80   Who, on my soul, hath willfully betrayed
        The lives of those that he did lead to fight
        Against that great magician, damned Glendower—
        Whose daughter, as we hear, that Earl of March
        Hath lately married. Shall our coffers, then,
85   Be emptied to redeem a traitor home?

---

55 **God save the mark** (a ritual phrase originally used to invoke a bless-
ing, but here expressing scorn)   56 **sovereignest** best   57 **parmacity**
spermaceti (medicinal substance found in sperm whales)   61 **tall** stal-
wart   65 **indirectly** absently   67 **Come current** (1) be accepted (i.e.,
as of true coin) (2) intrude   74 **To do him wrong** i.e., to be held against
him   75 **so** provided

Shall we buy treason, and indent° with fears°
When they have lost and forfeited themselves?
No, on the barren mountains let him starve!
For I shall never hold that man my friend
Whose tongue shall ask me for one penny cost　　90
To ransom home revolted Mortimer.

Hotspur. Revolted Mortimer?
　He never did fall off, my sovereign liege,
　But by the chance of war. To prove that true
　Needs no more but one tongue for all those wounds,　　95
　Those mouthèd wounds,° which valiantly he took
　When on the gentle Severn's sedgy bank,
　In single opposition hand to hand,
　He did confound° the best part of an hour
　In changing hardiment° with great Glendower.　　100
　Three times they breathed,° and three times did they
　　drink,
　Upon agreement, of swift Severn's flood;
　Who° then affrighted with their bloody looks
　Ran fearfully among the trembling reeds
　And hid his crisp° head in the hollow bank,　　105
　Bloodstainèd with these valiant combatants.
　Never did bare and rotten policy°
　Color° her working with such deadly wounds;
　Nor never could the noble Mortimer
　Receive so many, and all willingly.　　110
　Then let not him be slanderèd with revolt.°

King. Thou dost belie° him, Percy, thou dost belie him!
　He never did encounter with Glendower.
　I tell thee, he durst as well have met the devil alone
　As Owen Glendower for an enemy.　　115

86 **indent** bargain　86 **fears** (1) cowards (2) traitors, i.e., those who by
"fear" have yielded to the enemy and so become traitors "to be feared"
96 **mouthèd wounds** i.e., wounds that speak for him (based on the
likeness of a bloody flesh wound to a mouth)　99 **confound** spend
100 **changing hardiment** battling　101 **breathed** paused for breath
103 **Who** i.e., the river　105 **crisp** (used punningly to mean both
"curled" [of a man's head] and "rippling" [of a river]; "head" also re-
fers punningly to a river's force)　107 **policy** cunning　108 **Color** (1)
disguise (2) redden (i.e., with blood)　111 **revolt** treason　112 **belie**
misrepresent

Art thou not ashamed? But, sirrah,° henceforth
Let me not hear you speak of Mortimer.
Send me your prisoners with the speediest means,
Or you shall hear in such a kind from me
120   As will displease you. My Lord Northumberland,
We license your departure with your son.
Send us your prisoners, or you will hear of it.
                    Exit King, [with Blunt, and train].

Hotspur. And if° the devil come and roar for them,
   I will not send them. I will after straight
125   And tell him so, for I will ease my heart,
   Albeit I make a hazard of° my head.

Northumberland. What, drunk with choler?° Stay, and
      pause awhile.
   Here comes your uncle.

                    Enter Worcester.

Hotspur.   Speak of Mortimer?
   Zounds, I will speak of him, and let my soul
130   Want mercy if I do not join with him!
   Yea, on his part I'll empty all these veins,
   And shed my dear blood drop by drop in the dust,
   But I will lift the downtrod Mortimer
   As high in the air as this unthankful king,
135   As this ingrate and cank'red° Bolingbroke.°

Northumberland. Brother, the King hath made your
      nephew mad.

Worcester. Who struck this heat up after I was gone?

Hotspur. He will forsooth have all my prisoners;
   And when I urged the ransom once again
140   Of my wife's brother, then his cheek looked pale,
   And on my face he turned an eye of death,
   Trembling even at the name of Mortimer.

Worcester. I cannot blame him. Was not he pro-
      claimed

116 **sirrah** (term of address to an inferior, here insulting)   123 **And if** if
126 **make a hazard of** risk   127 **choler** anger   135 **cank'red** infected
135 **Bolingbroke** i.e., the king

By Richard that dead is, the next of blood?°

Northumberland. He was, I heard the proclamation: 145
And then it was when the unhappy king
(Whose wrongs in us° God pardon!) did set forth
Upon his Irish expedition;
From whence he intercepted° did return
To be deposed, and shortly murderèd. 150

Worcester. And for whose death we in the world's wide
mouth
Live scandalized and foully spoken of.

Hotspur. But soft, I pray you, did King Richard then
Proclaim my brother Edmund Mortimer
Heir to the crown?

Northumberland.　　He did, myself did hear it. 155

Hotspur. Nay, then I cannot blame his cousin king,
That wished him on the barren mountains starve.
But shall it be that you, that set the crown
Upon the head of this forgetful man,
And for his sake wear the detested blot 160
Of murderous subornation°—shall it be
That you a world of curses undergo,
Being the agents or base second means,
The cords, the ladder, or the hangman rather?
O, pardon me that I descend so low 165
To show the line° and the predicament°
Wherein you range under this subtle king!
Shall it for shame be spoken in these days,
Or fill up chronicles in time to come,
That men of your nobility and power 170
Did gage° them both in an unjust behalf
(As both of you, God pardon it, have done)
To put down Richard, that sweet lovely rose,

---

144 **next of blood** i.e., heir to the throne　147 **in us** at our hands　149 **intercepted** interrupted　161 **murderous subornation** confederacy in murder　166 **line** degree, station (but also "hangman's rope" [cf. line 164] and "tether" [cf. line 167])　166 **predicament** category (but also "perilous position")　171 **gage** pledge

And plant this thorn, this canker° Bolingbroke?
175 And shall it in more shame be further spoken
That you are fooled, discarded, and shook off
By him for whom these shames ye underwent?
No, yet time serves wherein you may redeem
Your banished honors and restore yourselves
180 Into the good thoughts of the world again;
Revenge the jeering and disdained contempt
Of this proud king, who studies day and night
To answer all the debt he owes to you
Even with the bloody payment of your deaths.°
Therefore I say—

185 *Worcester.*   Peace, cousin, say no more;
And now I will unclasp a secret book,
And to your quick-conceiving° discontents
I'll read you matter deep and dangerous,
As full of peril and adventurous spirit
190 As to o'erwalk a current roaring loud
On the unsteadfast footing of a spear.

Hotspur. If he fall in, good night, or sink, or swim!°
Send danger from the east unto the west,
So honor cross it from the north to south,
195 And let them grapple. O, the blood more stirs
To rouse a lion than to start a hare!

Northumberland. Imagination of some great exploit
Drives him beyond the bounds of patience.

Hotspur. By heaven, methinks it were an easy leap
200 To pluck bright honor from the pale-faced moon,
Or dive into the bottom of the deep,
Where fathom line could never touch the ground,
And pluck up drownèd honor by the locks,
So° he that doth redeem her thence might wear
205 Without corrival° all her dignities;
But out upon this half-faced fellowship!°

174 **canker** dog-rose (an inferior rose, but with suggestions of "cankerworm"
and "ulcer")   183–84 **debt ... deaths** pronounced enough alike in Elizabethan speech to invite puns, as here   187 **quick-conceiving** eagerly respon-
sive   192 **good ... swim** i.e., the man is doomed whether he sinks at once
or is swept away by the current   204 **So** provided   205 **corrival** partner
206 **out ... fellowship** down with this half-and-half sharing (of honors)

Worcester. He apprehends a world of figures° here,
  But not the form of what he should attend.
  Good cousin, give me audience for a while.

Hotspur. I cry you mercy.°   210

Worcester. Those same noble Scots that are your
  prisoners—

Hotspur. I'll keep them all.
  By God, he shall not have a Scot of them!
  No, if a Scot° would save his soul, he shall not.
  I'll keep them, by this hand!

Worcester.   You start away   215
  And lend no ear unto my purposes.
  Those prisoners you shall keep.

Hotspur.   Nay, I will! That's flat!
  He said he would not ransom Mortimer,
  Forbade my tongue to speak of Mortimer,
  But I will find him when he lies asleep,   220
  And in his ear I'll hollo "Mortimer."
  Nay, I'll have a starling shall be taught to speak
  Nothing but "Mortimer," and give it him
  To keep his anger still in motion.

Worcester. Hear you, cousin, a word.   225

Hotspur. All studies° here I solemnly defy°
  Save how to gall and pinch this Bolingbroke;
  And that same sword-and-buckler° Prince of Wales,
  But that I think his father loves him not
  And would be glad he met with some mischance,   230
  I would have him poisonèd with a pot of ale.°

Worcester. Farewell, kinsman: I'll talk to you
  When you are better tempered to attend.

---

207 **figures** (1) figures of speech (2) airy fancies (as opposed to substantial "form," line 208)   210 **cry you mercy** beg your pardon   214 **Scot** (pun on "scot," meaning "small payment")   226 **studies** interests   226 **defy** reject   228 **sword-and-buckler** "low-down" (sword and shield were arms of the lower classes)   231 **ale** (a further glance at Hal's presumed low tastes, gentlemen's drink being wine)

Northumberland. Why, what a wasp-stung and impa-
    tient fool
235 Art thou to break into this woman's mood,
    Tying thine ear to no tongue but thine own!

Hotspur. Why, look you, I am whipped and scourged
    with rods,
    Nettled, and stung with pismires,° when I hear
    Of this vile politician, Bolingbroke.
240 In Richard's time—what do you call the place?
    A plague upon it! It is in Gloucestershire;
    'Twas where the madcap duke his uncle kept,°
    His uncle York—where I first bowed my knee
    Unto this king of smiles, this Bolingbroke—
245 'Sblood!—when you and he came back from Ravens-
    purgh°—

Northumberland. At Berkeley Castle.

Hotspur. You say true.
    Why, what a candy deal° of courtesy
    This fawning greyhound then did proffer me!
250 "Look when his infant fortune came to age,"
    And "gentle Harry Percy," and "kind cousin"—
    O, the devil take such cozeners!°—God forgive me!
    Good uncle, tell your tale; I have done.

Worcester. Nay, if you have not, to it again.
    We will stay your leisure.

255 *Hotspur.*   I have done, i' faith.

Worcester. Then once more to your Scottish prisoners:
    Deliver them up without their ransom straight,
    And make the Douglas' son your only mean
    For powers in Scotland—which, for divers reasons
260 Which I shall send you written, be assured
    Will easily be granted. [*To Northumberland*] You,
    my lord,

---

238 **pismires** ants   242 **kept** dwelt   245 **Ravenspurgh** harbor in York-
shire (where Hotspur's father had gone to take sides with Bolingbroke—
who was returning from exile on the Continent—against the absent King
Richard II)   248 **candy deal** sugared bit   252 **cozeners** cheats (with
pun on "cousin" of previous line)

Your son in Scotland being thus employed,
Shall secretly into the bosom creep
Of that same noble prelate well-beloved,
The Archbishop.   265

Hotspur. Of York, is it not?

Worcester. True; who bears hard°
His brother's death at Bristow,° the Lord Scroop.
I speak not this in estimation,°
As what I think might be, but what I know   270
Is ruminated, plotted, and set down,
And only stays but to behold the face
Of that occasion that shall bring it on.

Hotspur. I smell it.° Upon my life, it will do well.

Northumberland. Before the game is afoot thou still
    let'st slip.°   275

Hotspur. Why, it cannot choose but be a noble plot.
And then the power of Scotland and of York
To join with Mortimer, ha?

Worcester.   And so they shall.

Hotspur. In faith, it is exceedingly well aimed.

Worcester. And 'tis no little reason bids us speed   280
To save our heads by raising of a head;°
For, bear ourselves as even as we can,
The King will always think him in our debt,
And think we think ourselves unsatisfied,
Till he hath found a time to pay us home.°   285
And see already how he doth begin
To make us strangers to his looks of love.

Hotspur. He does, he does! We'll be revenged on him.

Worcester. Cousin, farewell. No further go in this
Than I by letters shall direct your course.   290

---

267 **bears hard** (because his brother had been executed by Henry)
268 **Bristow** Bristol 269 **in estimation** as a guess 274 **smell it** i.e.,
like a hound catching the scent 275 **let'st slip** let loose (the dogs)
281 **head** army 285 **home** i.e., with a "home" thrust

When time is ripe, which will be suddenly,
I'll steal to Glendower and Lord Mortimer,
Where you and Douglas, and our pow'rs at once,
As I will fashion it, shall happily meet,
To bear our fortunes in our own strong arms,
Which now we hold at much uncertainty.

Northumberland. Farewell, good brother. We shall
thrive, I trust.

Hotspur. Uncle, adieu. O, let the hours be short
Till fields and blows and groans applaud our sport!
                                        Exeunt.

[ACT 2

Scene 1. *Rochester. An inn yard.*]

Enter a Carrier with a lantern in his hand.

First Carrier. Heigh-ho! An it be not four by the day,°
I'll be hanged. Charles' wain° is over the new chimney, and yet our horse not packed. What, ostler!

Ostler. [*Within*] Anon, anon.

First Carrier. I prithee, Tom, beat° Cut's saddle, put   5
a few flocks in the point;° poor jade is wrung in the
withers° out of all cess.°

Enter another Carrier.

Second Carrier. Peas and beans are as dank here as a
dog, and that is the next° way to give poor jades the
bots.° This house is turned upside down since Robin   10
Ostler died.

First Carrier. Poor fellow never joyed since the price
of oats rose; it was the death of him.

Second Carrier. I think this be the most villainous
house in all London road for fleas, I am stung like   15
a tench.°

2.1.1 **by the day** in the morning   2 **Charles' wain** the Great Bear
5 **beat** i.e., to soften it   6 **a few flocks in the point** a little padding in the
pommel   6–7 **wrung in the withers** rubbed raw at the shoulders   7 **out
of all cess** to excess   9 **next** nearest   10 **bots** worms   16 **tench** fish
with red spots (as if flea-bitten)

First Carrier. Like a tench? By the mass, there is ne'er
   a king christen could be better bit than I have been°
   since the first cock.°

20 *Second Carrier.* Why, they will allow us ne'er a jordan,° and then we leak in your chimney,° and your
   chamber-lye° breeds fleas like a loach.°

First Carrier. What, ostler! Come away and be hanged!
   Come away!

25 *Second Carrier.* I have a gammon° of bacon and two
   razes° of ginger, to be delivered as far as Charing
   Cross.

First Carrier. God's body! The turkeys in my pannier°
   are quite starved. What, ostler! A plague on thee,
30   hast thou never an eye in thy head? Canst not hear?
   And 'twere not as good deed as drink to break the
   pate on thee, I am a very villain. Come, and be
   hanged! Hast no faith in thee?

Enter Gadshill.

Gadshill. Good morrow, carriers, what's o'clock?

35 *First Carrier.* I think it be two o'clock.

Gadshill. I prithee lend me thy lantern to see my gelding in the stable.

First Carrier. Nay, by God, soft!° I know a trick worth
   two of that, i' faith.

40 *Gadshill.* I pray thee lend me thine.

Second Carrier. Ay, when? Canst tell?° Lend me thy
   lantern, quoth he? Marry, I'll see thee hanged first!

17–18 **there . . . been** i.e., not even a Christian king (though kings get the
best of everything) could have surpassed my record in fleabites   19 **the
first cock** midnight   20–21 **jordan** chamberpot   21 **chimney** fireplace
22 **chamber-lye** urine   22 **loach** fish that breeds often   25 **gammon**
haunch   26 **razes** roots   28 **pannier** basket   38 **soft** i.e., "listen to
him!"   41 **Ay, when? Canst tell?** (standard retort to an inopportune
request)

Gadshill. Sirrah carrier, what time do you mean to come to London?

Second Carrier. Time enough to go to bed with a   45
candle,° I warrant thee. Come, neighbor Mugs, we'll call up the gentlemen, they will along with company, for they have great charge.°   *Exeunt [Carriers].*

Gadshill. What, ho! Chamberlain!

Enter Chamberlain.

Chamberlain. "At hand,° quoth pickpurse."   50

Gadshill. That's even as fair as "at hand, quoth the chamberlain"; for thou variest no more from picking of purses than giving direction doth from laboring: thou layest the plot how.

Chamberlain. Good morrow, Master Gadshill. It holds   55
current° that I told you yesternight: there's a franklin° in the Wild° of Kent hath brought three hundred marks° with him in gold, I heard him tell it to one of his company last night at supper—a kind of auditor,° one that hath abundance of charge too,   60
God knows what. They are up already and call for eggs and butter, they will away presently.

Gadshill. Sirrah, if they meet not with Saint Nicholas' clerks,° I'll give thee this neck.

Chamberlain. No, I'll none of it; I pray thee keep that   65
for the hangman; for I know thou worshippest Saint Nicholas as truly as a man of falsehood may.

Gadshill. What talkest thou to me of the hangman? If I hang, I'll make a fat pair of gallows; for if I hang,

---

45–46 **Time . . . candle** (evasively spoken, the carriers being suspicious of Gadshill)   48 **charge** luggage   50 **At hand** (a popular tag meaning "Ready, sir!" but relevant here to the Chamberlain's filching way of life, as Gadshill points out)   56 **current** true   56–57 **franklin** rich farmer   57 **Wild** weald, open country   57–58 **three hundred marks** £200 (Elizabethan value)   60 **auditor** revenue officer   63–64 **Saint Nicholas' clerks** highwaymen (St. Nicholas was reckoned the patron of all travelers, including traveling thieves)

70   old Sir John hangs with me, and thou knowest he is
     no starveling. Tut! There are other Troyans° that
     thou dream'st not of, the which for sport sake are
     content to do the profession some grace; that would
     (if matters should be looked into) for their own
75   credit sake make all whole. I am joined with no foot-
     landrakers,° no long-staff sixpenny strikers,° none
     of these mad mustachio purple-hued maltworms;°
     but with nobility and tranquillity,° burgomasters and
     great oneyers,° such as can hold in,° such as will
80   strike sooner than speak,° and speak sooner than
     drink, and drink sooner than pray—and yet, zounds,
     I lie, for they pray continually to their saint, the com-
     monwealth, or rather, not pray to her, but prey on
     her, for they ride up and down on her and make her
85   their boots.°

     Chamberlain. What, the commonwealth their boots?
          Will she hold out water in foul way?°

     Gadshill. She will, she will! Justice hath liquored° her.
          We steal as in a castle, cocksure. We have the re-
90   ceipt of fernseed,° we walk invisible.

     Chamberlain. Nay, by my faith, I think you are more
          beholding to the night than to fernseed for your
          walking invisible.

     Gadshill. Give me thy hand. Thou shalt have a share
95   in our purchase,° as I am a true man.

     Chamberlain. Nay, rather let me have it, as you are a
          false thief.

     71 **Troyans** good fellows   75–76 **foot-landrakers** footloose vagabonds
     76 **long-staff sixpenny strikers** men who would pull you from your
     horse with long staves even to steal sixpence   77 **mustachio purple-
     hued maltworms** big-mustached purple-faced drunkards   78 **tranquil-
     lity** (Gadshill's witty coinage, on the analogy of "nobility": people who
     don't have to scrounge their living)   79 **oneyers** ones (?)   79 **hold in**
     keep confidence   80 **speak** i.e., say "hands up"   85 **boots** (with pun on
     "boots/booty")   87 **in foul way** on muddy roads   88 **liquored** (1)
     greased (as with boots) (2) made her drunk   89–90 **receipt of fernseed**
     recipe of fernseed (popularly supposed to render one invisible)   95 **pur-
     chase** (euphemism for loot)

Gadshill. Go to; "homo" is a common name to all
   men.° Bid the ostler bring my gelding out of the
   stable. Farewell, you muddy knave.   [*Exeunt.*]   *100*

[Scene 2. *The highway, near Gad's Hill.*]

Enter Prince, Poins, and Peto, etc.

Poins. Come, shelter, shelter! I have removed Falstaff's
   horse, and he frets° like a gummed velvet.

Prince. Stand close.   [*They step aside.*]

Enter Falstaff.

Falstaff. Poins! Poins, and be hanged! Poins!

Prince. [*Comes forward*] Peace, ye fat-kidneyed rascal!   *5*
   What a brawling dost thou keep!

Falstaff. Where's Poins, Hal?

Prince. He is walked up to the top of the hill; I'll go
   seek him.   [*Steps aside.*]

Falstaff. I am accursed to rob in that thief's company.   *10*
   The rascal hath removed my horse and tied him I
   know not where. If I travel but four foot by the
   squire° further afoot, I shall break my wind. Well,
   I doubt not but to die a fair death for all this, if I
   scape hanging for killing that rogue. I have forsworn   *15*
   his company hourly any time this two and twenty
   years, and yet I am bewitched with the rogue's company. If the rascal have not given me medicines to
   make me love him, I'll be hanged. It could not be
   else: I have drunk medicines. Poins! Hal! A plague   *20*

98–99 **homo ... men** the Latin for man, *homo* is a term that covers
all men, true (i.e., honest) or false   2.2.2 **frets** chafes (with pun on the
fretting or fraying of velvet as the gum used to stiffen it wore away)
13 **squire** rule

upon you both! Bardolph! Peto! I'll starve° ere I'll
rob a foot further. And 'twere not as good a deed
as drink to turn true man and to leave these rogues,
I am the veriest varlet that ever chewed with a tooth.
25   Eight yards of uneven ground is threescore and ten
miles afoot with me, and the stony-hearted villains
know it well enough. A plague upon it when thieves
cannot be true one to another! (*They whistle.*)
Whew! A plague upon you all! Give me my horse,
30   you rogues! Give me my horse and be hanged!

Prince. [*Comes forward*] Peace, ye fat-guts! Lie down,
lay thine ear close to the ground, and list if thou
canst hear the tread of travelers.

Falstaff. Have you any levers to lift me up again, being
35   down? 'Sblood, I'll not bear mine own flesh so far
afoot again for all the coin in thy father's exchequer.
What a plague mean ye to colt° me thus?

Prince. Thou liest, thou art not colted, thou art uncolted.°

40   *Falstaff.* I prithee, good Prince Hal, help me to my
horse, good king's son.

Prince. Out, ye rogue! Shall I be your ostler?

Falstaff. Hang thyself in thine own heir-apparent garters!° If I be ta'en, I'll peach° for this. And I have
45   not ballads made on you all, and sung to filthy tunes,
let a cup of sack be my poison. When a jest is so
forward—and afoot too—I hate it.

Enter Gadshill [*and Bardolph*].

Gadshill. Stand!

Falstaff. So I do, against my will.

___

21 **starve** die   37 **colt** trick   38–39 **uncolted** i.e., unhorsed   43–44 **heir-
apparent garters** (Falstaff adapts a proverbial phrase to fit a crown
prince)   44 **peach** inform on you

Poins. O, 'tis our setter;° I know his voice. [*Comes*　50
forward] Bardolph, what news?

Bardolph. Case ye, case ye! On with your vizards!
There's money of the King's coming down the hill;
'tis going to the King's exchequer.

Falstaff. You lie, ye rogue! 'Tis going to the King's　55
tavern.

Gadshill. There's enough to make us all—

Falstaff. To be hanged.

Prince. Sirs, you four shall front them in the narrow
lane; Ned Poins and I will walk lower: if they scape　60
from your encounter, then they light on us.

Peto. How many be there of them?

Gadshill. Some eight or ten.

Falstaff. Zounds, will they not rob us?

Prince. What, a coward, Sir John Paunch?　　65

Falstaff. Indeed, I am not John of Gaunt° your grandfather, but yet no coward, Hal.

Prince. Well, we leave that to the proof.°

Poins. Sirrah Jack, thy horse stands behind the hedge.
When thou need'st him, there thou shalt find him.　70
Farewell and stand fast.

Falstaff. Now cannot I strike him, if I should be
hanged.

Prince. [*Aside to Poins*] Ned, where are our disguises?

Poins. [*Aside to Prince*] Here, hard by. Stand close.　75
　　　　　　　　　　[*Exeunt Prince and Poins.*]

---

50 **setter** one who makes arrangements for a robbery　66 **John of
Gaunt** Hal's grandfather (but in reply to "Sir John Paunch" Falstaff puns
on "gaunt/thin" which Hal evidently is [cf. 2.4.244–48])　68 **proof** test

Falstaff. Now, my masters, happy man be his dole,° say I. Every man to his business.

Enter the Travelers.

Traveler. Come, neighbor. The boy shall lead our horses down the hill; we'll walk afoot awhile and
80 ease our legs.

Thieves. Stand!

Traveler. Jesus bless us!

Falstaff. Strike! Down with them! Cut the villains' throats! Ah, whoreson caterpillars!° Bacon-fed
85 knaves! They hate us youth. Down with them! Fleece them!

Traveler. O, we are undone, both we and ours forever!

Falstaff. Hang ye, gorbellied° knaves, are ye undone? No, ye fat chuffs;° I would your store° were here!
90 On, bacons, on! What, ye knaves, young men must live. You are grandjurors,° are ye? We'll jure ye, faith!   *Here they rob them and bind them. Exeunt.*

Enter the Prince and Poins [disguised].

Prince. The thieves have bound the true men. Now could thou and I rob the thieves and go merrily to
95 London, it would be argument° for a week, laughter for a month, and a good jest forever.

Poins. Stand close! I hear them coming.
     [They stand aside.]

Enter the thieves again.

Falstaff. Come, my masters, let us share, and then to horse before day. And the Prince and Poins be not
100 two arrant° cowards, there's no equity stirring.°

76 **happy man be his dole** may happiness be our lot   84 **whoreson caterpillars** miserable parasites   88 **gorbellied** great-bellied   89 **chuffs** misers   89 **store** total wealth   91 **grandjurors** i.e., men of substance (as required for service on a grand jury)   95 **be argument** make conversation   100 **arrant** thorough   100 **no equity stirring** i.e., no justice left alive

There's no more valor in that Poins than in a wild
duck.

Prince. Your money!

Poins. Villains!

{ *As they are sharing, the Prince
and Poins set upon them.
They all run away, and Falstaff, after a blow or two,
runs away too, leaving the
booty behind them.* }

Prince. Got with much ease. Now merrily to horse. The   105
thieves are all scattered, and possessed with fear so
strongly that they dare not meet each other: each
takes his fellow for an officer. Away, good Ned. Falstaff sweats to death and lards the lean earth as he
walks along. Were't not for laughing, I should pity   110
him.°

Poins. How the fat rogue roared!   *Exeunt.*

[Scene 3. *Northumberland. Warkworth Castle.*]

Enter Hotspur solus,° *reading a letter.*

Hotspur. "But, for mine own part, my lord, I could be
well contented to be there, in respect of the love I
bear your house."° He could be contented—why is
he not then? In respect of the love he bears our
house! He shows in this he loves his own barn better   5
than he loves our house. Let me see some more. "The
purpose you undertake is dangerous"—why, that's
certain! 'Tis dangerous to take a cold, to sleep, to
drink; but I tell you, my lord fool, out of this nettle,
danger, we pluck this flower, safety. "The purpose   10
you undertake is dangerous, the friends you have

105–11 **Got . . . him** (printed as verse by Pope and many later editors, with
line breaks after "horse/fear/other/officer/death/along/him")   2.3.s.d. **solus** alone (Latin)   3 **house** family

named uncertain, the time itself unsorted,° and your
whole plot too light for the counterpoise of so great
an opposition." Say you so, say you so? I say unto
15   you again, you are a shallow, cowardly hind,° and
you lie. What a lack-brain is this! By the Lord, our
plot is a good plot as ever was laid; our friends true
and constant: a good plot, good friends, and full of
expectation; an excellent plot, very good friends.
20   What a frosty-spirited rogue is this! Why, my Lord
of York° commends the plot and the general course
of the action. Zounds, and I were now by this rascal,
I could brain him with his lady's fan. Is there not my
father, my uncle, and myself; Lord Edmund Mor-
25   timer, my Lord of York, and Owen Glendower? Is
there not, besides, the Douglas? Have I not all their
letters to meet me in arms by the ninth of the next
month, and are they not some of them set forward
already? What a pagan° rascal is this, an infidel! Ha!
30   you shall see now, in very sincerity of fear and cold
heart will he to the King and lay open all our proceedings. Oh, I could divide myself and go to buffets°
for moving such a dish of skim milk with so honorable an action! Hang him, let him tell the King! We
35   are prepared. I will set forward tonight.

Enter his Lady.

How now, Kate? I must leave you within these two
hours.

Lady. O my good lord, why are you thus alone?
For what offense have I this fortnight been
40   A banished woman from my Harry's bed?
Tell me, sweet lord, what is't that takes from thee
Thy stomach,° pleasure, and thy golden sleep?
Why dost thou bend thine eyes upon the earth,
And start so often when thou sit'st alone?

---

12 **unsorted** unsuitable   15 **hind** menial   20–21 **my Lord of York** the
Archbishop of York (cf. 1.3.264ff)   29 **pagan** faithless   32 **divide . . .
buffets** split myself into two, and set the halves fighting   42 **stomach**
appetite

Why hast thou lost the fresh blood in thy cheeks   45
And given my treasures and my rights of thee
To thick-eyed musing and cursed° melancholy?
In thy faint slumbèrs I by thee have watched,°
And heard thee murmur tales of iron wars,
Speak terms of manage to thy bounding steed,   50
Cry "Courage! To the field!" And thou hast talked
Of sallies and retires, of trenches, tents,
Of palisadoes,° frontiers,° parapets,
Of basilisks,° of cannon, culverin,°
Of prisoners' ransom, and of soldiers slain,   55
And all the currents° of a heady° fight.
Thy spirit within thee hath been so at war,
And thus hath so bestirred thee in thy sleep,
That beads of sweat have stood upon thy brow
Like bubbles in a late-disturbèd stream,   60
And in thy face strange motions have appeared,
Such as we see when men restrain their breath
On some great sudden hest.° O, what portents are
    these?
Some heavy business hath my lord in hand,
And I must know it, else he loves me not.   65

Hotspur. What, ho!

[*Enter a Servant.*]

                    Is Gilliams with the packet gone?

Servant. He is, my lord, an hour ago.

Hotspur. Hath Butler brought those horses from the
    sheriff?

Servant. One horse, my lord, he brought even now.

Hotspur. What horse? A roan, a crop-ear, is it not?   70

Servant. It is, my lord.

---

47 **cursed** peevish   48 **watched** lain awake   53 **palisadoes** defenses
made of stakes   53 **frontiers** fortifications   54 **basilisks, culverin**
(sizes and types of cannon)   56 **currents** occurrences   56 **heady** violent   63 **hest** (1) command? (2) resolution?

Hotspur. That roan shall be my throne. Well, I will
    back him straight. O Esperance!° Bid Butler lead
    him forth into the park.°

[*Exit Servant.*]

75 *Lady.* But hear you, my lord.

Hotspur. What say'st thou, my lady?

Lady. What is it carries you away?°

Hotspur. Why, my horse, my love—my horse!

Lady. Out, you mad-headed ape! A weasel hath not
80   such a deal of spleen° as you are tossed with. In
    faith, I'll know your business, Harry, that I will! I
    fear my brother Mortimer doth stir about his title
    and hath sent for you to line° his enterprise; but if
    you go°—

85 *Hotspur.* So far afoot, I shall be weary, love.

Lady. Come, come, you paraquito,° answer me directly
    unto this question that I ask. In faith, I'll break thy
    little finger, Harry, and if thou wilt not tell me all
    things true.°

90 *Hotspur.* Away, away, you trifler! Love? I love thee not;
    I care not for thee, Kate. This is no world
    To play with mammets° and to tilt° with lips.
    We must have bloody noses and cracked crowns,°
    And pass them current too. Gods me,° my horse!
95   What say'st thou, Kate? What wouldst thou have
        with me?

---

73 **Esperance** hope (part of the Percy motto)   72–74 **That ... park**
(Pope and many later editors print as verse, with line breaks after
"throne/Esperance/park"   77 **away** (1) i.e., from home (2) from your
usual self   80 **spleen** caprice   83 **line** strengthen   79–84 **Out ... go**
(printed by Pope and many later editors as verse, but with a variety
of lineations)   86 **paraquito** parrot   86–89 **Come ... true** (printed
by Pope and many later editors as verse, with line breaks after
"me/ask/Harry/true"   92 **mammets** dolls   92 **tilt** duel   93 **crowns** (1)
heads (2) coins—which when "cracked" were hard to "pass current"
(possibly there is an allusion to the "crown" of kingship, which, though
not genuine when usurped, may be passed current by force)   94 **Gods
me** God save me

Lady. Do you not love me? Do you not indeed?
　Well, do not then; for since you love me not,
　I will not love myself. Do you not love me?
　Nay, tell me if you speak in jest or no.

Hotspur. Come, wilt thou see me ride?   *100*
　And when I am a-horseback, I will swear
　I love thee infinitely. But hark you, Kate:
　I must not have you henceforth question me
　Whither I go, nor reason whereabout.
　Whither I must, I must, and—to conclude,   *105*
　This evening must I leave you, gentle Kate.
　I know you wise—but yet no farther wise
　Than Harry Percy's wife; constant you are—
　But yet a woman; and for secrecy,
　No lady closer—for I well believe   *110*
　Thou wilt not utter what thou dost not know,
　And so far will I trust thee, gentle Kate—

Lady. How? So far?

Hotspur. Not an inch further. But hark you, Kate:
　Whither I go, thither shall you go too;   *115*
　Today will I set forth, tomorrow you.
　Will this content you, Kate?

Lady.　　　　　　　　　　　It must of force.° *Exeunt.*

[Scene 4. *Eastcheap. The tavern.°*]

Enter Prince and Poins.

Prince. Ned, prithee come out of that fat° room and
　lend me thy hand to laugh a little.

Poins. Where hast been, Hal?

---

117 **of force** of necessity   2.4.s.d. **tavern** (the tavern is said to be in
Eastcheap, but it is never explicitly named; references to a boar in
Henry IV [*Part Two*] suggest it is the Boar's Head)   1 **fat** hot

Prince. With three or four loggerheads° amongst three
5   or fourscore hogsheads. I have sounded the very
bass-string of humility. Sirrah, I am sworn brother
to a leash° of drawers° and can call them all by their
christen names, as Tom, Dick, and Francis. They
take it already upon their salvation° that, though I
10 be but Prince of Wales, yet I am the king of courtesy,
and tell me flatly I am no proud Jack° like Falstaff,
but a Corinthian,° a lad of mettle, a good boy (by
the Lord, so they call me!), and when I am King of
England I shall command all the good lads in East-
15 cheap. They call drinking deep, dyeing scarlet;° and
when you breathe in your watering,° they cry "hem!"
and bid you play it off.° To conclude, I am so good
a proficient in one quarter of an hour that I can drink
with any tinker in his own language during my life.
20 I tell thee, Ned, thou hast lost much honor that thou
wert not with me in this action. But, sweet Ned—
to sweeten which name of Ned, I give thee this
pennyworth of sugar,° clapped even now into my
hand by an under-skinker,° one that never spake
25 other English in his life than "Eight shillings and
sixpence," and "You are welcome," with this shrill
addition, "Anon,° anon, sir! Score° a pint of bas-
tard° in the Half-moon,"° or so—but, Ned, to drive
away the time till Falstaff come, I prithee do thou
30 stand in some by-room while I question my puny
drawer to what end he gave me the sugar; and do
thou never leave calling "Francis!" that his tale to
me may be nothing but "Anon!" Step aside, and I'll
show thee a precedent.°

---

4 **loggerheads** blockheads   7 **leash** trio   7 **drawers** tapsters   9 **take . . . salvation** pledge their salvation   11 **Jack** fellow   12 **Corinthian** gay blade   15 **dyeing scarlet** i.e., from the complexion it gives a man   16 **breathe in your watering** pause for breath while drinking   17 **play it off** down it   23 **sugar** i.e., for sweetening wine (cf. 1.2.117)   24 **under-skinker** under-tapster   27 **Anon** i.e., (I'm coming) at once   27 **Score** charge   27–28 **bastard** Spanish wine   28 **Half-moon** one of the inn's rooms   34 **precedent** example

Poins. Francis!   35

Prince. Thou art perfect.

Poins. Francis!   *[Poins steps aside.]*

          Enter [Francis, a] Drawer.

Francis. Anon, anon, sir. Look down into the Pom-
    garnet,° Ralph.

Prince. Come hither, Francis.   40

Francis. My Lord?

Prince. How long hast thou to serve,° Francis?

Francis. Forsooth, five years, and as much as to—

Poins. [*Within*] Francis!

Francis. Anon, anon, sir.   45

Prince. Five year! By'r Lady,° a long lease for the clink-
    ing of pewter. But, Francis, darest thou be so valiant
    as to play the coward with thy indenture° and show
    it a fair pair of heels and run from it?

Francis. O Lord, sir, I'll be sworn upon all the books   50
    in England I could find in my heart—

Poins. [*Within*] Francis!

Francis. Anon, sir.

Prince. How old art thou, Francis?

Francis. Let me see: about Michaelmas° next I shall   55
    be—

Poins. [*Within*] Francis!

Francis. Anon, sir. Pray stay a little, my lord.

Prince. Nay, but hark you, Francis. For the sugar thou
    gavest me—'twas a pennyworth, was't not?   60

38–39 **Pomgarnet** Pomegranate (another of the inn's rooms)   42 **serve**
i.e., as an apprentice (apprenticeship ran for seven years)   46 **By'r Lady**
by Our Lady (mild oath)   48 **indenture** contract   55 **Michaelmas** September 29

Francis. O Lord! I would it had been two!

Prince. I will give thee for it a thousand pound. Ask me when thou wilt, and thou shalt have it.

Poins. [*Within*] Francis!

65 · *Francis.* Anon, anon.

Prince. Anon, Francis?° No, Francis; but tomorrow, Francis; or, Francis, a Thursday; or indeed, Francis, when thou wilt. But, Francis—

Francis. My lord?

70 *Prince.* Wilt thou rob this leathern-jerkin, crystal-button, knot-pated, agate-ring, puke-stocking, caddis-garter, smooth-tongue, Spanish-pouch?°

Francis. O Lord, sir, who do you mean?

Prince. Why then, your brown bastard is your only
75 drink; for look you, Francis, your white canvas doublet will sully. In Barbary, sir, it cannot come to so much.°

Francis. What, sir?

Poins. [*Within*] Francis!

80 *Prince.* Away, you rogue! Dost thou not hear them call?

> *Here they both call him. The Drawer stands amazed, not knowing which way to go.*

> *Enter Vintner.°*

Vintner. What, stand'st thou still, and hear'st such a calling? Look to the guests within. [*Exit Francis.*]

---

66 **Anon, Francis?** (Hal pretends to take Francis' "anon"—at once—to Poins as meaning he wants the thousand pounds at once)   70–72 **this . . . Spanish-pouch** i.e., the innkeeper, whose middle-class appearance Hal details: leather jacket with crystal buttons, short hair, agate ring, wool stockings, plain worsted (not fancy) garters, ingratiating (and probably unctuous) speech, money pouch of Spanish leather   74–77 **Why . . . much** (semi-nonsense; but the implication seems clear that Francis must stick to his trade)   80 s.d. **Vintner** the innkeeper

My lord, old Sir John, with half a dozen more, are
at the door. Shall I let them in?

Prince. Let them alone awhile, and then open the door.   85
[*Exit Vintner.*] Poins!

Poins. [*Within*] Anon, anon, sir.

Enter Poins.

Prince. Sirrah, Falstaff and the rest of the thieves are at
the door. Shall we be merry?

Poins. As merry as crickets, my lad. But hark ye; what   90
cunning match have you made with this jest of the
drawer? Come, what's the issue?°

Prince. I am now of all humors that have showed themselves humors since the old days of goodman Adam
to the pupil age of this present twelve o'clock at   95
midnight.°

[*Enter Francis.*]

What's o'clock, Francis?

Francis. Anon, anon, sir.   [*Exit.*]

Prince. That ever this fellow should have fewer words
than a parrot, and yet the son of a woman! His in-   100
dustry is upstairs and downstairs, his eloquence the
parcel of a reckoning.° I am not yet of Percy's mind,
the Hotspur of the North: he that kills me some six
or seven dozen of Scots at a breakfast, washes his
hands, and says to his wife, "Fie upon this quiet   105
life! I want work." "O my sweet Harry," says she,
"how many hast thou killed today?" "Give my roan
horse a drench,"° says he, and answers "Some fourteen," an hour after, "a trifle, a trifle." I prithee call in
Falstaff. I'll play Percy, and that damned brawn°   110

92 **issue** outcome, point (of the jest)   93–96 **I ... midnight** I am ready
for every kind of gaiety that men have invented since the beginning of the
world   100–02 **His industry ... reckoning** his whole activity is running up and down stairs, his whole conversation the totaling of bills
108 **drench** dose of medicine   110 **brawn** fat boar

shall play Dame Mortimer his wife. "Rivo!"° says
the drunkard. Call in Ribs, call in Tallow.

Enter Falstaff, [Gadshill, Bardolph, and Peto;
Francis follows with wine].

Poins. Welcome, Jack. Where hast thou been?

Falstaff. A plague of° all cowards, I say, and a ven-
115   geance too! Marry and amen! Give me a cup of sack,
        boy. Ere I lead this life long, I'll sew netherstocks,°
        and mend them and foot them too. A plague of all
        cowards! Give me a cup of sack, rogue. Is there no
        virtue extant?   *He drinketh.*

120 *Prince.* Didst thou never see Titan° kiss a dish of butter
        (pitiful-hearted Titan!) that melted at the sweet tale
        of the sun's? If thou didst, then behold that com-
        pound.

Falstaff. You rogue, here's lime° in this sack too! There
125   is nothing but roguery to be found in villainous man.
        Yet a coward is worse than a cup of sack with lime
        in it—a villainous coward! Go thy ways, old Jack,
        die when thou wilt; if manhood, good manhood, be
        not forgot upon the face of the earth, then am I a
130   shotten herring.° There lives not three good men un-
        hanged in England; and one of them is fat, and grows
        old. God help the while! A bad world, I say. I would
        I were a weaver; I could sing psalms° or anything. A
        plague of all cowards, I say still!

135 *Prince.* How now, woolsack? What mutter you?

Falstaff. A king's son! If I do not beat thee out of thy

---

111 **Rivo** (drinking cry of uncertain meaning)   114 **of** on   116 **nether-
stocks** stockings   120 **Titan** the sun (of which Hal is possibly reminded
by Falstaff's broad face, and his melting effect on the sack)   124 **lime**
(added to make poor wine seem dry and clear)   130 **shotten herring** herring that has cast its roe (and is therefore long and lean)
132–33 **God . . . psalms** (Falstaff reassumes his role of comic Puritan:
English weavers were often psalm-singing Protestants who had fled from
the Roman Catholic continent)

kingdom with a dagger of lath° and drive all thy
subjects afore thee like a flock of wild geese, I'll never
wear hair on my face more. You Prince of Wales?

Prince. Why, you whoreson round man, what's the   *140*
matter?

Falstaff. Are not you a coward? Answer me to that—
and Poins there?

Poins. Zounds, ye fat paunch, and ye call me coward,
by the Lord, I'll stab thee.   *145*

Falstaff. I call thee coward? I'll see thee damned ere I
call thee coward, but I would give a thousand pound
I could run as fast as thou canst. You are straight
enough in the shoulders; you care not who sees your
back. Call you that backing of your friends? A plague   *150*
upon such backing, give me them that will face me.
Give me a cup of sack. I am a rogue if I drunk today.

Prince. O villain, thy lips are scarce wiped since thou
drunk'st last.

Falstaff. All is one for that. (*He drinketh.*) A plague   *155*
of all cowards, still say I.

Prince. What's the matter?

Falstaff. What's the matter? There be four of us here
have ta'en a thousand pound this day morning.

Prince. Where is it, Jack, where is it?   *160*

Falstaff. Where is it? Taken from us it is. A hundred
upon poor four of us!

Prince. What, a hundred, man?

Falstaff. I am a rogue if I were not at half-sword° with
a dozen of them two hours together. I have scaped   *165*
by miracle. I am eight times thrust through the dou-

---

137 **dagger of lath** wooden dagger (by this phrase Falstaff associates
himself with a character called "the Vice" in the old religious plays, who
drove the devil offstage by beating him with a wooden dagger)   164 **at
half-sword** infighting at close quarters

blet,° four through the hose;° my buckler cut
through and through; my sword hacked like a hand-
saw—*ecce signum!*° I never dealt° better since I was
170   a man. All would not do. A plague of all cowards!
Let them speak. If they speak more or less than
truth, they are villains and the sons of darkness.°

Prince. Speak, sirs. How was it?

Gadshill. We four set upon some dozen—

175   *Falstaff.* Sixteen at least, my lord.

Gadshill. And bound them.

Peto. No, no, they were not bound.

Falstaff. You rogue, they were bound, every man of
them, or I am a Jew else—an Ebrew Jew.

180   *Gadshill.* As we were sharing, some six or seven fresh
men set upon us—

Falstaff. And unbound the rest, and then come in the
other.°

Prince. What, fought you with them all?

185   *Falstaff.* All? I know not what you call all, but if I
fought not with fifty of them, I am a bunch of radish!° If there were not two or three and fifty° upon
poor old Jack, then am I no two-legged creature.

Prince. Pray God you have not murd'red some of them.

190   *Falstaff.* Nay, that's past praying for. I have peppered
two of them. Two I am sure I have paid,° two rogues
in buckram suits. I tell thee what, Hal—if I tell thee
a lie, spit in my face, call me horse. Thou knowest

166–67 **doublet** Elizabethan upper garment   167 **hose** Elizabethan breeches
169 **ecce signum** behold the evidence (Latin; spoken as he shows his sword)
169 **dealt** i.e., dealt blows   172 **sons of darkness** i.e., damned (but cf. also
1.2.24)   183 **other** others   186–87 **bunch of radish** (again an object long
and lean)   187 **three and fifty** (fifty-three was the number of Spanish ships
popularly reputed to have opposed Sir Richard Grenville at the battle of the
Azores in 1591; Falstaff thus humorously claims for his fight the status of a national epic)   191 **paid** settled with

my old ward:° here I lay, and thus I bore my point.
Four rogues in buckram let drive at me.   195

Prince. What, four? Thou saidst but two even now.

Falstaff. Four, Hal. I told thee four.

Poins. Ay, ay, he said four.

Falstaff. These four came all afront and mainly° thrust
at me. I made me no more ado but took all their   200
seven points in my target, thus.

Prince. Seven? Why, there were but four even now.

Falstaff. In buckram?

Poins. Ay, four, in buckram suits.

Falstaff. Seven, by these hilts, or I am a villain else.   205

Prince. [*Aside to Poins*] Prithee let him alone. We shall
have more anon.

Falstaff. Dost thou hear me, Hal?

Prince. Ay, and mark° thee too, Jack.

Falstaff. Do so, for it is worth the list'ning to. These   210
nine in buckram that I told thee of—

Prince. So, two more already.

Falstaff. Their points being broken—

Poins. Down fell their hose.°

Falstaff. Began to give me ground; but I followed me   215
close, came in, foot and hand, and with a thought°
seven of the eleven I paid.

Prince. O monstrous! Eleven buckram men grown out
of two!

Falstaff. But, as the devil would have it, three misbe-   220

---

194 **ward** fencing posture   199 **mainly** mightily   209 **mark** pay close
attention to   214 **Down fell their hose** (Poins wittily takes "points" in
the sense of laces holding the breeches to the doublet)   216 **with a
thought** quick as a thought

gotten knaves in Kendal green came at my back and
let drive at me; for it was so dark, Hal, that thou
couldest not see thy hand.

Prince. These lies are like their father° that begets them
225   —gross as a mountain, open, palpable. Why, thou
clay-brained guts, thou knotty-pated° fool, thou
whoreson obscene greasy tallow-catch°—

Falstaff. What, art thou mad? Art thou mad? Is not
the truth the truth?

230 *Prince.* Why, how couldst thou know these men in Kendal green when it was so dark thou couldst not see
thy hand? Come, tell us your reason. What sayest
thou to this?

Poins. Come, your reason, Jack, your reason.

235 *Falstaff.* What, upon compulsion? Zounds, and I were
at the strappado° or all the racks in the world, I
would not tell you on compulsion. Give you a reason on compulsion? If reasons° were as plentiful as
blackberries, I would give no man a reason upon
240 compulsion, I.

Prince. I'll be no longer guilty of this sin; this sanguine°
coward, this bed-presser, this horseback-breaker,
this huge hill of flesh—

Falstaff. 'Sblood, you starveling, you eel-skin, you dried
245 neat's tongue,° you bull's pizzle,° you stockfish°—
O for breath to utter what is like thee!—you tailor's
yard, you sheath, you bowcase, you vile standing
tuck!°

Prince. Well, breathe awhile, and then to it again; and

---

224 **lies . . . father** i.e. (1) Falstaff, who invents them (2) the Devil, who
is the "Father of lies"   226 **knotty-pated** blockheaded   227 **tallow-
catch** (1) pan to catch drippings under roasting meat? (2) tallow-keech,
i.e., roll of fat for making candles?   236 **strappado** instrument of torture   238 **reasons** (pronounced like "raisins," and hence comparable to
blackberries)   241 **sanguine** ruddy (and hence valorous-seeming)
245 **neat's tongue** ox-tongue   245 **pizzle** penis   245 **stockfish** dried
codfish   247–48 **standing tuck** upright rapier

when thou hast tired thyself in base comparisons,   250
hear me speak but this.

Poins. Mark, Jack.

Prince. We two saw you four set on four, and bound
them and were masters of their wealth. Mark now
how a plain tale shall put you down. Then did we   255
two set on you four and, with a word,° outfaced you
from your prize, and have it; yea, and can show it
you here in the house. And, Falstaff, you carried your
guts away as nimbly, with as quick dexterity, and
roared for mercy, and still run and roared, as ever   260
I heard bullcalf. What a slave art thou to hack thy
sword as thou hast done, and then say it was in fight!
What trick, what device, what starting hole° canst
thou now find out to hide thee from this open and
apparent shame?   265

Poins. Come, let's hear, Jack. What trick hast thou
now?

Falstaff. By the Lord, I knew ye as well as he that made
ye. Why, hear you, my masters. Was it for me to
kill the heir apparent? Should I turn upon the true   270
prince? Why, thou knowest I am as valiant as Her-
cules, but beware instinct. The lion will not touch
the true prince.° Instinct is a great matter. I was now
a coward on instinct. I shall think the better of myself, and thee, during my life—I for a valiant lion,   275
and thou for a true prince. But, by the Lord, lads,
I am glad you have the money. Hostess, clap to
the doors. Watch tonight, pray tomorrow.° Gallants,
lads, boys, hearts of gold, all the titles of good fellowship come to you! What, shall we be merry? Shall   280
we have a play extempore?

---

256 **with a word** (1) in brief? (2) with a mere shout to scare you?
263 **starting hole** hiding place   272–73 **The lion ... prince** (a traditional belief about lions)   278 **Watch ... tomorrow** cf. Matthew 26:41
"Watch and pray, that ye enter not into temptation." (Falstaff puns on
"watch," which means "carouse" as well as "keep vigil")

Prince. Content—and the argument° shall be thy running away.

Falstaff. Ah, no more of that, Hal, and thou lovest me!

Enter Hostess.

285 *Hostess.* O Jesu, my lord the Prince!

Prince. How now, my lady the hostess? What say'st thou to me?

Hostess. Marry, my lord, there is a nobleman of the court at door would speak with you. He says he comes from your father.

290

Prince. Give him as much as will make him a royal man,° and send him back again to my mother.

Falstaff. What manner of man is he?

Hostess. An old man.

295 *Falstaff.* What doth gravity° out of his bed at midnight? Shall I give him his answer?

Prince. Prithee do, Jack.

Falstaff. Faith, and I'll send him packing.   *Exit.*

Prince. Now, sirs. By'r Lady, you fought fair; so did you, Peto; so did you, Bardolph. You are lions too, you ran away upon instinct, you will not touch the true prince; no—fie!

300

Bardolph. Faith, I ran when I saw others run.

Prince. Faith, tell me now in earnest, how came Falstaff's sword so hacked?

305

Peto. Why, he hacked it with his dagger, and said he would swear truth out of England but he would make you believe it was done in fight, and persuaded us to do the like.

---

282 **argument** subject   291–92 **royal man** cf. "noble" in the previous speech, but with a pun on the "royal," a coin worth ten shillings, which was of greater value than the "noble," worth six shillings eight pence 295 **gravity** i.e., sober age

Bardolph. Yea, and to tickle our noses with speargrass   *310*
to make them bleed, and then to beslubber our garments with it and swear it was the blood of true men.
I did that° I did not this seven year before—I
blushed to hear his monstrous devices.

Prince. O villain! Thou stolest a cup of sack eighteen   *315*
years ago and wert taken with the manner,° and ever
since thou hast blushed extempore. Thou hadst fire°
and sword on thy side, and yet thou ran'st away.
What instinct hadst thou for it?

Bardolph. My lord, do you see these meteors?° Do you   *320*
behold these exhalations?°

Prince. I do.

Bardolph. What think you they portend?

Prince. Hot livers and cold purses.°

Bardolph. Choler,° my lord, if rightly taken.   *325*

Prince. No, if rightly taken, halter.

Enter Falstaff.

Here comes lean Jack; here comes bare-bone. How
now, my sweet creature of bombast?° How long is't
ago, Jack, since thou sawest thine own knee?

Falstaff. My own knee? When I was about thy years,   *330*
Hal, I was not an eagle's talent° in the waist; I could
have crept into any alderman's thumb-ring. A plague
of sighing and grief, it blows a man up like a bladder.
There's villainous news abroad. Here was Sir John
Bracy from your father: you must to the court in   *335*

---

313 **that** what   316 **taken with the manner** caught with the goods
317 **fire** i.e., the alcoholic hue of Bardolph's face   320, 321 **meteors,
exhalations** i.e., the pimples and other features of Bardolph's face, spoken of as if they were meteorological portents   324 **Hot livers and cold
purses** (the two notable results of excessive drink)   325 **Choler** anger
(Bardolph implies that he is choleric, and therefore no coward; Hal proceeds to understand "choler" as "collar," which in Bardolph's case will
be—if "rightly taken"—the hangman's noose)   328 **bombast** cotton
stuffing   331 **talent** talon

the morning. That same mad fellow of the north,
Percy, and he of Wales that gave Amamon the bas-
tinado, and made Lucifer cuckold, and swore the
devil his true liegeman upon the cross of a Welsh
340　hook°—what a plague call you him?

Poins. Owen Glendower.

Falstaff. Owen, Owen—the same; and his son-in-law
Mortimer, and old Northumberland, and that
sprightly Scot of Scots, Douglas, that runs a-horse-
345　back up a hill perpendicular—

Prince. He that rides at high speed and with his pistol
kills a sparrow flying.

Falstaff. You have hit it.

Prince. So did he never the sparrow.

350　*Falstaff.* Well, that rascal hath good metal° in him; he
will not run.

Prince. Why, what a rascal art thou then, to praise him
so for running!

Falstaff. A-horseback, ye cuckoo! But afoot he will not
355　budge a foot.

Prince. Yes, Jack, upon instinct.

Falstaff. I grant ye, upon instinct. Well, he is there too,
and one Mordake, and a thousand bluecaps° more.
Worcester is stol'n away tonight; thy father's beard
360　is turned white with the news; you may buy land
now as cheap as stinking mack'rel.

Prince. Why then, it is like, if there come a hot June,
and this civil buffeting hold, we shall buy maidenheads as they buy hobnails, by the hundreds.°

337–40 **he of Wales . . . hook** (Falstaff alludes to Glendower's supposed
magical powers: he has cudgeled a devil named Amamon, made horns
grow on Lucifer, and forced the devil to swear allegiance to him on the
cross of a weapon that has no cross)　350 **good metal** (with pun on
"mettle," spirit, courage)　358 **bluecaps** Scots　362–64 **if there . . .
hundreds** (the Prince applies the analogy of selling cheap what won't
keep to the reactions of virgins as they see all the men going off to war)

Falstaff. By the mass, lad, thou sayest true; it is like we   365
shall have good trading that way. But tell me, Hal,
art not thou horrible afeard? Thou being heir apparent, could the world pick thee out three such enemies again as that fiend Douglas, that spirit Percy,
and that devil Glendower? Art thou not horribly   370
afraid? Doth not thy blood thrill° at it?

Prince. Not a whit, i' faith. I lack some of thy instinct.

Falstaff. Well, thou wilt be horribly chid tomorrow
when thou comest to thy father. If thou love me,
practice an answer.   375

Prince. Do thou stand for my father and examine me
upon the particulars of my life.

Falstaff. Shall I? Content. This chair shall be my state,°
this dagger my scepter, and this cushion my crown.

Prince. Thy state is taken for° a joined-stool, thy golden   380
scepter for a leaden dagger, and thy precious rich
crown for a pitiful bald crown.

Falstaff. Well, and the fire of grace be not quite out of
thee, now shalt thou be moved. Give me a cup of
sack to make my eyes look red, that it may be   385
thought I have wept; for I must speak in passion,
and I will do it in King Cambyses' vein.°

Prince. Well, here is my leg.

Falstaff. And here is my speech. Stand aside, nobility.°

Hostess. O Jesu, this is excellent sport, i' faith!   390

Falstaff. Weep not, sweet queen,° for trickling tears are
vain.

---

371 **thrill** shiver (with fear)   378 **state** chair of state   380 **taken for**
(either "seen to be merely," or, alternatively, this is a meditative comment, possibly an aside, in the detached vein of 1.2.199 and 2.4.481, with
"thy" referring to the King)   387 **King Cambyses' vein** i.e., the old
ranting style of Preston's *King Cambyses* (1569)   389 **nobility** (addressed to his motley ragamuffins)   391 **queen** (addressed to the Hostess, who is evidently tearful with laughter; probably with a standard pun
on *quean* = tart, prostitute)

Hostess. O, the Father, how he holds his countenance!°

Falstaff. For God's sake, lords, convey my tristful°
queen!
For tears do stop the floodgates of her eyes.

395 *Hostess.* O Jesu, he doth it as like one of these harlotry°
players as ever I see!

Falstaff. Peace, good pintpot. Peace, good tickle-brain.
Harry, I do not only marvel where thou spendest thy
time, but also how thou art accompanied. For
400 though the camomile,° the more it is trodden on, the
faster it grows, so° youth, the more it is wasted, the
sooner it wears. That thou art my son I have partly
thy mother's word, partly my own opinion, but
chiefly a villainous trick° of thine eye and a foolish
405 hanging of thy nether lip that doth warrant me. If
then thou be son to me, here lies the point: why,
being son to me, art thou so pointed at? Shall the
blessed sun of heaven prove a micher and eat blackberries?° A question not to be asked. Shall the son°
410 of England prove a thief and take purses? A question
to be asked. There is a thing, Harry, which thou
hast often heard of, and it is known to many in our
land by the name of pitch. This pitch (as ancient
writers do report) doth defile; so doth the company
415 thou keepest. For, Harry, now I do not speak to
thee in drink, but in tears; not in pleasure, but in
passion; not in words only, but in woes also: and
yet there is a virtuous man whom I have often noted
in thy company, but I know not his name.

---

392 **holds his countenance** keeps a straight face   393 **tristful** sad
395 **harlotry** rascally   400 **camomile** aromatic herb (Falstaff proceeds
to satirize the highflown style of the court by using a manner of speech
called euphuism—from John Lily's fictional narrative, *Euphues* [1578]
which introduced it—based on similes drawn from natural history, intri-
cate balance, antithesis, and repetition of sounds, words, and ideas)
401 **so** (some editors emend to "yet," but the imperfect logical correspon-
dence of "though . . . so" may be part of Falstaff's mockery)   404 **trick**
mannerism (possibly a twitch)   408–09 **prove . . . blackberries** be a
truant from duty and go blackberrying   409 **son** (with pun on "sun," the
royal symbol)

Prince. What manner of man, and it like your Majesty?   *420*

Falstaff. A goodly portly° man, i' faith, and a corpulent;° of a cheerful look, a pleasing eye, and a most
noble carriage; and, as I think, his age some fifty,
or, by'r Lady, inclining to threescore; and now I remember me, his name is Falstaff. If that man should   *425*
be lewdly given,° he deceiveth me; for, Harry, I see
virtue in his looks. If then the tree may be known by
the fruit,° as the fruit by the tree, then, peremptorily°
I speak it, there is virtue in that Falstaff. Him keep
with, the rest banish. And tell me now, thou naughty   *430*
varlet, tell me where hast thou been this month?

Prince. Dost thou speak like a king? Do thou stand for
me, and I'll play my father.

Falstaff. Depose me? If thou dost it half so gravely, so
majestically, both in word and matter, hang me up   *435*
by the heels for a rabbit-sucker° or a poulter's hare.

Prince. Well, here I am set.

Falstaff. And here I stand. Judge, my masters.

Prince. Now, Harry, whence come you?

Falstaff. My noble lord, from Eastcheap.   *440*

Prince. The complaints I hear of thee are grievous.

Falstaff. 'Sblood, my lord, they are false! Nay, I'll
tickle ye for a young prince,° i' faith.

Prince. Swearest thou, ungracious boy? Henceforth
ne'er look on me. Thou art violently carried away   *445*
from grace. There is a devil haunts thee in the likeness of an old fat man; a tun° of man is thy companion. Why dost thou converse with that trunk of

---

421 **portly** stately   421–22 **corpulent** well filled out   426 **lewdly given**
inclined to evil-doing   427–28 **If . . . fruit** cf. Matthew 12:33: "The tree
is known by his fruit"   428 **peremptorily** decisively   436 **rabbit-
sucker** suckling rabbit   442–43 **I'll . . . prince** I'll act a prince that will
amuse you   447 **tun** hogshead

humors,° that bolting-hutch° of beastliness, that
450   swoll'n parcel of dropsies,° that huge bombard° of
sack, that stuffed cloakbag of guts, that roasted
Manningtree° ox with the pudding in his belly, that
reverend vice,° that gray iniquity,° that father
ruffian,° that vanity° in years? Wherein is he good,
455   but to taste sack and drink it? Wherein neat and
cleanly, but to carve a capon and eat it? Wherein
cunning, but in craft?° Wherein crafty, but in
villainy? Wherein villainous, but in all things?
Wherein worthy, but in nothing?

460   *Falstaff.* I would your Grace would take me with you.°
Whom means your Grace?

Prince. That villainous abominable misleader of youth,
Falstaff, that old white-bearded Satan.

Falstaff. My lord, the man I know.

465   *Prince.* I know thou dost.

Falstaff. But to say I know more harm in him than in
myself were to say more than I know. That he is old,
the more the pity, his white hairs do witness it; but
that he is, saving your reverence, a whoremaster,
470   that I utterly deny. If sack and sugar be a fault, God
help the wicked! If to be old and merry be a sin,
then many an old host that I know is damned. If to
be fat be to be hated, then Pharaoh's lean kine° are
to be loved. No, my good lord: banish Peto, banish
475   Bardolph, banish Poins; but for sweet Jack Falstaff,
kind Jack Falstaff, true Jack Falstaff, valiant Jack

448–49 **trunk of humors** receptacle of body fluids (with allusion to the
diseases that were thought to be the product of these fluids)   449 **bolting-
hutch** sifting-bin (where impurities collect)   450 **dropsies** internal fluids   450 **bombard** leather wine vessel   452 **Manningtree** town in
Essex (where at annual fairs plays were acted and, evidently, great oxen
were stuffed and barbecued)   453–54 **vice, iniquity, ruffian, vanity**
(names intended to associate Falstaff with characters of the old morality
plays, all of whom were corrupters of virtue. But unlike Falstaff, who
ought to know better, *they* were young)   456–57 **Wherein cunning, but
in craft** i.e., wherein skillful but in underhanded skills   460 **take me
with you** let me follow your meaning   473 **kine** cows (cf. Genesis
41:19–21)

Falstaff, and therefore more valiant being, as he is,
old Jack Falstaff, banish not him thy Harry's company, banish not him thy Harry's company, banish
plump Jack, and banish all the world!   480

Prince. I do, I will.   [*A knocking heard.*
        Exeunt Hostess, Francis, and Bardolph.]

        Enter Bardolph, running.

Bardolph. O, my lord, my lord! The sheriff with a most
monstrous watch° is at the door.

Falstaff. Out, ye rogue! Play out the play, I have much   485
to say in the behalf of that Falstaff.

        Enter the Hostess.

Hostess. O Jesu, my lord, my lord!

Prince. Heigh, heigh, the devil rides upon a fiddlestick!
What's the matter?

Hostess. The sheriff and all the watch are at the door.
They are come to search the house. Shall I let   490
them in?

Falstaff. Dost thou hear, Hal? Never call a true piece
of gold a counterfeit. Thou art essentially made without seeming so.°

Prince. And thou a natural coward without instinct.   495

Falstaff. I deny your major.° If you will deny the sheriff, so; if not, let him enter. If I become not a cart° as
well as another man, a plague on my bringing up!
I hope I shall as soon be strangled with a halter as
another.   500

Prince. Go hide thee behind the arras.° The rest walk
up above. Now, my masters, for a true face and good
conscience.

483 **watch** group of constables   492–94 **Never ... so** (a difficult passage, perhaps meaning that Falstaff, as a true piece of gold despite appearances, should not be turned over to the sheriff by a royal friend who is
also true gold despite appearances)   496 **major** i.e., major premise, with
pun on "mayor"   497 **cart** hangman's cart   501 **arras** wall-hanging

Falstaff. Both which I have had; but their date is out,
505   and therefore I'll hide me.   *Exit.*

Prince. Call in the sheriff.
          [*Exeunt all but the Prince and Peto.*]
          Enter Sheriff and the Carrier.

Now, master sheriff, what is your will with me?

Sheriff. First, pardon me, my lord. A hue and cry
   Hath followed certain men unto this house.

510   *Prince.* What men?

Sheriff. One of them is well known, my gracious lord—
   A gross fat man.

Carrier.   As fat as butter.

Prince. The man, I do assure you, is not here,
   For I myself at this time have employed him.°
515   And, sheriff, I will engage my word to thee
   That I will by tomorrow dinner time
   Send him to answer thee, or any man,
   For anything he shall be charged withal;
   And so let me entreat you leave the house.

520   *Sheriff.* I will, my lord. There are two gentlemen
   Have in this robbery lost three hundred marks.

Prince. It may be so. If he have robbed these men,
   He shall be answerable; and so farewell.

Sheriff. Good night, my noble lord.

525   *Prince.* I think it is good morrow, is it not?

Sheriff. Indeed, my lord, I think it be two o'clock.
          Exit [*with Carrier*].

Prince. This oily rascal is known as well as Paul's. Go
   call him forth.

513–14 **The man ... him** (Hal's reply is equivocal: Falstaff is not
"here," in the heir-apparent's presence, but "employed" behind the arras)

Peto. Falstaff! Fast asleep behind the arras, and snort-
　　ing° like a horse.　　　　　　　　　　　　　　　　*530*

Prince. Hark how hard he fetches breath. Search his
　　pockets.
　　　He searcheth his pocket and findeth certain papers.
　　What hast thou found?

Peto. Nothing but papers, my lord.

Prince. Let's see what they be. Read them.　　　　*535*

[*Peto reads*] "Item, A capon　.　.　.　.　2s. 2d.
　　　　　　　Item, Sauce　.　.　.　.　.　4d.
　　　　　　　Item, Sack two gallons　.　.　5s. 8d.
　　　　　　　Item, Anchovies and sack
　　　　　　　　　after supper　.　.　.　2s. 6d　　*540*
　　　　　　　Item, Bread　.　.　.　.　.　　ob."°

Prince. O monstrous! But one halfpennyworth of bread
　　to this intolerable deal° of sack! What there is else,
　　keep close; we'll read it at more advantage. There
　　let him sleep till day. I'll to the court in the morn-　*545*
　　ing. We must all to the wars, and thy place shall be
　　honorable. I'll procure this fat rogue a charge of
　　foot,° and I know his death will be a march of twelve
　　score.° The money shall be paid back again with
　　advantage.° Be with me betimes° in the morning,　*550*
　　and so good morrow, Peto.

Peto. Good morrow, good my lord.　　　　*Exeunt.*

529–30 **snorting** snoring　541 **ob.** obolus, halfpenny　543 **deal** lot
547–48 **charge of foot** company of infantry　548–49 **twelve score**
twelve score paces　550 **advantage** interest　550 **betimes** early

[ACT 3

Scene 1. *Wales. A room.*]

*Enter Hotspur, Worcester, Lord Mortimer, Owen
Glendower.*

Mortimer. These promises are fair, the parties sure,
And our induction° full of prosperous hope.

Hotspur. Lord Mortimer, and cousin Glendower, will
you sit down? And uncle Worcester. A plague upon
it! I have forgot the map.

Glendower. No, here it is. Sit, cousin Percy, sit, good
cousin Hotspur, for by that name as oft as Lancaster
doth speak of you, his cheek looks pale, and with
a rising sigh he wisheth you in heaven.

Hotspur. And you in hell, as oft as he hears Owen
Glendower spoke of.°

Glendower. I cannot blame him. At my nativity
The front of heaven was full of fiery shapes
Of burning cressets,° and at my birth
The frame and huge foundation of the earth
Shakèd like a coward.

5

10

15

3.1.2 **induction** beginning   3-11 **Lord . . . spoke of** (many editors revise to
read as verse, with line breaks after "down/it/is/Hotspur/you/sigh/hell/of";
or, leaving Hotspur's lines as prose, revise Glendower's speech to read
as verse with breaks after "Percy/name/you sigh/heaven")   14 **cressets**
beacons

Hotspur. Why, so it would have done at the same season
    if your mother's cat had but kittened, though your-
    self had never been born.

Glendower. I say the earth did shake when I was born.   *20*

Hotspur. And I say the earth was not of my mind,
    If you suppose as fearing you it shook.

Glendower. The heavens were all on fire, the earth did
    tremble.

Hotspur. O, then the earth shook to see the heavens on
    fire,
    And not in fear of your nativity.   *25*
    Diseasèd nature oftentimes breaks forth
    In strange eruptions; oft the teeming earth
    Is with a kind of colic pinched and vexed
    By the imprisoning of unruly wind
    Within her womb, which, for enlargement striving,   *30*
    Shakes the old beldame° earth and topples down
    Steeples and mossgrown towers. At your birth
    Our grandam earth, having this distemp'rature,°
    In passion° shook.

Glendower.   Cousin, of many men
    I do not bear these crossings. Give me leave   *35*
    To tell you once again that at my birth
    The front of heaven was full of fiery shapes,
    The goats ran from the mountains, and the herds
    Were strangely clamorous to the frighted fields.
    These signs have marked me extraordinary,   *40*
    And all the courses of my life do show
    I am not in the roll of common men.
    Where is he living, clipped in with° the sea
    That chides the banks of England, Scotland, Wales,
    Which calls me pupil or hath read to° me?   *45*
    And bring him out that is but woman's son
    Can trace° me in the tedious ways of art°
    And hold me pace in deep experiments.

31 **beldame** grandmother (cf. "grandam," line 33)   33 **distemp'rature**
physical disorder   34 **passion** pain   43 **clipped in with** embraced
by   45 **read to** tutored   47 **trace** follow   47 **art** magic

Hotspur. I think there's no man speaks better Welsh.°
50   I'll to dinner.

Mortimer. Peace, cousin Percy; you will make him
     mad.

Glendower. I can call spirits from the vasty deep.

Hotspur. Why, so can I, or so can any man;
     But will they come when you do call for them?

55   *Glendower.* Why, I can teach you, cousin, to command
     the devil.

Hotspur. And I can teach thee, coz, to shame the
     devil—
     By telling truth. Tell truth and shame the devil.
     If thou have power to raise him, bring him hither,
60   And I'll be sworn I have power to shame him hence.
     O, while you live, tell truth and shame the devil!

Mortimer. Come, come, no more of this unprofitable
     chat.

Glendower. Three times hath Henry Bolingbroke made
     head
     Against my power; thrice from the banks of Wye
65   And sandy-bottomed Severn have I sent him
     Bootless° home and weather-beaten back.

Hotspur. Home without boots, and in foul weather too?
     How scapes he agues,° in the devil's name?

Glendower. Come, here is the map. Shall we divide our
     right°
70   According to our threefold order ta'en?

Mortimer. The Archdeacon hath divided it
     Into three limits° very equally.
     England, from Trent and Severn hitherto,
     By south and east is to my part assigned;

---

49 **speaks better Welsh** (1) brags better (2) talks more unintelligibly
66 **Bootless** profitless (probably trisyllabic)   68 **agues** i.e., catching
cold   69 **our right** i.e., the kingdom they hope to win   72 **limits**
regions

All westward, Wales beyond the Severn shore,　　*75*
And all the fertile land within that bound,
To Owen Glendower; and, dear coz, to you
The remnant northward lying off from Trent.
And our indentures tripartite° are drawn,
Which being sealèd interchangeably°　　*80*
(A business that this night may execute),
Tomorrow, cousin Percy, you and I
And my good Lord of Worcester will set forth
To meet your father and the Scottish power,
As is appointed us, at Shrewsbury.　　*85*
My father Glendower is not ready yet,
Nor shall we need his help these fourteen days.
[*To Glendower*] Within that space you may have
　　drawn together
Your tenants, friends, and neighboring gentlemen.

Glendower. A shorter time shall send me to you, lords;　　*90*
And in my conduct shall your ladies come,
From whom you now must steal and take no leave,
For there will be a world of water shed
Upon the parting of your wives and you.

Hotspur. Methinks my moiety,° north from Burton
　　here,　　*95*
In quantity equals not one of yours.
See how this river comes me cranking° in
And cuts me from the best of all my land
A huge half-moon, a monstrous cantle° out.
I'll have the current in this place dammed up,　　*100*
And here the smug° and silver Trent shall run
In a new channel fair and evenly.
It shall not wind with such a deep indent
To rob me of so rich a bottom° here.

Glendower. Not wind? It shall, it must! You see it doth.　　*105*

Mortimer. Yea, but mark how he bears his course, and

---

79 **indentures tripartite** three-way agreements　80 **interchangeably**
i.e., by all three parties　95 **moiety** share　97 **cranking** winding
99 **cantle** piece　101 **smug** smooth　104 **bottom** valley

runs me up with like advantage° on the other side,
gelding the opposèd continent° as much as on the
other side it takes from you.°

Worcester. Yea, but a little charge° will trench° him
110   here
And on this north side win this cape of land;
And then he runs straight and even.

Hotspur. I'll have it so, a little charge will do it.

Glendower. I'll not have it alt'red.

115 *Hotspur.* Will not you?

Glendower. No, nor you shall not.

Hotspur. Who shall say me nay?

Glendower. Why, that will I.

Hotspur. Let me not understand you then; speak it in
120   Welsh.

Glendower. I can speak English, lord, as well as you;
For I was trained up in the English court,
Where, being but young, I framèd to the harp
Many an English ditty lovely well,
125   And gave the tongue a helpful ornament°—
A virtue that was never seen in you.

Hotspur. Marry, and I am glad of it with all my heart!
I had rather be a kitten and cry mew
Than one of these same meter ballad-mongers.°
130   I had rather hear a brazen canstick turned°
Or a dry wheel grate on the axletree,
And that would set my teeth nothing on edge,
Nothing so much as mincing° poetry.

---

107 **advantage** i.e., disadvantage   108 **gelding the opposèd continent**
cutting out of the opposite bank   106–09 **Yea . . . you** (revised by most
editors to four or five lines of verse, with little agreement about lineation)
110 **charge** cost   110 **trench** make a new course for   125 **gave . . . or-
nament** (1) ornamented the words with music? (2) benefited the English
language by my poems?   129 **meter ballad-mongers** singers of dog-
gerel ballads   130 **canstick turned** i.e., candlestick in process of being
burnished (and therefore raucously scraped)   133 **mincing** affected

'Tis like the forced gait of a shuffling nag.

Glendower. Come, you shall have Trent turned.   *135*

Hotspur. I do not care. I'll give thrice so much land
To any well-deserving friend;
But in the way of bargain, mark ye me,
I'll cavil on the ninth part of a hair.
Are the indentures drawn? Shall we be gone?   *140*

Glendower. The moon shines fair; you may away by
     night.
I'll haste the writer, and withal
Break with° your wives of your departure hence.
I am afraid my daughter will run mad,
So much she doteth on her Mortimer.   *Exit.*   *145*

Mortimer. Fie, cousin Percy, how you cross my father!

Hotspur. I cannot choose. Sometime he angers me
With telling me of the moldwarp° and the ant,
Of the dreamer Merlin and his prophecies,
And of a dragon and a finless fish,   *150*
A clip-winged griffin and a moulten raven,
A couching° lion and a ramping° cat,
And such a deal of skimble-skamble° stuff
As puts me from my faith. I tell you what—
He held me last night at least nine hours   *155*
In reckoning up the several devils' names
That were his lackeys. I cried "hum," and "Well,
     go to!"
But marked him not a word. O, he is as tedious
As a tired horse, a railing wife;
Worse than a smoky house. I had rather live   *160*
With cheese and garlic in a windmill far
Than feed on cates° and have him talk to me
In any summer house in Christendom.

143 **Break with** inform   148 **moldwarp** mole, i.e, Henry   152 **couch-
ing, ramping** (Hotspur ridicules heraldic crouching and rearing beasts;
evidently Glendower talked of ancient prophecies which held that the
kingdom of the mole should be divided by the lion, dragon and wolf,
which were the crests of Percy, Glendower, and Mortimer)   153 **skim-
ble-skamble** meaningless   162 **cates** delicacies

Mortimer. In faith, he is a worthy gentleman,
165   Exceedingly well read and profited
    In strange concealments,° valiant as a lion,
    And wondrous affable, and as bountiful
    As mines of India. Shall I tell you, cousin?
    He holds your temper in a high respect
170   And curbs himself even of his natural scope°
    When you come 'cross his humor.° Faith, he does.
    I warrant you that man is not alive
    Might so have tempted him as you have done
    Without the taste of danger and reproof.
175   But do not use it oft, let me entreat you.

Worcester. In faith, my lord, you are too willful-blame,°
    And since your coming hither have done enough
    To put him quite besides his patience.
    You must needs learn, lord, to amend this fault.
    Though sometimes it show greatness, courage,
180   blood°—
    And that's the dearest grace it renders you—
    Yet oftentimes it doth present° harsh rage,
    Defect of manners, want of government,°
    Pride, haughtiness, opinion,° and disdain;
185   The least of which haunting a nobleman
    Loseth men's hearts, and leaves behind a stain
    Upon the beauty of all parts besides,
    Beguiling them of commendation.

Hotspur. Well, I am schooled. Good manners be your
    speed!°
190   Here come our wives, and let us take our leave.

        Enter Glendower with the Ladies.

Mortimer. This is the deadly spite° that angers me—
    My wife can speak no English, I no Welsh.

165–66 **profited . . . concealments** expert in secret arts   170 **scope** tendencies   171 **come 'cross his humor** clash with his temperament   176 **too willful-blame** blamable for too much willfulness   180 **blood** spirit   182 **present** indicate   183 **government** self-control   184 **opinion** arrogance   189 **be your speed** bring you success   191 **spite** misfortune

Glendower. My daughter weeps; she'll not part with
    you,
She'll be a soldier too, she'll to the wars.

Mortimer. Good father, tell her that she and my aunt
    Percy   *195*
Shall follow in your conduct speedily.
    Glendower speaks to her in Welsh, and she answers
                            him in the same.

Glendower. She is desperate here.
    A peevish self-willed harlotry,° one that no per-
    suasion can do good upon.
                            The Lady speaks in Welsh.

Mortimer. I understand thy looks. That pretty Welsh°   *200*
    Which thou pourest down from these swelling
        heavens°
I am too perfect in; and, but for shame,
In such a parley° should I answer thee.
                            The Lady again in Welsh.
I understand thy kisses, and thou mine,
And that's a feeling disputation.°   *205*
But I will never be a truant, love,
Till I have learnt thy language; for thy tongue
Makes Welsh as sweet as ditties highly penned,°
Sung by a fair queen in a summer's bow'r,
With ravishing division,° to her lute.   *210*

Glendower. Nay, if you melt, then will she run mad.
                        The Lady speaks again in Welsh.

Mortimer. O, I am ignorance itself in this!

Glendower. She bids you on the wanton° rushes lay
    you down
And rest your gentle head upon her lap,
And she will sing the song that pleaseth you   *215*

---

198 **harlotry** ninny, fool 200 **That pretty Welsh** i.e., her tears
201 **heavens** i.e., her eyes 203 **parley** meeting (of tears) 205 **feeling disputation** dialogue by (1) touching (2) the feelings 208
highly penned i.e., lofty 210 **division** musical variation 213 **wanton**
luxurious

And on your eyelids crown the god of sleep,°
Charming your blood with pleasing heaviness,
Making such difference 'twixt wake and sleep
As is the difference betwixt day and night
220 The hour before the heavenly-harnessed team°
Begins his golden progress in the east.

Mortimer. With all my heart I'll sit and hear her sing.
By that time will our book,° I think, be drawn.

Glendower. Do so, and those musicians that shall play
to you
225 Hang in the air a thousand leagues from hence,
And straight they shall be here: sit, and attend.

Hotspur. Come, Kate, thou art perfect in lying down.
Come, quick, quick, that I may lay my head in thy
lap.

230 *Lady Percy.* Go, ye giddy goose.   *The music plays.*

Hotspur. Now I perceive the devil understands Welsh,
And 'tis no marvel he is so humorous,°
By'r Lady, he is a good musician.

Lady Percy. Then should you be nothing but musical,
235 For you are altogether governed by humors.
Lie still, ye thief, and hear the lady sing in Welsh.

Hotspur. I had rather hear Lady, my brach,° howl in
Irish.

Lady Percy. Wouldst thou have thy head broken?

240 *Hotspur.* No.

Lady Percy. Then be still.

Hotspur. Neither! 'Tis a woman's fault.

Lady Percy. Now God help thee!

Hotspur. To the Welsh lady's bed.

---

216 **crown the god of sleep** i.e., give sleep sovereignty 220 **the heavenly-harnessed team** the horses of the sun 223 **book** agreement 232 **humorous** capricious 237 **brach** bitch-hound

Lady Percy. What's that?   245

Hotspur. Peace! She sings.
                    Here the Lady sings a Welsh song.
        Come, Kate, I'll have your song too.

Lady Percy. Not mine, in good sooth.°

Hotspur. Not yours, in good sooth? Heart, you swear
        like a comfit-maker's° wife. "Not you, in good   250
        sooth!" and "as true as I live!" and "as God shall
        mend me!" and "as sure as day!"
        And givest such sarcenet surety° for thy oaths
        As if thou never walk'st further than Finsbury.°
        Swear me, Kate, like a lady as thou art,   255
        A good mouth-filling oath, and leave "in sooth"
        And such protest of pepper gingerbread°
        To velvet guards° and Sunday citizens.
        Come, sing.

Lady Percy. I will not sing.   260

Hotspur. 'Tis the next way to turn tailor° or be red-
        breast-teacher.° And the indentures be drawn, I'll
        away within these two hours; and so come in when
        ye will.   *Exit.*

Glendower. Come, come, Lord Mortimer. You are as
        slow   265
        As hot Lord Percy is on fire to go.
        By this our book is drawn; we'll but seal,
        And then to horse immediately.

Mortimer.   With all my heart.
                                              Exeunt.

---

248 **sooth** truth   250 **comfit-maker's** confectioner's   253 **sarcenet surety**
flimsy security ("sarcenet"—a thin silk)   254 **Finsbury** favorite resort
near London (frequented by the middle-class groups whom Hotspur satirizes)   257 **pepper gingerbread** i.e., insubstantial, crumbling in the
mouth   258 **velvet guards** i.e., shopkeepers, who favored velvet trim-
mings for Sunday wear   261 **tailor** (like weavers, tailors were famed for
singing at their work)   261–62 **red-breast-teacher** singing master to
songbirds

[Scene 2. *London. The palace.*]

Enter the King, Prince of Wales, and others.

King. Lords, give us leave: the Prince of Wales and I
    Must have some private conference; but be near at
      hand,
    For we shall presently have need of you.
                            Exeunt Lords.
    I know not whether God will have it so
5   For some displeasing service I have done,
    That, in his secret doom,° out of my blood°
    He'll breed revengement and a scourge for me;
    But thou dost in thy passages° of life
    Make me believe that thou art only marked
10   For the hot vengeance and the rod of heaven
    To punish my mistreadings.° Tell me else,
    Could such inordinate° and low desires,
    Such poor, such bare, such lewd, such mean at-
      tempts,
    Such barren pleasures, rude society,
15   As thou art matched withal° and grafted to,
    Accompany the greatness of thy blood
    And hold their level with thy princely heart?

Prince. So please your Majesty, I would I could
    Quit° all offenses with as clear excuse
20   As well° as I am doubtless I can purge
    Myself of many I am charged withal.
    Yet such extenuation let me beg

3.2.6 **doom** judgment 6 **blood** i.e., heirs 8 **passages** courses 9–11
thou ... mistreadings i.e., (1) heaven is punishing me through you (2)
heaven will punish you to punish me   12 **inordinate** i.e., out of order (for
one of your rank)   15 **withal** with   19 **Quit** clear myself of   20 **As well**
and as well

As, in reproof of many tales devised,
Which oft the ear of greatness needs must hear
By smiling pickthanks and base newsmongers,   25
I may, for some things true wherein my youth
Hath faulty wand'red and irregular,
Find pardon on my true submission.°

King. God pardon thee! Yet let me wonder, Harry,
  At thy affections,° which do hold a wing   30
  Quite from the flight of all thy ancestors.
  Thy place in council thou hast rudely lost,
  Which by thy younger brother is supplied,
  And art almost an alien to the hearts
  Of all the court and princes of my blood.   35
  The hope and expectation of thy time°
  Is ruined, and the soul of every man
  Prophetically do forethink thy fall.
  Had I so lavish of my presence been,
  So common-hackneyed in the eyes of men,   40
  So stale and cheap to vulgar company,
  Opinion,° that did help me to the crown,
  Had still kept loyal to possession°
  And left me in reputeless banishment,
  A fellow of no mark nor likelihood.   45
  By being seldom seen, I could not stir
  But, like a comet, I was wond'red at;
  That men would tell their children, "This is he!"
  Others would say, "Where? Which is Bolingbroke?"
  And then I stole all courtesy from heaven,°   50
  And dressed myself in such humility
  That I did pluck allegiance from men's hearts,
  Loud shouts and salutations from their mouths
  Even in the presence of the crownèd King.

22–28 **Yet ... submission** yet let me beg such extenuation that when
I have confuted many manufactured charges (which the ear of greatness
is bound to hear from informers and tattletales) I may be pardoned for
some true faults of which my youth has been guilty   30 **affections**
tastes   36 **time** reign   42 **Opinion** public opinion   43 **possession** i.e.,
Richard II   50 **I ... heaven** I took a godlike graciousness on myself

55   Thus did I keep my person fresh and new,
    My presence, like a robe pontifical,
    Ne'er seen but wond'red at; and so my state,
    Seldom but sumptuous, showed like a feast
    And won by rareness such solemnity.
60   The skipping King, he ambled up and down
    With shallow jesters and rash bavin° wits,
    Soon kindled and soon burnt; carded° his state;
    Mingled his royalty with cap'ring fools;
    Had his great name profanèd with their scorns
65   And gave his countenance, against his name,°
    To laugh at gibing boys and stand the push°
    Of every beardless vain comparative;°
    Grew a companion to the common streets,
    Enfeoffed himself to popularity;°
70   That, being daily swallowed by men's eyes,
    They surfeited with honey and began
    To loathe the taste of sweetness, whereof a little
    More than a little is by much too much.
    So, when he had occasion to be seen,
75   He was but as the cuckoo is in June,
    Heard, not regarded—seen, but with such eyes
    As, sick and blunted with community,°
    Afford no extraordinary gaze,
    Such as is bent on sunlike majesty
80   When it shines seldom in admiring eyes;
    But rather drowsed and hung their eyelids down,
    Slept in his face, and rend'red such aspect
    As cloudy° men use to their adversaries,
    Being with his presence glutted, gorged, and full.
85   And in that very line, Harry, standest thou;
    For thou hast lost thy princely privilege
    With vile participation.° Not an eye
    But is aweary of thy common sight,

---

61 **bavin** brushwood (which flares and burns out)   62 **carded** debased
65 **his name** i.e., (1) his kingly title (2) his kingly authority   66 **stand
the push** put up with the impudence   67 **comparative** deviser of insulting comparisons   69 **Enfeoffed ... popularity** bound himself to
low company   77 **with community** by familiarity (with the king)
83 **cloudy** sullen (but also with reference to "clouds" obscuring the royal
"sun")   87 **participation** companionship

Save mine, which hath desired to see thee more;
Which now doth that I would not have it do—   90
Make blind itself with foolish tenderness.°

Prince. I shall hereafter, my thrice-gracious lord,
Be more myself.

King.   For all the world,
As thou art to this hour was Richard then
When I from France set foot at Ravenspurgh;   95
And even as I was then is Percy now.
Now, by my scepter, and my soul to boot,
He hath more worthy interest° to the state
Than thou the shadow of succession;
For of no right, nor color° like to right,   100
He doth fill fields with harness° in the realm,
Turns head against the lion's armèd jaws,
And, being no more in debt to years than thou,
Leads ancient lords and reverend bishops on
To bloody battles and to bruising arms.   105
What never-dying honor hath he got
Against renownèd Douglas! whose high deeds,
Whose hot incursions and great name in arms
Holds from all soldiers chief majority°
And military title capital°   110
Through all the kingdoms that acknowledge Christ.
Thrice hath this Hotspur, Mars in swathling clothes,
This infant warrior, in his enterprises
Discomfited great Douglas; ta'en him once,
Enlargèd him, and made a friend of him,   115
To fill the mouth of deep defiance up°
And shake the peace and safety of our throne.
And what say you to this? Percy, Northumberland,
The Archbishop's grace of York, Douglas, Mortimer
Capitulate° against us and are up.°   120
But wherefore do I tell these news to thee?

91 **tenderness** i.e., tears   98 **worthy interest** claim based on worth (as
compared with a "shadow" claim by inheritance)   100 **color** pretense
101 **harness** armor   109 **majority** preeminence   110 **capital** topmost
116 **To fill . . . up** to deepen the noise of defiance   120 **Capitulate** (1)
make a "head" or armed force? (2) draw up "heads" of an argument?
120 **up** in arms

Why, Harry, do I tell thee of my foes,
Which art my nearest and dearest° enemy?
Thou that art like enough, through vassal fear,
125   Base inclination, and the start of spleen,
To fight against me under Percy's pay,
To dog his heels and curtsy at his frowns,
To show how much thou art degenerate.

Prince. Do not think so, you shall not find it so.
130   And God forgive them that so much have swayed
Your Majesty's good thoughts away from me.
I will redeem all this on Percy's head
And, in the closing of some glorious day,
Be bold to tell you that I am your son,
135   When I will wear a garment all of blood,
And stain my favors° in a bloody mask,
Which, washed away, shall scour my shame with it.
And that shall be the day, whene'er it lights,
That this same child of honor and renown,
140   This gallant Hotspur, this all-praisèd knight,
And your unthought-of Harry chance to meet.
For every honor sitting on his helm,
Would they were multitudes, and on my head
My shames redoubled! For the time will come
145   That I shall make this northern youth exchange
His glorious deeds for my indignities.
Percy is but my factor,° good my lord,
To engross° up glorious deeds on my behalf;
And I will call him to so strict account
150   That he shall render every glory up,
Yea, even the slightest worship of his time,°
Or I will tear the reckoning from his heart.
This in the name of God I promise here;
The which if he be pleased I shall perform,
155   I do beseech your Majesty may salve
The long-grown wounds of my intemperance.
If not, the end of life cancels all bands,°

123 **dearest** (1) most loved (2) costliest   136 **favors** features   147 **factor** agent   148 **engross** hoard   151 **worship of his time** honor he has gained in his lifetime   157 **bands** bonds, promises

And I will die a hundred thousand deaths
Ere break the smallest parcel° of this vow.

King. A hundred thousand rebels die in this!   160
Thou shalt have charge and sovereign trust herein.

Enter Blunt.

How now, good Blunt? Thy looks are full of speed.

Blunt. So hath the business° that I come to speak of.
Lord Mortimer of Scotland hath sent word   165
That Douglas and the English rebels met
The eleventh of this month at Shrewsbury.
A mighty and a fearful head they are,
If promises be kept on every hand,
As ever off'red foul play in a state.

King. The Earl of Westmoreland set forth today;   170
With him my son, Lord John of Lancaster:
For this advertisement is five days old.
On Wednesday next, Harry, you shall set forward;
On Thursday we ourselves will march. Our meeting
Is Bridgenorth; and, Harry, you shall march   175
Through Gloucestershire; by which account,
Our business valuèd,° some twelve days hence
Our general forces at Bridgenorth shall meet.
Our hands are full of business. Let's away:
Advantage feeds him° fat while men delay.   *Exeunt.*   180

[Scene 3. *Eastcheap. The tavern.*]

Enter Falstaff and Bardolph.

Falstaff. Bardolph, am I not fall'n away vilely since this
last action? Do I not bate?° Do I not dwindle? Why,

159 **parcel** item   163 **So hath the business** i.e., the business too has
speed (must be dealt with speedily)   177 **Our business valuèd** having
sized up what we have to do   180 **him** itself   3.3.2 **bate** lose weight

my skin hangs about me like an old lady's loose
gown! I am withered like an old apple-john.° Well,
5   I'll repent, and that suddenly, while I am in some
liking.° I shall be out of heart° shortly, and then I
shall have no strength to repent. And I have not forgotten what the inside of a church is made of, I am
a peppercorn,° a brewer's horse.° The inside of a
10   church! Company, villainous company, hath been
the spoil of me.

Bardolph. Sir John, you are so fretful you cannot live
long.

Falstaff. Why, there it is! Come, sing me a bawdy song,
15   make me merry. I was as virtuously given as a gentleman need to be, virtuous enough: swore little, diced
not above seven times a week, went to a bawdy house
not above once in a quarter of an hour, paid money
that I borrowed three or four times,° lived well, and
20   in good compass;° and now I live out of all order,
out of all compass.

Bardolph. Why, you are so fat, Sir John, that you must
needs be out of all compass—out of all reasonable
compass, Sir John.

25   *Falstaff.* Do thou amend thy face, and I'll amend my
life. Thou art our admiral,° thou bearest the lantern
in the poop—but 'tis in the nose of thee: thou art
the Knight of the Burning Lamp.

Bardolph. Why, Sir John, my face does you no harm.

30   *Falstaff.* No, I'll be sworn. I make as good use of it as
many a man doth of a death's-head° or a memento
mori.° I never see thy face but I think upon hellfire

4 **old apple-john** apple with shriveled skin   5–6 **am in some liking** (1)
am in the mood (2) still have some flesh left   6 **out of heart** (1) out of
the mood (2) out of shape   9 **peppercorn, brewer's horse** (Falstaff this
time picks objects *not* long and thin, but dry, withered, decrepit)
16–19 **diced … times** (probably spoken with significant pauses after
"diced not," "once," "borrowed")   20 **compass** order (but Bardolph
takes it in the sense of "size")   26 **admiral** flagship (recognizable by its
lantern)   31 **death's-head** ring with a skull   31–32 **memento mori** re-
minder of death

and Dives° that lived in purple; for there he is in his
robes, burning, burning. If thou wert any way given
to virtue, I would swear by thy face; my oath should   *35*
be "By this fire, that's God's angel."° But thou art
altogether given over, and wert indeed, but for the
light in thy face, the son of utter darkness. When
thou ran'st up Gad's Hill in the night to catch my
horse, if I did not think thou hadst been an ignis   *40*
fatuus° or a ball of wildfire,° there's no purchase in
money. O, thou art a perpetual triumph,° an everlasting bonfire-light! Thou hast saved me a thousand
marks in links° and torches, walking with thee in the
night betwixt tavern and tavern; but the sack that   *45*
thou hast drunk me would have bought me lights as
good cheap° at the dearest chandler's° in Europe.
I have maintained that salamander° of yours with
fire any time this two and thirty years. God reward
me for it!   *50*

Bardolph. 'Sblood, I would my face were in your belly!°

Falstaff. God-a-mercy! So should I be sure to be heart-
burned.

Enter Hostess.

How now, Dame Partlet° the hen? Have you en-
quired yet who picked my pocket?   *55*

Hostess. Why, Sir John, what do you think, Sir John?
Do you think I keep thieves in my house? I have
searched, I have enquired, so has my husband, man
by man, boy by boy, servant by servant. The tithe°
of a hair was never lost in my house before.   *60*

---

33 **Dives** uncharitable rich man who burns in hell (Luke 16:19–31)
36 **angel** (alluding to the Scriptural accounts of angels manifesting themselves as fire, or possibly to the seraphs, highest order of angels, who were
fire)   40–41 **ignis fatuus** will-o'-the-wisp   41 **ball of wildfire** fire-
work   42 **triumph** i.e., of the Roman kind, with torches   44 **links** flares
47 **good cheap** cheaply   47 **chandler's** candle maker's   48 **salamander**
lizard supposed to live in fire   51 **I . . . belly** (proverbial retort, to which
Falstaff's reply gives new life)   54 **Dame Partlet** (traditional name for a
hen, and well suited to the clucking Hostess)   59 **tithe** tenth part

Falstaff. Ye lie, hostess. Bardolph was shaved and lost many a hair, and I'll be sworn my pocket was picked. Go to, you are a woman, go!

Hostess. Who, I? No;° I defy thee! God's light, I was
65 never called so in mine own house before!

Falstaff. Go to, I know you well enough.

Hostess. No, Sir John; you do not know me, Sir John. I know you, Sir John. You owe me money, Sir John, and now you pick a quarrel to beguile me of it. I
70 bought you a dozen of shirts to your back.

Falstaff. Dowlas,° filthy dowlas! I have given them away to bakers' wives; they have made bolters° of them.

Hostess. Now, as I am a true woman, holland° of eight
75 shillings an ell.° You owe money here besides, Sir John, for your diet and by-drinkings,° and money lent you, four and twenty pound.

Falstaff. He had his part of it; let him pay.

Hostess. He? Alas, he is poor; he hath nothing.

80 *Falstaff.* How? Poor? Look upon his face. What call you rich?° Let them coin his nose, let them coin his cheeks. I'll not pay a denier.° What, will you make a younker° of me? Shall I not take mine ease in mine inn but I shall have my pocket picked? I have lost a
85 seal ring of my grandfather's worth forty mark.

Hostess. O Jesu, I have heard the Prince tell him, I know not how oft, that that ring was copper!

Falstaff. How? The Prince is a Jack,° a sneak-up.°

64 **No** (the Hostess suspects that any word or phrase of Falstaff's may contain hidden innuendoes about her moral character; she sometimes retorts with comments containing amusing innuendoes about herself that she is too ignorant to understand)   71 **Dowlas** coarse linen   72 **bolters** sieves   74 **holland** fine linen   75 **ell** one and a quarter yards   76 **by-drinkings** drinks between meals   81 **rich** (referring to its red gold-and-copper hues)   82 **denier** tenth of a penny   83 **younker** greenhorn   88 **Jack** rascal   88 **sneak-up** sneak

'Sblood, and he were here, I would cudgel him like
a dog if he would say so.   90

*Enter the Prince [and Poins], marching, and
Falstaff meets them, playing upon his truncheon°
like a fife.*

How now, lad? Is the wind in that door,° i' faith?
Must we all march?

Bardolph. Yea, two and two,° Newgate fashion.

Hostess. My lord, I pray you hear me.

Prince. What say'st thou, Mistress Quickly? How doth   95
thy husband? I love him well, he is an honest man.

Hostess. Good my lord, hear me.

Falstaff. Prithee let her alone and list to me.

Prince. What say'st thou, Jack?

Falstaff. The other night I fell asleep here behind the   100
arras and had my pocket picked. This house is turned
bawdy house; they pick pockets.

Prince. What didst thou lose, Jack?

Falstaff. Wilt thou believe me, Hal, three or four bonds
of forty pound apiece and a seal ring of my grand-   105
father's.

Prince. A trifle, some eightpenny matter.

Hostess. So I told him, my lord, and I said I heard your
Grace say so; and, my lord, he speaks most vilely of
you, like a foulmouthed man as he is, and said he   110
would cudgel you.

Prince. What! He did not?

Hostess. There's neither faith, truth, nor womanhood
in me else.

90s.d. **truncheon** cudgel   91 **Is ... door** i.e., is that how things are going   93 **two and two** i.e., bound in pairs like prisoners on the way to
(Newgate) prison

115   *Falstaff.* There's no more faith in thee than in a stewed
        prune,° nor no more truth in thee than in a drawn°
        fox; and for womanhood, Maid Marian may be the
        deputy's wife of the ward to thee.° Go, you thing, go!

      Hostess. Say, what thing, what thing?

120   *Falstaff.* What thing? Why, a thing to thank God on.

      Hostess. I am no thing to thank God on, I would thou
        shouldst know it! I am an honest man's wife, and,
        setting thy knighthood aside, thou art a knave to
        call me so.

125   *Falstaff.* Setting thy womanhood aside, thou art a beast
        to say otherwise.

      Hostess. Say, what beast, thou knave, thou?

      Falstaff. What beast? Why, an otter.

      Prince. An otter, Sir John? Why an otter?

130   *Falstaff.* Why, she's neither fish nor flesh; a man knows
        not where to have her.

      Hostess. Thou art an unjust man in saying so. Thou
        or any man knows where to have me, thou knave,
        thou!

135   *Prince.* Thou say'st true, hostess, and he slanders thee
        most grossly.

      Hostess. So he doth you, my lord, and said this other
        day you ought° him a thousand pound.

      Prince. Sirrah, do I owe you a thousand pound?

140   *Falstaff.* A thousand pound, Hal? A million! Thy love
        is worth a million, thou owest me thy love.

115–16 **stewed prune** (evidently chosen by Falstaff because stewed
prunes were associated with bawdy houses)   116 **drawn** drawn from his
lair and trying every trick to get back to it   117–18 **Maid Marian . . .
thee** a disreputable female in country May games is chaste as the wife of
the ward's most respectable citizen in comparison with you   138 **ought**
owed

Hostess. Nay, my lord, he called you Jack and said he
   would cudgel you.

Falstaff. Did I, Bardolph?

Bardolph. Indeed, Sir John, you said so.   *145*

Falstaff. Yea, if he said my ring was copper.

Prince. I say 'tis copper. Darest thou be as good as thy
   word now?

Falstaff. Why, Hal, thou knowest, as thou art but man,
   I dare; but as thou art Prince, I fear thee as I fear   *150*
   the roaring of the lion's whelp.

Prince. And why not as the lion?

Falstaff. The King himself is to be feared as the lion.
   Dost thou think I'll fear thee as I fear thy father? Nay,
   and I do, I pray God my girdle break.   *155*

Prince. O, if it should, how would thy guts fall about
   thy knees! But, sirrah, there's no room for faith,
   truth, nor honesty in this bosom of thine. It is all
   filled up with guts and midriff. Charge an honest
   woman with picking thy pocket? Why, thou whore-   *160*
   son, impudent, embossed° rascal,° if there were
   anything in thy pocket but tavern reckonings, mem-
   orandums of bawdy houses, and one poor pennyworth of sugar candy to make thee long-winded—
   if thy pocket were enriched with any other injuries°   *165*
   but these, I am a villain. And yet you will stand to
   it; you will not pocket up wrong. Art thou not
   ashamed?

Falstaff. Dost thou hear, Hal? Thou knowest in the
   state of innocency Adam fell, and what should poor   *170*
   Jack Falstaff do in the days of villainy? Thou seest
   I have more flesh than another man, and therefore
   more frailty. You confess then, you picked my
   pocket?

161 **embossed** (1) swollen (2) foaming at the mouth (of a deer)   161 **rascal** (1) rogue (2) lean young deer   165 **injuries** i.e., things whose loss
you call injuries

175 *Prince.* It appears so by the story.

Falstaff. Hostess, I forgive thee, go make ready breakfast, love thy husband, look to thy servants, cherish
thy guests. Thou shalt find me tractable to any honest reason. Thou seest I am pacified still. Nay, prithee
180 be gone.   *Exit Hostess.*
Now, Hal, to the news at court. For the robbery, lad
—how is that answered?

Prince. O my sweet beef, I must still be good angel to
thee. The money is paid back again.

185 *Falstaff.* O, I do not like that paying back! 'Tis a double
labor.

Prince. I am good friends with my father, and may do
anything.

Falstaff. Rob me the exchequer the first thing thou
190 doest, and do it with unwashed hands° too.

Bardolph. Do, my lord.

Prince. I have procured thee, Jack, a charge of foot.

Falstaff. I would it had been of horse. Where shall I
find one that can steal well? O for a fine thief° of the
195 age of two and twenty or thereabouts! I am heinously
unprovided. Well, God be thanked for these rebels,
they offend none but the virtuous: I laud them, I
praise them.

Prince. Bardolph!

200 *Bardolph.* My lord?

Prince. Go bear this letter to Lord John of Lancaster,
To my brother John; this to my lord of Westmore-
land.   [*Exit Bardolph.*]
Go, Peto, to horse, to horse; for thou and I
Have thirty miles to ride yet ere dinner time.
               [*Exit Peto.*]

190 **with unwashed hands** with no delay   194 **thief** i.e., to steal a horse

Jack, meet me tomorrow in the Temple Hall   *205*
At two o'clock in the afternoon.
There shalt thou know thy charge, and there receive
Money and order for their furniture.°
The land is burning, Percy stands on high,
And either we or they must lower lie.   [*Exit.*] *210*

Falstaff. Rare words! Brave world! Hostess, my break-
    fast, come.
O, I could wish this tavern were my drum!°   [*Exit.*]

[ACT 4

Scene 1. *The rebel camp, near Shrewsbury.*]

[*Enter Hotspur, Worcester, and Douglas.*]

Hotspur. Well said, my noble Scot. If speaking truth
    In this fine age were not thought flattery,
    Such attribution° should the Douglas have
    As not a soldier of this season's stamp
5   Should go so general current° through the world.
    By God, I cannot flatter, I do defy°
    The tongues of soothers!° But a braver place
    In my heart's love hath no man than yourself.
    Nay, task me° to my word; approve me, lord.

10 *Douglas.* Thou art the king of honor.
    No man so potent breathes upon the ground
    But I will beard° him.

            Enter one with letters.

Hotspur.   Do so, and 'tis well.—
    What letters hast thou there?—I can but thank you.

Messenger. These letters come from your father.

4.1.3 **attribution** recognition   5 **go so general current** be as widely accepted (the image is of a coin of recent mintage: "this season's stamp")
6 **defy** despite   7 **soothers** flatterers   9 **task me** try me, test me
12 **beard** oppose

Hotspur. Letters from him? Why comes he not himself?   15

Messenger. He cannot come, my lord, he is grievous
  sick.

Hotspur. Zounds! How has he the leisure to be sick
  In such a justling° time? Who leads his power?
  Under whose government° come they along?

Messenger. His letters bears° his mind, not I, my lord.   20

Worcester. I prithee tell me, doth he keep his bed?

Messenger. He did, my lord, four days ere I set forth,
  And at the time of my departure thence
  He was much feared° by his physicians.

Worcester. I would the state of time had first been
    whole   25
  Ere he by sickness had been visited.
  His health was never better worth than now.

Hotspur. Sick now? Droop now? This sickness doth
    infect
  The very lifeblood of our enterprise.
  'Tis catching hither, even to our camp.   30
  He writes me here that inward sickness—
  And that his friends by deputation°
  Could not so soon be drawn; nor did he think it meet
  To lay so dangerous and dear a trust
  On any soul removed but on his own.   35
  Yet doth he give us bold advertisement,
  That with our small conjunction° we should on,
  To see how fortune is disposed to us;
  For, as he writes, there is no quailing now,
  Because the King is certainly possessed°   40
  Of all our purposes. What say you to it?

Worcester. Your father's sickness is a maim to us.

---

18 **justling** jostling, unquiet   19 **government** command   20 **bears** (a
singular verb with plural subject is not uncommon in Elizabethan English)   24 **feared** feared for   32 **deputation** a deputy   37 **conjunction**
combination of forces   40 **possessed** informed

Hotspur. A perilous gash, a very limb lopped off.
  And yet, in faith, it is not! His present want
45 Seems more than we shall find it. Were it good
  To set° the exact wealth of all our states
  All at one cast? To set so rich a main°
  On the nice° hazard of one doubtful hour?
  It were not good; for therein should we read
50 The very bottom and the soul° of hope,
  The very list,° the very utmost bound
  Of all our fortunes.

Douglas.   Faith, and so we should.
  Where now remains a sweet reversion,°
  We may boldly spend upon the hope of what is to
    come in.
55 A comfort of retirement° lives in this.

Hotspur. A rendezvous, a home to fly unto,
  If that the devil and mischance look big°
  Upon the maidenhead of our affairs.

Worcester. But yet I would your father had been here.
60 The quality and hair° of our attempt
  Brooks° no division. It will be thought
  By some that know not why he is away,
  That wisdom, loyalty, and mere dislike
  Of our proceedings kept the Earl from hence.
65 And think how such an apprehension
  May turn the tide of fearful° faction
  And breed a kind of question in our cause.
  For well you know we of the off'ring side°
  Must keep aloof from strict arbitrament,°
70 And stop all sight-holes, every loop° from whence
  The eye of reason may pry in upon us.
  This absence of your father's draws° a curtain

46 **set** risk   47 **main** (1) stake (in gambling) (2) army   48 **nice** precarious   50 **soul** (1) essence (2) sole (cf. "bottom")   51 **list** limit   53 **reversion** inheritance still to be received   55 **A comfort of retirement** a
security to fall back on   57 **big** menacingly   60 **hair** nature   61 **Brooks**
allows of   66 **fearful** timid   68 **we of the off'ring side** we who take the
offensive   69 **arbitrament** evaluation   70 **loop** loophole   72 **draws**
draws aside

That shows the ignorant a kind of fear
Before not dreamt of.

Hotspur.   You strain too far.
 I rather of his absence make this use: *75*
 It lends a luster and more great opinion,°
 A larger dare to our great enterprise,
 Than if the Earl were here; for men must think,
 If we, without his help, can make a head°
 To push against a kingdom, with his help   *80*
 We shall o'erturn it topsy-turvy down.
 Yet all goes well; yet all our joints are whole.

Douglas. As heart can think. There is not such a word
 Spoke of in Scotland as this term of fear.

    Enter Sir Richard Vernon.

Hotspur. My cousin Vernon, welcome, by my soul.   *85*

Vernon. Pray God my news be worth a welcome, lord.
 The Earl of Westmoreland, seven thousand strong,
 Is marching hitherwards; with him Prince John.

Hotspur. No harm. What more?

Vernon.   And further, I have learned
 The King himself in person is set forth,   *90*
 Or hitherwards intended speedily,
 With strong and mighty preparation.

Hotspur. He shall be welcome too. Where is his son,
 The nimble-footed madcap Prince of Wales,
 And his comrades, that daffed° the world aside   *95*
 And bid it pass?

Vernon.   All furnished, all in arms;
 All plumed like estridges° that with the wind
 Bated° like eagles having lately bathed;
 Glittering in golden coats like images;
 As full of spirit as the month of May   *100*
 And gorgeous as the sun at midsummer;

---

76 **opinion** prestige 79 **a head** (1) an army (2) headway 95 **daffed**
thrust 97 **estridges** ostriches (ostrich plumes are the emblem of the
Prince of Wales) 98 **Bated** shook their wings

Wanton° as youthful goats, wild as young bulls.
I saw young Harry with his beaver° on,
His cushes° on his thighs, gallantly armed,
105 Rise from the ground like feathered Mercury,
And vaulted with such ease into his seat
As if an angel dropped down from the clouds
To turn and wind° a fiery Pegasus
And witch the world with noble horsemanship.

Hotspur. No more, no more! Worse than the sun in
110   March,
This praise doth nourish agues.° Let them come.
They come like sacrifices in their trim,
And to the fire-eyed maid° of smoky war
All hot and bleeding will we offer them.
115 The mailèd Mars shall on his altars sit
Up to the ears in blood. I am on fire
To hear this rich reprisal° is so nigh,
And yet not ours. Come, let me taste my horse,
Who is to bear me like a thunderbolt
120 Against the bosom of the Prince of Wales.
Harry to Harry shall, hot horse to horse,
Meet, and ne'er part till one drop down a corse.
O that Glendower were come!

Vernon.   There is more news.
I learned in Worcester, as I rode along,
125 He cannot draw his power this fourteen days.

Douglas. That's the worst tidings that I hear of yet.

Worcester. Ay, by my faith, that bears a frosty sound.

Hotspur. What may the King's whole battle° reach
unto?

Vernon. To thirty thousand.

Hotspur.   Forty let it be.
130 My father and Glendower being both away,

102 **Wanton** exuberant   103 **beaver** helmet   104 **cushes** thigh armor
108 **wind** wheel about   111 **agues** chills and fever (the spring sun
was believed to set them going)   113 **maid** Bellona, goddess of war
117 **reprisal** prize   128 **battle** army

The powers of us may serve so great a day.
Come, let us take a muster speedily.
Doomsday is near. Die all, die merrily.

Douglas. Talk not of dying. I am out of fear
Of death or death's hand for this one half year.   135
                                             Exeunt.

[Scene 2. *A road near Coventry.*]

Enter Falstaff [and] Bardolph.

Falstaff. Bardolph, get thee before to Coventry; fill me
a bottle of sack. Our soldiers shall march through.
We'll to Sutton Co'fil' tonight.

Bardolph. Will you give me money, captain?

Falstaff. Lay out,° lay out.   5

Bardolph. This bottle makes an angel.°

Falstaff. And if it do, take it for thy labor; and if it
make twenty, take them all; I'll answer the coinage.
Bid my lieutenant Peto meet me at town's end.

Bardolph. I will, captain. Farewell.   *Exit.*   10

Falstaff. If I be not ashamed of my soldiers, I am a
soused gurnet.° I have misused the King's press°
damnably. I have got, in exchange of a hundred and
fifty soldiers, three hundred and odd pounds. I press
me none but good householders, yeomen's sons;° in-   15

4.2.5 **Lay out** i.e., pay out of your own pocket 6 **angel** coin worth, at
various times, six shillings eight pence to ten shillings (Bardolph means
that Falstaff now owes him an angel, but Falstaff jokingly takes "make"
in the literal sense—as if the bottle were minting angels; he tells Bardolph to take them all and he will guarantee they are not counterfeit)
12 **soused gurnet** pickled fish 12 **press** power of conscription
15 **good householders, yeomen's sons** i.e., men of some means, who
could pay to be let off

quire me out contracted bachelors, such as had been
asked twice on the banes°—such a commodity of
warm° slaves as had as lief hear the devil as a drum,
such as fear the report of a caliver° worse than a
20   struck fowl or a hurt wild duck. I pressed me none
but such toasts-and-butter, with hearts in their bellies no bigger than pins' heads, and they have bought
out their services; and now my whole charge consists
of ancients,° corporals, lieutenants, gentlemen of
25   companies°—slaves as ragged as Lazarus° in the
painted cloth,° where the glutton's dogs licked his
sores; and such as indeed were never soldiers, but
discarded unjust° serving-men, younger sons to
younger brothers, revolted° tapsters, and ostlers
30   trade-fall'n;° the cankers° of a calm world and a long
peace; ten times more dishonorable ragged than an
old fazed ancient;° and such have I to fill up the
rooms of them as have bought out their services that
you would think that I had a hundred and fifty tat-
35   tered prodigals lately come from swine-keeping, from
eating draff° and husks. A mad fellow met me on the
way, and told me I had unloaded all the gibbets and
pressed the dead bodies. No eye hath seen such scare-
crows. I'll not march through Coventry with them,
40   that's flat. Nay, and the villains march wide betwixt
the legs, as if they had gyves° on, for indeed I had
the most of them out of prison. There's not a shirt
and a half in all my company, and the half-shirt is
two napkins tacked together and thrown over the
45   shoulders like a herald's coat without sleeves; and
the shirt, to say the truth, stol'n from my host at
Saint Albans, or the red-nose innkeeper of Daventry.

---

17 **asked twice on the banes** i.e., on the verge of marriage (banns [banes]
were announcements of intent to marry, published usually three times at
weekly intervals)   18 **warm** comfortable   19 **caliver** musket   24 **ancients**
ensigns   24–25 **gentlemen of companies** lesser officers   25 **Lazarus** the
beggar in the Dives parable (Luke 16:19–31)   26 **painted cloth** painted
wall-hanging   28 **unjust** dishonest   29 **revolted** runaway   30 **trade-
fall'n** unemployed   30 **cankers** parasites   32 **fazed ancient** tattered flag
36 **draff** pig-swill (the prodigal son, in Luke 15:15–16, was so hungry he
longed for draff)   41 **gyves** fetters

But that's all one; they'll find linen enough on every
hedge.°

Enter the Prince [and the] Lord of Westmoreland.

Prince. How now, blown° Jack?° How now, quilt?   *50*

Falstaff. What, Hal? How now, mad wag? What a devil
dost thou in Warwickshire? My good Lord of Westmoreland, I cry you mercy. I thought your honor
had already been at Shrewsbury.

Westmoreland. Faith, Sir John, 'tis more than time that   *55*
I were there, and you too, but my powers are there
already. The King, I can tell you, looks for us all, we
must away all night.

Falstaff. Tut, never fear me: I am as vigilant as a cat
to steal cream.   *60*

Prince. I think, to steal cream indeed, for thy theft hath
already made thee butter. But tell me, Jack, whose
fellows are these that come after?

Falstaff. Mine, Hal, mine.

Prince. I did never see such pitiful rascals.   *65*

Falstaff. Tut, tut, good enough to toss;° food for powder, food for powder, they'll fill a pit as well as better.
Tush, man, mortal men, mortal men.

Westmoreland. Ay, but, Sir John, methinks they are ex-
ceeding poor and bare, too beggarly.   *70*

Falstaff. Faith, for their poverty, I know not where
they had that, and for their bareness, I am sure they
never learned that of me.

Prince. No, I'll be sworn, unless you call three fingers°
in the ribs bare. But, sirrah, make haste. Percy is   *75*
already in the field.   *Exit.*

---

49 **hedge** i.e., where linen was put out to dry   50 **blown** (1) swelled (2)
short of wind   50 **Jack** (1) Falstaff's name (2) soldier's quilted jacket
66 **toss** i.e., on the end of a pike   74 **three fingers** i.e., of fat

Falstaff. What, is the King encamped?

Westmoreland. He is, Sir John. I fear we shall stay too
    long.

Falstaff. Well, to the latter end of a fray and the begin-
    ning of a feast fits a dull fighter and a keen guest.

Exeunt.°

[Scene 3. *The rebel camp, near Shrewsbury.*]

Enter Hotspur, Worcester, Douglas, Vernon.

Hotspur. We'll fight with him tonight.

Worcester.   It may not be.

Douglas. You give him then advantage.

Vernon.   Not a whit.

Hotspur. Why say you so? Looks he not for supply?°

Vernon. So do we.

Hotspur.   His is certain, ours is doubtful.

5 *Worcester.* Good cousin, be advised; stir not tonight.

Vernon. Do not, my lord.

Douglas.   You do not counsel well.
    You speak it out of fear and cold heart.

Vernon. Do me no slander, Douglas. By my life—
    And I dare well maintain it with my life—
10   If well-respected° honor bid me on,
    I hold as little counsel with weak fear

---

81 s.d. **Exeunt** (the quarto's "Exeunt," implying that Westmoreland goes
off with Falstaff, may be wrong. Falstaff's last speech sounds as if Westmoreland had departed, and Falstaff winks at the audience)   4.3.3 **supply** reinforcement   10 **well-respected** well-considered

As you, my lord, or any Scot that this day lives.
Let it be seen tomorrow in the battle
Which of us fears.

Douglas.   Yea, or tonight.

Vernon.   Content.

Hotspur. Tonight, say I.   15

Vernon. Come, come, it may not be.
I wonder much, being men of such great leading° as
    you are,
That you foresee not what impediments
Drag back our expedition.° Certain horse
Of my cousin Vernon's are not yet come up.   20
Your uncle Worcester's horse came but today;
And now their pride and mettle is asleep,
Their courage with hard labor tame and dull,
That not a horse is half the half of himself.

Hotspur. So are the horses of the enemy   25
In general journey-bated° and brought low.
The better part of ours are full of rest.

Worcester. The number of the King exceedeth ours.
For God's sake, cousin, stay till all come in.
                    The trumpet sounds a parley.

Enter Sir Walter Blunt.

Blunt. I come with gracious offers from the King,   30
If you vouchsafe me hearing and respect.

Hotspur. Welcome, Sir Walter Blunt, and would to God
You were of our determination.°
Some of us love you well; and even those some
Envy your great deservings and good name,   35
Because you are not of our quality,°
But stand against us like an enemy.

17 **leading** generalship   19 **expedition** i.e., hastening into battle   26
journey-bated travel-weakened   33 **determination** party   36 **quality**
company

Blunt. And God defend° but still I should stand so,
        So long as out of limit° and true rule
40   You stand against anointed majesty.
        But to my charge.° The King hath sent to know
        The nature of your griefs, and whereupon
        You conjure from the breast of civil peace
        Such bold hostility, teaching his duteous land
45   Audacious cruelty. If that the King
        Have any way your good deserts forgot,
        Which he confesseth to be manifold,
        He bids you name your griefs, and with all speed
        You shall have your desires with interest,
50   And pardon absolute for yourself and these
        Herein misled by your suggestion.°

Hotspur. The King is kind, and well we know the King
        Knows at what time to promise, when to pay.
        My father and my uncle and myself
55   Did give him that same royalty he wears;
        And when he was not six and twenty strong,
        Sick in the world's regard, wretched and low,
        A poor unminded outlaw sneaking home,
        My father gave him welcome to the shore;
60   And when he heard him swear and vow to God
        He came but to be Duke of Lancaster,
        To sue his livery and beg his peace,°
        With tears of innocency and terms of zeal,
        My father, in kind heart and pity moved,
65   Swore him assistance, and performed it too.
        Now when the lords and barons of the realm
        Perceived Northumberland did lean to him,
        The more and less came in with cap and knee;°
        Met him in boroughs, cities, villages,
70   Attended him on bridges, stood in lanes,°

---

38 **defend** forbid   39 **limit** i.e., a subject's proper limits   41 **charge**
message   51 **suggestion** instigation   62 **sue . . . peace** sue for the deliv-
ery of his lands (which Richard II had arrogated to the crown) and make
his peace with the king   68 **with cap and knee** i.e., with cap off and
bended knee (in token of allegiance)   70 **lanes** facing rows

Laid gifts before him, proffered him their oaths,
Gave him their heirs as pages, followed him
Even at the heels in golden multitudes.
He presently, as greatness knows itself,°
Steps me a little higher than his vow   75
Made to my father, while his blood was poor,
Upon the naked shore at Ravenspurgh;
And now, forsooth, takes on him to reform
Some certain edicts and some strait° decrees
That lie too heavy on the commonwealth;   80
Cries out upon abuses, seems to weep
Over his country's wrongs; and by this face,
This seeming brow of justice, did he win
The hearts of all that he did angle for;
Proceeded further—cut me off the heads   85
Of all the favorites that the absent king
In deputation° left behind him here
When he was personal° in the Irish war.

Blunt. Tut! I came not to hear this.

Hotspur.   Then to the point.
In short time after, he deposed the King;   90
Soon after that deprived him of his life;
And in the neck of that° tasked° the whole state;
To make that worse, suff'red his kinsman March
(Who is, if every owner were well placed,
Indeed his king) to be engaged in Wales,   95
There without ransom to lie forfeited;
Disgraced me in my happy victories,
Sought to entrap me by intelligence;°
Rated° mine uncle from the council board;
In rage, dismissed my father from the court;   100
Broke oath on oath, committed wrong on wrong;
And in conclusion drove us to seek out
This head° of safety, and withal to pry

---

74 **as greatness knows itself** as greatness begins to feel its strength
79 **strait** strict 87 **In deputation** as deputies 88 **personal** personally
engaged 92 **in the neck of that** i.e., next 92 **tasked** taxed 98 **intelligence** spies 99 **Rated** scolded (cf. 1.3.14–20) 103 **head** army

Into his title, the which we find
105   Too indirect° for long continuance.

Blunt. Shall I return this answer to the King?

Hotspur. Not so, Sir Walter. We'll withdraw awhile.
     Go to the King; and let there be impawned
     Some surety for a safe return again,
110   And in the morning early shall mine uncle
     Bring him our purposes; and so farewell.

Blunt. I would you would accept of grace and love.

Hotspur. And may be so we shall.

Blunt.   Pray God you do. [*Exeunt.*]

[Scene 4. *York. The Archbishop's palace.*]

Enter [*the*] *Archbishop of York* [*and*] *Sir Michael.*

Archbishop. Hie, good Sir Michael; bear this sealèd
          brief°
     With wingèd haste to the Lord Marshal;
     This to my cousin Scroop; and all the rest
     To whom they are directed. If you knew
5   How much they do import, you would make haste.

Sir Michael. My good lord, I guess their tenor.

Archbishop. Like enough you do.
     Tomorrow, good Sir Michael, is a day
     Wherein the fortune of ten thousand men
10   Must bide the touch;° for, sir, at Shrewsbury,
     As I am truly given to understand,
     The King with mighty and quick-raisèd power
     Meets with Lord Harry; and I fear, Sir Michael,

---

105 **indirect** (1) not in the direct line (from Richard) (2) morally
oblique 4.4.1 **brief** message 10 **bide the touch** stand the test (as metal
is tested by the touchstone to know if it is gold)

What with the sickness of Northumberland,
Whose power was in the first proportion,°   15
And what with Owen Glendower's absence thence,
Who with them was a rated sinew° too
And comes not in, overruled by prophecies—
I fear the power of Percy is too weak
To wage an instant trial with the King.   20

Sir Michael. Why, my good lord, you need not fear;
There is Douglas and Lord Mortimer.

Archbishop. No, Mortimer is not there.

Sir Michael. But there is Mordake, Vernon, Lord Harry
Percy,
And there is my Lord of Worcester, and a head   25
Of gallant warriors, noble gentlemen.

Archbishop. And so there is; but yet the King hath
drawn
The special head° of all the land together—
The Prince of Wales, Lord John of Lancaster,
The noble Westmoreland and warlike Blunt,   30
And many moe corrivals° and dear° men
Of estimation and command in arms.

Sir Michael. Doubt not, my lord, they shall be well opposed.

Archbishop. I hope no less, yet needful 'tis to fear;
And, to prevent the worst, Sir Michael, speed.   35
For if Lord Percy thrive not, ere the King
Dismiss his power, he means to visit us,
For he hath heard of our confederacy,
And 'tis but wisdom to make strong against him.
Therefore make haste. I must go write again   40
To other friends; and so farewell, Sir Michael.
                                        Exeunt.

---

15 **proportion** magnitude 17 **rated sinew** highly valued strength
28 **head** army 31 **moe corrivals** more associates 31 **dear** important

[ACT 5

Scene 1. *The King's camp, near Shrewsbury.*]

*Enter the King, Prince of Wales, Lord John of
Lancaster, Earl of Westmoreland,° Sir Walter
Blunt, Falstaff.*

King. How bloodily the sun begins to peer
    Above yon bulky hill! The day looks pale
    At his distemp'rature.°

Prince.   The southern wind
    Doth play the trumpet° to his° purposes
5   And by his hollow whistling in the leaves
    Foretells a tempest and a blust'ring day.

King. Then with the losers let it sympathize,
    For nothing can seem foul to those that win.

The trumpet sounds. Enter Worcester [and Vernon].

    How now, my Lord of Worcester? 'Tis not well
10   That you and I should meet upon such terms

5.1.s.d. **Earl of Westmoreland** (in 5.2.28 we learn that Westmoreland
has been held as the "surety" of 4.3.109, but at this point Shakespeare apparently had not decided who was the hostage)   **3 his distemp'rature**
the sun's apparent ailment   **4 play the trumpet** (1) act the announcer
(2) blow as if playing a trumpet   **4 his** the sun's

As now we meet. You have deceived our trust
And made us doff our easy robes of peace
To crush our old limbs in ungentle steel.
This is not well, my lord; this is not well.
What say you to it? Will you again unknit   15
This churlish knot of all-abhorrèd war,
And move in that obèdient orb° again
Where you did give a fair and natural light,
And be no more an exhaled meteor,°
A prodigy of fear, and a portent   20
Of broachèd° mischief to the unborn times?

Worcester. Hear me, my liege.
For mine own part, I could be well content
To entertain the lag-end of my life
With quiet hours, for I protest   25
I have not sought the day of this dislike.

King. You have not sought it! How come it then?

Falstaff. Rebellion lay in his way, and he found it.

Prince. Peace, chewet,° peace!

Worcester. It pleased your Majesty to turn your looks   30
Of favor from myself and all our house;
And yet I must remember° you, my lord,
We were the first and dearest of your friends.
For you my staff of office did I break
In Richard's time, and posted day and night   35
To meet you on the way and kiss your hand
When yet you were in place and in account
Nothing so strong and fortunate as I.
It was myself, my brother, and his son
That brought you home and boldly did outdare   40
The dangers of the time. You swore to us,
And you did swear that oath at Doncaster,
That you did nothing purpose 'gainst the state,

---

17 **obedient orb** orbit of obedience   19 **exhaled meteor** wandering
body (not subject to orbit, and thought an omen or "prodigy")   21 **broachèd**
opened   29 **chewet** (1) jackdaw, i.e., chatterer (2) meat pie   32 **remember** remind

Nor claim no further than your new-fall'n° right,
45   The seat of Gaunt, dukedom of Lancaster.
To this we swore our aid. But in short space
It rained down fortune show'ring on your head,
And such a flood of greatness fell on you—
What with our help, what with the absent King,
50   What with the injuries of a wanton time,
The seeming sufferances that you had borne,
And the contrarious winds that held the King
So long in his unlucky Irish wars
That all in England did repute him dead—
55   And from this swarm of fair advantages
You took occasion to be quickly wooed
To gripe° the general sway into your hand;
Forgot your oath to us at Doncaster;
And, being fed by us, you used us so
60   As that ungentle gull,° the cuckoo's bird,°
Useth the sparrow—did oppress our nest,
Grew by our feeding to so great a bulk
That even our love durst not come near your sight
For fear of swallowing; but with nimble wing
65   We were enforced for safety sake to fly
Out of your sight and raise this present head;
Whereby we stand opposèd by such means
As you yourself have forged against yourself
By unkind usage, dangerous° countenance,
70   And violation of all faith and troth
Sworn to us in your younger enterprise.

King. These things, indeed, you have articulate,°
Proclaimed at market crosses, read in churches,
To face° the garment of rebellion
75   With some fine color° that may please the eye
Of fickle changelings and poor discontents,

---

44 **new-fall'n** i.e., by the death of his father, John of Gaunt   57 **gripe**
grab   60 **gull, bird** nestling (the cuckoo lays its eggs in other birds'
nests, and the young cuckoos when hatched speedily destroy the other
nestlings)   69 **dangerous** menacing   72 **articulate** spelled out   74 **face**
trim   75 **color** (1) hue (2) rhetorical coloring (hence, pretext)

Which gape and rub the elbow° at the news
Of hurlyburly innovation.°
And never yet did insurrection want
Such water colors to impaint his cause,   *80*
Nor moody beggars, starving for a time
Of pell-mell havoc and confusion.

Prince. In both your armies there is many a soul
Shall pay full dearly for this encounter,
If once they join in trial. Tell your nephew   *85*
The Prince of Wales doth join with all the world
In praise of Henry Percy. By my hopes,
This present enterprise set off his head,°
I do not think a braver gentleman,
More active-valiant or more valiant-young,   *90*
More daring or more bold, is now alive
To grace this latter age with noble deeds.
For my part, I may speak it to my shame,
I have a truant been to chivalry;
And so I hear he doth account me too.   *95*
Yet this before° my father's majesty—
I am content that he shall take the odds
Of his great name and estimation,
And will, to save the blood on either side,
Try fortune with him in a single fight.   *100*

King. And, Prince of Wales, so dare we venture thee;
Albeit,° considerations infinite
Do make against it. No, good Worcester, no!
We love our people well; even those we love
That are misled upon your cousin's part;   *105*
And, will they take the offer of our grace,°
Both he, and they, and you, yea, every man
Shall be my friend again, and I'll be his.
So tell your cousin, and bring me word
What he will do. But if he will not yield,   *110*
Rebuke and dread correction wait on us,°

---

77 **rub the elbow** i.e., hug themselves with delight   78 **innovation**
revolution   88 **set off his head** removed from his record   96 **this before** let me say this in the presence of   102 **Albeit** on the other
hand   106 **grace** pardon   111 **wait on us** are in our service

And they shall do their office.° So be gone.
We will not now be troubled with reply.
We offer fair; take it advisedly.

                    Exit Worcester [with Vernon].

115 *Prince.* It will not be accepted, on my life.
The Douglas and the Hotspur both together
Are confident against the world in arms.

King. Hence, therefore, every leader to his charge;
For, on their answer, will we set on them,
120 And God befriend us as our cause is just!

                    Exeunt. Manent° *Prince [and] Falstaff.*

Falstaff. Hal, if thou see me down in the battle and
bestride me, so!° 'Tis a point of friendship.

Prince. Nothing but a colossus can do thee that friendship. Say thy prayers, and farewell.

125 *Falstaff.* I would 'twere bedtime, Hal, and all well.

Prince. Why, thou owest God a death.°   [*Exit.*]

Falstaff. 'Tis not due yet: I would be loath to pay him
before his day. What need I be so forward with him
that calls not on me? Well, 'tis no matter; honor
130 pricks° me on. Yea, but how if honor prick° me off
when I come on? How then? Can honor set to a leg?
No. Or an arm? No. Or take away the grief of a
wound? No. Honor hath no skill in surgery then?
No. What is honor? A word. What is in that word
135 honor? What is that honor? Air—a trim° reckoning! Who hath it? He that died a Wednesday. Doth
he feel it? No. Doth he hear it? No. 'Tis insensible
then? Yea, to the dead. But will it not live with the
living? No. Why? Detraction° will not suffer it.
140 Therefore I'll none of it. Honor is a mere scutch-
eon°—and so ends my catechism.   *Exit.*

---

112 **office** duty   120 s.d. **Manent** remain (Latin)   122 **so** i.e., I shan't
object   126 **death** (pronounced like "debt," in which sense Falstaff
takes it)   130 **pricks** spurs   130 **prick** check (as a casualty)   135 **trim**
fine (spoken ironically)   139 **Detraction** slander   140–41 **scutcheon**
painted shield with coat of arms identifying a dead nobleman

[*Scene 2. The rebel camp, near Shrewsbury.*]

Enter Worcester [*and*] *Sir Richard Vernon.*

Worcester. O no, my nephew must not know, Sir Richard,
    The liberal and kind offer of the King.

Vernon. 'Twere best he did.

Worcester.   Then are we all undone.
    It is not possible, it cannot be,
    The King should keep his word in loving us.   5
    He will suspect us still and find a time
    To punish this offense in other faults.
    Supposition all our lives shall be stuck full of eyes;°
    For treason is but trusted like the fox,
    Who, never so tame, so cherished and locked up,   10
    Will have a wild trick° of his ancestors.
    Look how we can, or sad or° merrily,
    Interpretation will misquote our looks,
    And we shall feed like oxen at a stall,
    The better cherished still the nearer death.   15
    My nephew's trespass may be well forgot;
    It hath the excuse of youth and heat of blood,
    And an adopted name of privilege°—
    A hare-brained Hotspur, governed by a spleen.
    All his offenses live upon my head   20
    And on his father's. We did train° him on;
    And, his corruption being ta'en° from us,
    We, as the spring of all, shall pay for all.
    Therefore, good cousin, let not Harry know,
    In any case, the offer of the King.   25

5.2.8 **Supposition . . . eyes** suspicion will always be spying on us
11 **trick** (1) trait (2) wile   12 **or sad or** either sad or   18 **an . . . privilege** a nickname which carries a privilege (to be impulsive) with it
21 **train** (1) draw (2) aim   22 **ta'en** taken (like an infection)

Enter Hotspur [and Douglas]

Vernon. Deliver° what you will, I'll say 'tis so.
  Here comes your cousin.

Hotspur.   My uncle is returned.
  Deliver up my Lord of Westmoreland.°
  Uncle, what news?

30 *Worcester.* The King will bid you battle presently.

Douglas. Defy him by the Lord of Westmoreland.

Hotspur. Lord Douglas, go you and tell him so.

Douglas. Marry, and shall, and very willingly.   *Exit.*

Worcester. There is no seeming mercy in the King.

35 *Hotspur.* Did you beg any? God forbid!

Worcester. I told him gently of our grievances,
  Of his oath-breaking, which he mended thus,
  By now forswearing that he is forsworn.
  He calls us rebels, traitors, and will scourge
40 With haughty arms this hateful name in us.

Enter Douglas.

Douglas. Arm, gentlemen, to arms, for I have thrown
  A brave defiance in King Henry's teeth,
  And Westmoreland, that was engaged,° did bear it;
  Which cannot choose but bring him quickly on.

Worcester. The Prince of Wales stepped forth before
45   the King
  And, nephew, challenged you to single fight.

Hotspur. O, would the quarrel lay upon our heads,
  And that no man might draw short breath today
  But I and Harry Monmouth! Tell me, tell me,
50 How showed his tasking?° Seemed it in contempt?

---

26 **Deliver** report   28 **Westmoreland** (who has been hostage for the
safe return of Worcester and Vernon)   43 **engaged** held as hostage
50 **tasking** challenging

Vernon. No, by my soul. I never in my life
   Did hear a challenge urged more modestly,
   Unless a brother should a brother dare
   To gentle exercise and proof of arms.
   He gave you all the duties of a man;°   55
   Trimmed up your praises with a princely tongue;
   Spoke your deservings like a chronicle;°
   Making you ever better than his praise
   By still dispraising praise valued with you;°
   And, which became him like a prince indeed,   60
   He made a blushing cital of° himself,
   And chid his truant youth with such a grace
   As if he mast'red there a double spirit
   Of teaching and of learning instantly.°
   There did he pause; but let me tell the world,   65
   If he outlive the envy of this day,
   England did never owe° so sweet a hope,
   So much misconstrued in° his wantonness.

Hotspur. Cousin, I think thou art enamorèd
   On his follies. Never did I hear   70
   Of any prince so wild a liberty.°
   But be he as he will, yet once ere night
   I will embrace him with a soldier's arm,
   That° he shall shrink under my courtesy.
   Arm, arm with speed! And, fellows, soldiers, friends,   75
   Better consider what you have to do
   Than I, that have not well the gift of tongue,
   Can lift your blood up with persuasion.

             Enter a Messenger.

Messenger. My lord, here are letters for you.

Hotspur. I cannot read them now.—   80
   O gentlemen, the time of life is short!

---

55 **duties of a man** duties that one man can owe another   57 **like a chronicle** i.e., with the itemized detail characteristic of a chronicle history   59 **dispraising . . . you** i.e., because it must fall so far short of your deservings   61 **cital of** reference to   64 **instantly** simultaneously   67 **owe** own   68 **in** with respect to   71 **liberty** reckless freedom   74 **That** so that

To spend that shortness basely were too long
If life did ride upon a dial's point,
Still ending at the arrival of an hour.°
85 And if we live, we live to tread on kings;
If die, brave death, when princes die with us!
Now for our consciences, the arms are fair,
When the intent of bearing them is just.

                Enter another [Messenger].

Messenger. My lord, prepare. The King comes on
        apace.

90 Hotspur. I thank him that he cuts me from my tale,
For I profess not talking: only this—
Let each man do his best; and here draw I
A sword whose temper I intend to stain
With the best blood that I can meet withal
95 In the adventure of this perilous day.
Now, Esperance! Percy! and set on.
Sound all the lofty instruments of war,
And by that music let us all embrace;
For, heaven to earth,° some of us never shall
100 A second time do such a courtesy.
        Here they embrace. The trumpets sound. [Exeunt.]

        [Scene 3. *Shrewsbury. The battlefield.*]

        *The King enters with his power. Alarum to the
        battle. [Exeunt.] Then enter Douglas, and Sir
        Walter Blunt [disguised as the King].*

Blunt. What is thy name, that in battle thus thou
        crossest me?
What honor dost thou seek upon my head?

82–84 **To ... hour** if life were measured by a clock's hand, closing after
a single hour, it would still be too long if basely spent   99 **heaven to
earth** the odds are as great as heaven to earth

Douglas. Know then my name is Douglas,
  And I do haunt thee in the battle thus
  Because some tell me that thou art a king.   5

Blunt. They tell thee true.

Douglas. The Lord of Stafford dear today hath bought
  Thy likeness, for instead of thee, King Harry,
  This sword hath ended him: so shall it thee,
  Unless thou yield thee as my prisoner.   10

Blunt. I was not born a yielder, thou proud Scot;
  And thou shalt find a king that will revenge
  Lord Stafford's death.

  *They fight. Douglas kills Blunt. Then enter
                Hotspur.*

Hotspur. O Douglas, hadst thou fought at Holmedon
    thus,
  I never had triumphed upon a Scot.   15

Douglas. All's done, all's won: here breathless lies the
    King.

Hotspur. Where?

Douglas. Here.

Hotspur. This, Douglas? No. I know this face full well.
  A gallant knight he was, his name was Blunt;   20
  Semblably° furnished like the King himself.

Douglas. A fool° go with thy soul, whither it goes!
  A borrowed title hast thou bought too dear:
  Why didst thou tell me that thou wert a king?

Hotspur. The King hath many marching in his coats.   25

Douglas. Now, by my sword, I will kill all his coats;
  I'll murder all his wardrobe, piece by piece,
  Until I meet the King.

5.3.21 **Semblably** similarly   22 **fool** i.e., the title "fool"

Hotspur.   Up and away!
Our soldiers stand full fairly for the day.   [*Exeunt.*]

Alarum. Enter Falstaff solus.

30 *Falstaff.* Though I could scape shot-free° at London,
I fear the shot here. Here's no scoring° but upon the
pate. Soft! Who are you? Sir Walter Blunt. There's
honor for you! Here's no vanity!° I am as hot as
molten lead, and as heavy too. God keep lead out of
35 me. I need no more weight than mine own bowels.
I have led my rag-of-muffins where they are peppered.° There's not three of my hundred and fifty
left alive, and they are for the town's end, to beg
during life. But who comes here?

Enter the Prince.

Prince. What, stands thou idle here? Lend me thy
40   sword.
Many a nobleman lies stark and stiff
Under the hoofs of vaunting enemies, whose deaths
are yet unrevenged. I prithee lend me thy sword.

Falstaff. O Hal, I prithee give me leave to breathe
45   awhile. Turk Gregory° never did such deeds in arms
as I have done this day. I have paid° Percy, I have
made him sure.

  Prince. He is indeed, and living to kill thee.
I prithee lend me thy sword.

50 *Falstaff.* Nay, before God, Hal, if Percy be alive, thou
gets not my sword; but take my pistol if thou wilt.

Prince. Give it me. What, is it in the case?

30 **shot-free** without paying the bill   31 **scoring** (1) billing (2)
striking   33 **Here's no vanity** (spoken ironically: i.e., here *is* "vanity"—
futility, foolishness. But vanity also implies lightness, which is then
set against the "heaviness" of life: cf. "lead," "heavy," "weight")   36–37
I . . . peppered (a common practice of officers, who drew the dead
soldiers' pay)   45 **Turk Gregory** (in Shakespeare's time, "Turk" was
a byword for any ruthless man; "Gregory" may refer to the irascible Pope
Gregory VII, or to Elizabeth's enemy, Pope Gregory XIII. Pope and Turk
were regarded as the two great enemies of Protestant Christendom)   46 **paid** killed

Falstaff. Ay, Hal. 'Tis hot, 'tis hot.° There's that will
   sack a city.

> *The Prince draws it out and finds*
> *it to be a bottle of sack.*

Prince. What, is it a time to jest and dally now?   55
> *He throws the bottle at him. Exit.*

Falstaff. Well, if Percy be alive, I'll pierce° him. If he
   do come in my way, so; if he do not, if I come in his
   willingly, let him make a carbonado° of me. I like
   not such grinning honor as Sir Walter hath. Give
   me life; which if I can save, so; if not, honor comes   60
   -unlooked for, and there's an end.   [*Exit.*]

[Scene 4. *Shrewsbury. The battlefield.*]

> *Alarum. Excursions.° Enter the King, the Prince,*
> *Lord John of Lancaster, Earl of Westmoreland.*

King. I prithee, Harry, withdraw thyself, thou bleedest
   too much.
   Lord John of Lancaster, go you with him.

John. Not, I, my lord, unless I did bleed too.

Prince. I beseech your Majesty make up,°
   Lest your retirement do amaze° your friends.   5

King. I will do so. My Lord of Westmoreland, lead
   him to his tent.

Westmoreland. Come, my lord, I'll lead you to your
   tent.

Prince. Lead me, my lord? I do not need your help;
   And God forbid a shallow scratch should drive   10

53 **hot** i.e., he has fired it so often he has had to put it away to cool
56 **pierce** (pronounced "perse")   58 **carbonado** meat slashed open
for broiling 5.4.s.d.   **Excursions** sorties   4 **make up** move forward
5 **amaze** dismay

The Prince of Wales from such a field as this,
Where stained nobility lies trodden on,
And rebels' arms triumph in massacres!

John. We breathe° too long. Come, cousin Westmore-
        land,
15   Our duty this way lies. For God's sake, come.
                    [*Exeunt Lancaster and Westmoreland.*]

Prince. By God, thou hast deceived me, Lancaster!
I did not think thee lord of such a spirit.
Before, I loved thee as a brother, John,
But now I do respect thee as my soul.

20 *King.* I saw him hold Lord Percy at the point
With lustier maintenance than I did look for
Of such an ungrown warrior.

Prince. O, this boy lends mettle to us all!   *Exit.*

                    [*Enter Douglas.*]

Douglas. Another king? They grow like Hydra's°
        heads.
25   I am the Douglas, fatal to all those
That wear those colors on them. What art thou
That counterfeit'st the person of a king?

King. The King himself, who, Douglas, grieves at heart
So many of his shadows thou hast met,
30   And not the very King. I have two boys
Seek Percy and thyself about the field;
But, seeing thou fall'st on me so luckily,
I will assay thee, and defend thyself.

Douglas. I fear thou art another counterfeit;
35   And yet, in faith, thou bearest thee like a king.
But mine I am sure thou art, whoe'er thou be,
And thus I win thee.

        *They fight, the King being in danger. Enter Prince
                of Wales.*

14 **breathe** pause   24 **Hydra** a many-headed monster which grew two
heads for each one destroyed

Prince. Hold up thy head, vile Scot, or thou art like
    Never to hold it up again. The spirits
    Of valiant Shirley, Stafford, Blunt° are in my arms.   *40*
    It is the Prince of Wales that threatens thee,
    Who never promiseth but he means to pay.
                    They fight: Douglas flieth.
    Cheerly, my lord. How fares your Grace?
    Sir Nicholas Gawsey hath for succor sent,
    And so hath Clifton. I'll to Clifton straight.   *45*

King. Stay and breathe awhile.
    Thou hast redeemed thy lost opinion,°
    And showed thou mak'st some tender° of my life,
    In this fair rescue thou hast brought to me.

Prince. O God, they did me too much injury   *50*
    That ever said I heark'ned for your death.
    If it were so, I might have let alone
    The insulting hand of Douglas over you,
    Which would have been as speedy in your end
    As all the poisonous potions in the world,   *55*
    And saved the treacherous labor of your son.

King. Make up to Clifton; I'll to Sir Nicholas Gawsey.
                          Exit.

Enter Hotspur.

Hotspur. If I mistake not, thou art Harry Monmouth.

Prince. Thou speak'st as if I would deny my name.

Hotspur. My name is Harry Percy.   *60*

Prince. Why, then I see a very valiant rebel of the name.
    I am the Prince of Wales, and think not, Percy,
    To share with me in glory any more.
    Two stars keep not their motion in one sphere,°
    Nor can one England brook° a double reign   *65*
    Of Harry Percy and the Prince of Wales.

---

40 Shirley, Stafford, Blunt (those whom Douglas has killed wearing the
King's coats)   **47 opinion** reputation   **48 tender** value   **64 sphere** orbit   **65 brook** put up with

Hotspur. Nor shall it, Harry, for the hour is come
  To end the one of us; and would to God
  Thy name in arms were now as great as mine!

70 *Prince.* I'll make it greater ere I part from thee,
  And all the budding honors on thy crest
  I'll crop to make a garland for my head.

Hotspur. I can no longer brook thy vanities. *They fight.*

  Enter Falstaff.

Falstaff. Well said, Hal! To it, Hal! Nay, you shall find
75 no boy's play here, I can tell you.

  Enter Douglas. He fighteth with Falstaff, [who]
  falls down as if he were dead. [Exit Douglas.]
  The Prince killeth Percy.

Hotspur. O Harry, thou hast robbed me of my youth!
  I better brook the loss of brittle life
  Than those proud titles thou hast won of me.
  They wound my thoughts worse than thy sword my
    flesh.
80 But thoughts, the slaves of life, and life, time's fool,°
  And time, that takes survey of all the world,
  Must have a stop. O, I could prophesy,
  But that the earthy and cold hand of death
  Lies on my tongue. No, Percy, thou art dust,
85 And food for—   [*Dies.*]

Prince. For worms, brave Percy. Fare thee well, great
    heart.
  Ill-weaved ambition, how much art thou shrunk!
  When that this body did contain a spirit,
  A kingdom for it was too small a bound;
90 But now two paces of the vilest earth
  Is room enough. This earth that bears thee dead
  Bears not alive so stout° a gentleman.
  If thou wert sensible of courtesy,
  I should not make so dear° a show of zeal.

---

80 **slaves ... fool** i.e., because thoughts are dependent on life and because life is subservient to time   92 **stout** valiant   94 **dear** heartfelt

But let my favors° hide thy mangled face;   *95*
And, even in thy behalf, I'll thank myself
For doing these fair rites of tenderness.
Adieu, and take thy praise with thee to heaven.
Thy ignominy sleep with thee in the grave,
But not rememb'red in thy epitaph.   *100*
                    He spieth Falstaff on the ground.
What, old acquaintance? Could not all this flesh
Keep in a little life? Poor Jack, farewell!
I could have better spared a better man.
O, I should have a heavy miss° of thee
If I were much in love with vanity.°   *105*
Death hath not struck so fat a deer° today,
Though many dearer,° in this bloody fray.
Emboweled° will I see thee by-and-by;
Till then in blood by noble Percy lie.   *Exit.*

                Falstaff riseth up.

Falstaff. Emboweled? If thou embowel me today, I'll   *110*
give you leave to powder° me and eat me too tomorrow. 'Sblood, 'twas time to counterfeit, or that
hot termagant° Scot had paid me scot and lot° too.
Counterfeit? I lie; I am no counterfeit. To die is to
be a counterfeit, for he is but the counterfeit of a   *115*
man who hath not the life of a man; but to counterfeit
dying when a man thereby liveth, is to be no
counterfeit, but the true and perfect image of life
indeed. The better part of valor is discretion,° in the
which better part I have saved my life. Zounds, I am   *120*
afraid of this gunpowder Percy, though he be dead.
How if he should counterfeit too, and rise? By my
faith, I am afraid he would prove the better counterfeit. Therefore I'll make him sure; yea, and I'll swear

95 **favors** (probably Hal's ostrich plumes, his emblem as Prince of
Wales)   104 **heavy miss** "heavy" loss (in two senses)   105 **vanity** friv-
olity (and lightness)   106 **deer** (with pun on "dear")   107 **dearer** nobler, more valuable   108 **Emboweled** disemboweled (for embalming)
111 **powder** salt   113 **termagant** bloodthirsty   113 **paid me scot and
lot** killed me (literally, paid me in full; "scot" and "lot" were parish
taxes)   119 **The ... discretion** (Falstaff willfully misinterprets the
maxim that valor is the better for being accompanied by discretion)

125   I killed him. Why may not he rise as well as I? Noth-
       ing confutes me but eyes, and nobody sees me.
       Therefore, sirrah [*stabs him*], with a new wound in
       your thigh, come you along with me.

       He takes up Hotspur on his back. Enter Prince
       [and] John of Lancaster.

       Prince. Come, brother John; full bravely hast thou
          fleshed
       Thy maiden sword.

130   *John.*   But, soft! whom have we here?
       Did you not tell me this fat man was dead?

       Prince. I did; I saw him dead,
       Breathless and bleeding on the ground. Art thou
          alive,
       Or is it fantasy that plays upon our eyesight?
135   I prithee speak. We will not trust our eyes
       Without our ears. Thou art not what thou seem'st.

       Falstaff. No, that's certain. I am not a double man;°
       but if I be not Jack Falstaff, then am I a Jack.° There
       is Percy. If your father will do me any honor, so; if
140   not, let him kill the next Percy himself. I look to be
       either earl or duke, I can assure you.

       Prince. Why, Percy I killed myself, and saw thee dead!

       Falstaff. Didst thou? Lord, Lord, how this world is
       given to lying. I grant you I was down, and out of
145   breath, and so was he; but we rose both at an instant
       and fought a long hour by Shrewsbury clock. If I
       may be believed, so; if not, let them that should re-
       ward valor bear the sin upon their own heads. I'll
       take it upon my death, I gave him this wound in the
150   thigh. If the man were alive and would deny it,
       zounds! I would make him eat a piece of my sword.

       John. This is the strangest tale that ever I heard.

       Prince. This is the strangest fellow, brother John.

       137 **double man** (1) wraith (2) twofold man   138 **Jack** rascal

Come, bring your luggage nobly on your back.
For my part, if a lie may do thee grace,   *155*
I'll gild it with the happiest terms I have.
                         A retreat is sounded.
The trumpet sounds retreat; the day is ours.
Come, brother, let us to the highest of the field,
To see what friends are living, who are dead.
                Exeunt [Prince Henry and Prince John].

Falstaff. I'll follow,° as they say, for reward. He that   *160*
   rewards me, God reward him. If I do grow great,
   I'll grow less; for I'll purge,° and leave sack, and
   live cleanly, as a nobleman should do.
                         Exit [bearing off the body].

            [Scene 5. *Shrewsbury. The battlefield.*]

*The trumpets sound. Enter the King, Prince of
Wales, Lord John of Lancaster, Earl of Westmoreland, with Worcester and Vernon prisoners.*

King. Thus ever did rebellion find rebuke.
   Ill-spirited Worcester, did not we send grace,
   Pardon, and terms of love to all of you?
   And wouldst thou turn our offers contrary?
   Misuse the tenor of thy kinsman's trust?   *5*
   Three knights upon our party slain today,
   A noble earl, and many a creature else
   Had been alive this hour,
   If like a Christian thou hadst truly borne
   Betwixt our armies true intelligence.°   *10*

Worcester. What I have done my safety urged me to;
   And I embrace this fortune patiently,
   Since not to be avoided it falls on me.

160 **follow** i.e., as hounds do when the quarry is killed, to receive their
reward   162 **purge** repent   5.5.10 **intelligence** information

King. Bear Worcester to the death, and Vernon too;
15   Other offenders we will pause upon.
                    [*Exeunt Worcester and Vernon, guarded*].
        How goes the field?

Prince. The noble Scot, Lord Douglas, when he saw
        The fortune of the day quite turned from him,
        The noble Percy slain, and all his men
20   Upon the foot of fear, fled with the rest;
        And falling from a hill, he was so bruised
        That the pursuers took him. At my tent
        The Douglas is, and I beseech your Grace
        I may dispose of him.

King.   With all my heart.

25   *Prince.* Then, brother John of Lancaster, to you
        This honorable bounty shall belong.
        Go to the Douglas and deliver him
        Up to his pleasure, ransomless and free.
        His valors shown upon our crests today
30   Have taught us how to cherish such high deeds,
        Even in the bosom of our adversaries.

John. I thank your Grace for this high courtesy,
        Which I shall give away immediately.

King. Then this remains, that we divide our power.
35   You, son John, and my cousin Westmoreland,
        Towards York shall bend you with your dearest
            speed
        To meet Northumberland and the prelate Scroop,
        Who, as we hear, are busily in arms.
        Myself and you, son Harry, will towards Wales
40   To fight with Glendower and the Earl of March.
        Rebellion in this land shall lose his sway,
        Meeting the check of such another day;
        And since this business° so fair is done,
        Let us not leave till all our own be won.   *Exeunt.*

FINIS

43 **business** (trisyllabic)

Textual Note

The text for the present edition as a whole is the first quarto of 1598. This is generally believed to have been set from an earlier edition of the same year (Qo), of which today only four leaves are known—containing the text of the play from 1.3.199 to 2.2.112. Qo, so far as we have it, shows characteristics which relate it closely to an authorial manuscript, probably a corrected working manuscript rather than a fair copy. Q1 may therefore be regarded as still reasonably faithful to what Shakespeare wrote. The later quartos (Q2, 1599; Q3, 1604; Q4, 1608; Q5, 1613), each set from the one preceding, and the Folio (1623), set from Q5, have increasingly less authority.

Apart from spelling and punctuation, which are modernized in this edition, and regularization of speech prefixes, I have followed Q1, and, where it exists, Qo. With one exception (4.1.12–13), I preserve the lineation of these editions, printing therefore as prose a number of passages so printed in Q1 but now almost invariably divided into lines of verse. It is possible, even probable, that some of these passages were intended to be verse; but the wide differences exhibited by editors in lineating them persuade me to reserve this entertainment for readers who wish to engage in it. I have usually indicated in the footnotes one or more of the traditional patterns of lineation for each passage.

The table below records departures from Qo–Q1. The first reading (*italics*) is that which I have adopted in the text; the second is that of Q1. Almost all of the emendations were made in the quartos or in the First Folio, indicating that in Shakespeare's own day the passages in question were suspect; but because these early texts have no authority, they are not cited as sources.

Division into acts and scenes is here that of the Folio, save that I follow Capell and most other editors (including those of the Globe edition) in dividing the Folio's 5.2 into 5.2 and 5.3 and renumbering the subsequent scenes. In the quartos there is no indication of acts or scenes.

1.1.62 *a dear* deere   69 *blood did* bloud. Did   76 *In faith it is* [the quartos and folios give to the King]

1.2.82 *similes* smiles   166 *Bardolph, Peto* Haruey, Rossill [these are names that Shakespeare evidently meant originally to assign to Falstaff's associates: see below, 2.4.173–76, 180–81]

1.3.199–206 [Q0–Q4 do not assign to Hotspur, but give as part of Northumberland's speech]

2.2.16 *two and twenty* xxii

2.3.4 *respect* the respect   70 *A roan* Roane

2.4.34 *precedent* present   37 [assigned to Prince]   173–76 [assigned to Gadshill, Ross (=Russell: see above, 1.2.166), Falstaff, Ross]   180–81 [assigned to Ross]   244 *eel-skin* elsskin   341 *Owen* O   393 *tristful* trustfull

3.1.99 *cantle* scantle   132 *on* an

3.2.115 *Enlargèd* Enlargd

3.3.36 *that's* that   59 *tithe* tight   90s.d. *them* him   178 *guests* ghesse   206 *o'* of

4.1.20 *I, my lord* I my mind   54 *is* tis   107 *dropped* drop   125 *cannot* can   126 *yet* it

4.3.21 *horse* horses   28 *ours* our   82 *country's* Countrey

5.1.138 *will it* wil

5.2.3 *undone* vnder one   25s.d. *Hotspur* Percy

5.3.22 *A* Ah

5.4.67 *Nor* Now   75s.d. *who* he   157 *ours* our

The Sources of *Henry IV* [*Part One*]

So far as we know, the sources on which Shakespeare chiefly drew in writing *Henry IV* [*Part One*] were the following: (1) the pages on Henry's reign in Volume III of Raphael Holinshed's compilation of British history, *Chronicles of England, Scotland, and Ireland*, first published in 1577 but later reissued (1586–87) in an enlarged edition, which seems to have been the text actually consulted by Shakespeare; (2) the relevant stanzas in Book III of Samuel Daniel's long poem, *The First Four Books of the Civil Wars between the Two Houses of Lancaster and York* (1595); and (3) *The Famous Victories of Henry the Fifth, Containing the Honorable Battle of Agincourt*—an anonymous play of uncertain date, first printed in 1598, today extant in only one known copy. This has been called in recent years both "a decrepit potboiler"[1] and a work of "extraordinary power of expression," probably an apprentice-piece by Shakespeare.[2]

The relevant parts of Daniel and Holinshed are printed in the following section, together with the whole of the *Famous Victories*, so that every reader may watch for himself the workings of a first-rate dramatic imagination. There are brief comments on this process in the Introduction, but the reader who would understand in practical terms what is meant by "art" in phrases like "the art of playwriting" will want to compare minutely at least one act of *1 Henry IV* with the materials out of which it was made. In the case of the *Famous Victories*, comparisons with appropriate parts of *2 Henry IV* and *Henry V* will also be illuminating.

---

[1]Bullough, Geoffrey. *Narrative and Dramatic Sources of Shakespeare,* vol. 4 (New York: Columbia University Press, 1962), p. 168.
[2]Pitcher, S. M. *The Case for Shakespeare's Authorship of the Famous Victories* (New York: University Publishers, 1961), p. 5.

Spelling and punctuation have been modernized in reprinting these selections, some emendations have been silently made, and the text of the *Famous Victories*, following the lead of J. Q. Adams and S. M. Pitcher, is set as prose.

RAPHAEL HOLINSHED

From Chronicles of England, Scotland, and Ireland [1587 Edition]

[Uneasy Lies the Head that Wears a Crown]

. . . One night, as the King was going to bed, he was in
danger to have been destroyed; for some naughty traitorous
persons had conveyed into his bed a certain iron made with
smith's craft, like a caltrop, with three long pricks, sharp
and small, standing upright in such sort that when he had
laid him down and that the weight of his body should come
upon the bed, he should have been thrust in with those
pricks and peradventure slain; but as God would, the King,
not thinking of any such thing, chanced yet to feel and perceive the instrument before he laid him down and so escaped the danger. Howbeit, he was not so soon delivered
from fear; for he might well have his life in suspicion and
provide for the preservation of the same, sith perils of death
crept into his secret chamber and lay lurking in the bed of
down where his body was to be reposed and to take rest. Oh
what a suspected state therefore is that of a king holding his
regiment with the hatred of his people, the heartgrudgings
of his courtiers, and the peremptory practices of both together! Could he confidently compose or settle himself to
sleep for fear of strangling? Durst he boldly eat and drink
without dread of poisoning? Might he adventure to show
himself in great meetings or solemn assemblies without
mistrust of mischief against his person intended? What
pleasure or what felicity could he take in his princely pomp,
which he knew by manifest and fearful experience to be envied and maligned to the very death? . . .

[Trouble in Wales and Scotland]

. . . Owen Glendower, according to his accustomed manner, robbing and spoiling within the English borders, caused all the forces of the shire of Hereford to assemble together against them, under the conduct of Edmund Mortimer, Earl of March. But coming to try the matter by battle, whether by treason or otherwise, so it fortuned that the English power was discomfited, the Earl taken prisoner, and above a thousand of his people slain in the place. The shameful villainy used by the Welshwomen towards the dead carcasses was such as honest ears would be ashamed to hear and continent tongues to speak thereof. The dead bodies might not be buried without great sums of money given for liberty to convey them away.

The King was not hasty to purchase the deliverance of the Earl of March, because his title to the crown was well-enough known, and therefore suffered him to remain in miserable prison, wishing both the said Earl and all other of his lineage out of this life, with God and his saints in heaven so they had been out of the way, for then all had been well enough as he thought. But to let these things pass, the King this year sent his eldest daughter Blanch, accompanied with the Earl of Somerset, the Bishop of Worcester, the Lord Clifford, and others, into Almanie [i.e., Germany], which brought her to Colin [i.e., Cologne], and there with great triumph she was married to William, Duke of Bavier [i.e., Bavaria], son and heir to Lewis, the Emperor. About mid of August, the King, to chastise the presumptuous attempts of the Welshmen, went with a great power of men into Wales to pursue the captain of the Welsh rebel Owen Glendower, but in effect he lost his labor; for Owen conveyed himself out of the way into his known lurking places, and (as was thought) through art magic[al], he caused such foul weather of winds, tempest, rain, snow, and hail to be raised for the annoyance of the King's army that the like had not been heard of; in such sort, that the King was constrained to return home, having caused his people yet to spoil and burn first a great part of the country. The same time, the Lord Edmund of Langley, Duke of York, departed this life and was buried at Langley with his brethren.

The Scots, under the leading of Patric Hepborne of the Hales, the younger, entering into England was overthrown at Nesbit in the marches, as in the Scottish chronicle ye may find more at large. This battle was fought the two and twentieth of June, in this year of our Lord, 1402.

Archibald, Earl Douglas, sore displeased in his mind for this overthrow, procured a commission to invade England, and that to his cost, as ye may likewise read in the Scottish histories. For at a place called Homeldon, they were so fiercely assailed by the Englishmen, under the leading of the Lord Percy, surnamed Henry Hotspur, and George, Earl of March, that with violence of the English shot they were quite vanquished and put to flight, on the Rood Day in harvest, with a great slaughter made by the Englishmen. . . . There were slain of men of estimation: Sir John Swinton, Sir Adam Gordon, Sir John Leviston, Sir Alexander Ramsey of Dalhousie, and three and twenty knights, besides ten thousand of the commons; and of prisoners among others were these: Mordake, Earl of Fife, son to the Governor; Archibald, Earl Douglas, which in the fight lost one of his eyes; Thomas, Earl of Murray; Robert, Earl of Angus; (and as some writers have) the Earls of Athol and Menteith, with five hundred other of meaner degrees. . . .

Edmund Mortimer, Earl of March, prisoner with Owen Glendower, whether for irksomeness of cruel captivity or fear of death or for what other cause, it is uncertain, agreed to take part with Owen against the King of England and took to wife the daughter of the said Owen.

Strange wonders happened (as men reported) at the nativity of this man, for the same night he was born, all his father's horses in the stable were found to stand in blood up to the bellies.

[The Percys' Rebellion]

Henry, Earl of Northumberland, with his brother Thomas, Earl of Worcester, and his son, the Lord Henry Percy, surnamed Hotspur, which were to King Henry in the beginning of his reign both faithful friends and earnest aiders, began now to envy his wealth and felicity; and especially they were grieved because the King demanded of the Earl and his son such Scottish prisoners as were taken at Homeldon and Nesbit: for of all the captives which were taken in the conflicts fought in those two places, there were delivered to the King's possession only Mordake, Earl of Fife, the Duke of Albany's son, though the King did divers and sundry times require deliverance of the residue, and that with great threatenings; wherewith the Percys, being sore offended, for that they claimed them as their own proper prisoners and their peculiar prize, by the counsel of the Lord Thomas Percy, Earl of Worcester, whose study was ever (as some write) to procure malice and set things in a broil, came to the King unto Windsor (upon a purpose to prove him) and there required of him that, either by ransom or otherwise, he would cause to be delivered out of prison Edmund Mortimer, Earl of March, their cousin german, whom (as they reported) Owen Glendower kept in filthy prison, shackled with irons, only for that he took his part and was to him faithful and true.

The King began not a little to muse at this request and not without cause; for indeed it touched him somewhat near, sith this Edmund was son to Roger, Earl of March, son to the Lady Philip, daughter of Lionel, Duke of Clarence, the third son of King Edward the Third; which Edmund, at King Richard's going into Ireland, was proclaimed heir apparent to the crown and realm; whose aunt called Eleanor, the Lord Henry Percy had married; and therefore King Henry could not well hear that any man should be earnest about the advancement of that lineage. The King, when he had studied on the matter, made answer that the Earl of March was not taken prisoner for his cause nor in his service but willingly suffered himself to be taken, because he would not withstand the attempts of Owen Glendower and his [ac]complices, and therefore he would neither ransom him nor relieve him.

The Percys with this answer and fraudulent excuse were not a little fumed, insomuch that Henry Hotspur said openly: "Behold, the heir of the realm is robbed of his right, and yet the robber with his own will not redeem him." So in this fury the Percys departed, minding nothing more than to depose King Henry from the high type of his royalty and to place in his seat their cousin Edmund, Earl of March, whom they did not only deliver out of captivity but also (to the high displeasure of King Henry) entered in league with the foresaid Owen Glendower. Herewith they, by their deputies in the house of the Archdeacon of Bangor, divided the realm amongst them, causing a tripartite indenture to be made and sealed with their seals, by the covenants whereof: all England from Severn and Trent south and eastward was assigned to the Earl of March; all Wales and the lands beyond Severn westward were appointed to Owen Glendower; and all the remnant from Trent northward to the Lord Percy.

This was done (as some have said) through a foolish credit given to a vain prophecy, as though King Henry was the moldwarp, cursed of God's own mouth, and they three were the dragon, the lion, and the wolf, which should divide this realm between them. Such is the deviation (saith Hall [an earlier chronicler]) and not divination of those blind and fantastical dreams of the Welsh prophesiers. King Henry, not knowing of this new confederacy, and nothing less minding than that which after happened, gathered a great army to go again into Wales, whereof the Earl of Northumberland and his son were advertised by the Earl of Worcester, and with all diligence raised all the power they could make, and sent to the Scots which before were taken prisoners at Homeldon for aid of men, promising to the Earl of Douglas the town of Berwick and a part of Northumberland, and to other Scottish lords great lordships and seignories, if they obtained the upper hand. The Scots, in hope of gain and desirous to be revenged of their old griefs, came to the Earl with a great company well appointed.

The Percys, to make their part seem good, devised certain articles by the advice of Richard Scroop, Archbishop of York, brother to the Lord Scroop, whom King Henry had caused to be beheaded at Bristol. These articles being shown to diverse noblemen and other states of the realm, moved them to favor their purpose, insomuch that many of them did not only promise to the Percys aid and succor by words, but also by their writings and seals confirmed the same. Howbeit, when the matter came to trial, the most part of the confederates abandoned them and at the day of the conflict left them alone. Thus after that the conspirators had discovered themselves, the Lord Henry Percy, desirous to proceed in the enterprise, upon trust to be assisted by Owen Glendower, the Earl of March, and others, assembled an army of men-of-arms and archers forth of Cheshire and Wales. Incontinently, his uncle Thomas Percy, Earl of Worcester, that had the government of the Prince of Wales, who as then lay at London in secret manner, conveyed himself out of the Prince's house, and coming to Stafford (where he met his nephew), they increased their power by all ways and means they could devise. The Earl of Northumberland himself was not with them but, being sick, had promised upon his amendment to repair unto them (as some write) with all convenient speed.

These noblemen, to make their conspiracy to seem excusable, besides the articles above mentioned sent letters abroad, wherein was contained that their gathering of an army tended to none other end but only for the safeguard of their own persons and to put some better government in the commonwealth. For whereas taxes and taillages [i.e., imposts] were daily levied under pretense to be employed in defense of the realm, the same were vainly wasted and unprofitably consumed; and where through the slanderous reports of their enemies the King had taken a grievous displeasure with them, they durst not appear personally in the King's presence, until the prelates and barons of the realm had obtained of the King license for them to come and purge themselves before him, by lawful trial of their peers, whose judgment (as they pretended) they would in no wise refuse. Many that saw and heard these letters did commend their diligence and highly praised their assured fidelity and trustiness towards the commonwealth.

But the King, understanding their cloaked drift, devised (by what means he might) to quiet and appease the commons and deface their contrived forgeries; and therefore he wrote an answer to their libels that he marveled much, sith the Earl of Northumberland and the Lord Henry Percy, his son, had received the most part of the sums of money granted to him by the clergy and commonalty for defense of the marches, as he could evidently prove what should move them to complain and raise such manifest slanders. And whereas he understood that the Earls of Northumberland and Worcester and the Lord Percy had by their letters signified to their friends abroad that, by reason of the slanderous reports of their enemies, they durst not appear in his presence without the mediation of the prelates and nobles of the realm, so as they required pledges whereby they might safely come afore him to declare and allege what they had to say in proof of their innocency, he protested by letters sent forth under his seal that they might safely come and go, without all danger or any manner of endamagement to be offered to their persons.

But this could not satisfy those men but that, resolved to go forwards with their enterprise, they marched towards Shrewsbury upon hope to be aided (as men thought) by Owen Glendower and his Welshmen, publishing abroad throughout the countries on each side that King Richard was alive, whom if they wished to see, they willed them to repair in armor unto the castle of Chester, where (without all doubt) he was at that present and ready to come forward. This tale being raised, though it were most untrue, yet it bred variable motions in men's minds, causing them to waver so as they knew not to which part they should stick; and verily divers were well affected towards King Richard, specially such as had tasted of his princely bountifulness, of which there was no small number. And to speak a truth, no marvel it was if many envied the prosperous state of King Henry, sith it was evident enough to the world that he had with wrong usurped the crown, and not only violently deposed King Richard but also cruelly procured his death; for the which, undoubtedly, both he and his posterity tasted such troubles as put them still in danger of their states, till their direct succeeding line was quite rooted out by the contrary faction, as in Henry the Sixth and Edward the Fourth it may appear.

But now to return where we left. King Henry, advertised of the proceedings of the Percys, forthwith gathered about him such power as he might make, and being earnestly called upon by the Scot, the Earl of March [not Mortimer, but George Dunbar, Earl of March of Scotland], to make haste and give battle to his enemies, before their power by delaying of time should still too much increase, he passed forward with such speed that he was in sight of his enemies, lying in camp near to Shrewsbury, before they were in doubt of any such thing; for the Percys thought that he would have stayed at Burton-upon-Trent till his council had come thither to him to give their advice what he were best to do. But herein the enemy was deceived of his expectation, sith the King had great regard of expedition and making speed for the safety of his own person whereunto the Earl of March incited him, considering that in delay is danger and loss in lingering, as the poet in the like case saith:

> *Tolle moras, nocuit semper differre paratis,*
> *Dum trepidant nullo firmatae robore partes.*

By reason of the King's sudden coming in this sort, they stayed from assaulting the town of Shrewsbury, which enterprise they were ready at that instant to have taken in hand, and forthwith the Lord Percy (as a captain of high courage) began to exhort the captains and soldiers to prepare themselves to battle, sith the matter was grown to that point that by no means it could be avoided, so that (said he): "This day shall either bring us all to advancement and honor or else, if it shall chance us to be overcome, shall deliver us from the King's spiteful malice and cruel disdain; for playing the men (as we ought to do), better it is to die in battle for the commonwealth's cause than through cowardlike fear to prolong life, which after shall be taken from us by sentence of the enemy."

Hereupon the whole army, being in number about fourteen thousand chosen men, promised to stand with him so long as life lasted. There were with the Percys as chieftains of this army: the Earl of Douglas, a Scottish man; the Baron of Kinderton; Sir Hugh Browne and Sir Richard Vernon, knights; with diverse other stout and right valiant captains. Now when the two armies were encamped, the one against the other, the Earl of Worcester and the Lord Percy with their [ac]complices sent the articles (whereof I spake before) by Thomas Caiton and Thomas Salvain, esquiers to King Henry, under their hands and seals, which articles in effect charged him with manifest perjury, in that (contrary to his oath received upon the evangelists at Doncaster, when he first entered the realm after his exile) he had taken upon him the crown and royal dignity, imprisoned King Richard, caused him to resign his title and, finally, to be murdered. Diverse other matters they laid to his charge: as levying of taxes and taillages, contrary to his promise; infringing of laws and customs of the realm; and suffering the Earl of March to remain in prison without travailing to have him delivered. All which things they, as procurers and protectors of the commonwealth, took upon them to prove against him, as they protested unto the whole world.

King Henry, after he had read their articles, with the defiance which they annexed to the same, answered the esquiers that he was ready with dint of sword and fierce battle to prove their quarrel false and nothing else than a forged matter, not doubting but that God would aid and assist him in his righteous cause against the disloyal and false forsworn traitors. The next day in the morning early, being the even of Mary Magdalen, they set their battles in order on both sides, and now, whilest the warriors looked when the token of battle should be given, the Abbot of Shrewsbury and one of the clerks of the privy seal were sent from the King unto the Percys to offer them pardon if they would come to any reasonable agreement. By their persuasions, the Lord Henry Percy began to give ear unto the King's offer and so sent with them his uncle, the Earl of Worcester, to declare unto the King the causes of those troubles and to require some effectual reformation in the same.

[The Battle of Shrewsbury, July 21, 1403]

It was reported for a truth that now, when the King had condescended unto all that was reasonable at his hands to be required and seemed to humble himself more than was meet for his estate, the Earl of Worcester (upon his return to his nephew) made relation clean contrary to that the King had said, in such sort that he set his nephew's heart more in displeasure towards the King than ever it was before, driving him by that means to fight whether he would or not; then suddenly [he] blew the trumpets, the King's part crying S[aint] George upon them, the adversaries cried "Esperance Percy," and so the two armies furiously joined. The archers on both sides shot for the best game, laying on such load with arrows that many died and were driven down that never rose again.

The Scots (as some write), which had the fore ward on the Percys' side, intending to be revenged of their old displeasures done to them by the English nation, set so fiercely on the King's fore ward, led by the Earl of Stafford, that they made the same draw back, and had almost broken their adversaries' array. The Welshmen also, which before had lain lurking in the woods, mountains, and marshes, hearing of this battle toward, came to the aid of the Percys and refreshed the wearied people with new succors. The King, perceiving that his men were thus put to distress, what with the violent impression of the Scots and the tempestuous storms of arrows that his adversaries discharged freely against him and his people, it was no need to will him to stir; for suddenly, with his fresh battle, he approached and relieved his men, so that the battle began more fierce than before. Here the Lord Henry Percy and the Earl Douglas, a right stout and hardy captain, not regarding the shot of the King's battle nor the close order of the ranks, pressing forward together bent their whole forces towards the King's person, coming upon him with spears and swords so fiercely that the Earl of March the Scot [again George Dunbar], perceiving their purpose, withdrew the King from that side of the field (as some write) for his great benefit and safeguard (as it appeared), for they gave such a violent onset upon them that stood about the King's standard that, slaying his standard-bearer, Sir Walter Blunt, and overthrowing the standard, they made slaughter of all those that stood about it, as the Earl of Stafford, that day made by the King Constable of the realm, and diverse other.

The Prince that day holp his father like a lusty young

gentleman; for although he was hurt in the face with an arrow, so that diverse noblemen that were about him would have conveyed him forth of the field, yet he would not suffer them so to do, lest his departure from amongst his men might haply have stricken some fear into their hearts; and so, without regard of his hurt, he continued with his men and never ceased either to fight where the battle was most hot or to encourage his men where it seemed most need. This battle lasted three long hours with indifferent fortune on both parts, till at length the King, crying Saint George victory, brake the array of his enemies and adventured so far that (as some write) the Earl Douglas strake him down and at that instant slew Sir Walter Blunt and three others appareled in the King's suit and clothing, saying: "I marvel to see so many kings thus suddenly arise one in the neck of another." The King indeed was raised and did that day many a noble feat of arms, for as it is written, he slew that day with his own hands six and thirty persons of his enemies. The other on his part, encouraged by his doings, fought valiantly and slew the Lord Percy, called Sir Henry Hotspur. To conclude, the King's enemies were vanquished and put to flight, in which flight the Earl of Douglas, for haste, falling from the crag of a high mountain, brake one of his cullions and was taken, and for his valiantness, of the King frankly and freely delivered.

There was also taken the Earl of Worcester, the procurer and setter forth of all this mischief, Sir Richard Vernon, and the Baron of Kinderton, with diverse other. There were slain upon the King's part, besides the Earl of Stafford, to the number of ten knights: Sir Hugh Shirley, Sir John Clifton, Sir John Cokaine, Sir Nicholas Gawsey, Sir Walter Blunt, Sir John Claverley, Sir John Macy of Podington, Sir Hugh Mortimer, and Sir Robert Gawsey, all the which received the same morning the order of knighthood; Sir Thomas Wendesley was wounded to death and so passed out of this life shortly after. There died in all upon the King's side sixteen hundred, and four thousand were grievously wounded. On the contrary side were slain, besides the Lord Percy, the most part of the knights and esquiers of the county of Chester, to the number of two hundred, besides yeomen and footmen; in all there died of those that fought on the Percys' side about five thousand. This battle was fought on Mary Magdalen Even, being Saturday. Upon the Monday following, the Earl of Worcester, the Baron of Kinderton, and Sir Richard Vernon, knights, were condemned and beheaded. The Earl's head was sent to London, there to be set on the bridge.

[Reconciliation of Prince and King, 1411]

. . . The Lord Henry, Prince of Wales, eldest son to King Henry, got knowledge that certain of his father's servants were busy to give informations against him, whereby discord might arise betwixt him and his father; for they put into the King's head not only what evil rule (according to the course of youth) the Prince kept, to the offense of many, but also what great resort of people came to his house, so that the court was nothing furnished with such a train as daily followed the Prince. These tales brought no small suspicion into the King's head, lest his son would presume to usurp the Crown, he being yet alive, through which suspicious jealousy it was perceived that he favored not his son, as in times past he had done.

The Prince, sore offended with such persons as, by slanderous reports, sought not only to spot his good name abroad in the realm but to sow discord also betwixt him and his father, wrote his letters into every part of the realm to reprove all such slanderous devices of those that sought his discredit. And to clear himself the better, that the world might understand what wrong he had to be slandered in such wise, about the feast of Peter and Paul, to wit, the nine and twentieth day of June, he came to the court with such a number of noblemen and other his friends that wished him well, as the like train had been seldom seen repairing to the court at any one time in those days. He was appareled in a gown of blue satin full of small eyelet holes, at every hole the needle hanging by a silk thread with which it was sewed. About his arm he wore a hound's collar set full of SS of gold, and the tirets likewise being of the same metal.

The court was then at Westminster where, he being entered into the hall, not one of his company durst once advance himself further than the fire in the same hall, notwithstanding they were earnestly requested by the lords to come higher; but they, regarding what they had in commandment of the Prince, would not presume to do in any thing contrary thereunto. He himself, only accompanied with those of the King's house, was straight admitted to the presence of the King his father, who being at that time grievously diseased, yet caused himself in his chair to be borne into his privy chamber, where in the presence of three or four persons in whom he had confidence, he commanded the Prince to show what he had to say concerning the cause of his coming.

The Prince, kneeling down before his father, said: "Most redoubted and sovereign lord and father, I am at this time come to your presence as your liege man and as your natural son, in all things to be at your commandment. And where I understand you have in suspicion my demeanor against your Grace, you know very well that if I knew any man within this realm of whom you should stand in fear, my duty were to punish that person, thereby to remove that grief from your heart. Then how much more ought I to suffer death, to ease your Grace of that grief which you have of me, being your natural son and liege man; and to that end I have this day made myself ready by confession and receiving of the sacrament. And therefore I beseech you, most redoubted lord and dear father, for the honor of God, to ease your heart of all such suspicion as you have of me and to dispatch me here before your knees with this same dagger," and withal he delivered unto the King his dagger, in all humble reverence, adding further that his life was not so dear to him that he wished to live one day with his displeasure, "and therefore in thus ridding me out of life and yourself from all suspicion, here in presence of these lords and before God at the day of the general judgment, I faithfully protest clearly to forgive you."

The King, moved herewith, cast from him the dagger and, embracing the Prince, kissed him and with shedding tears confessed that indeed he had him partly in suspicion, though now (as he perceived) not with just cause, and therefore, from thenceforth no misreport should cause him to have him in mistrust, and this he promised of his honor. So by his great wisdom was the wrongful suspicion which his father had conceived against him removed and he restored to his favor. And further, where he could not but grievously complain of them that had slandered him so greatly, to the defacing not only of his honor but also putting him in danger of his life, he humbly besought the King that they might answer their unjust accusation; and in case they were found to have forged such matters upon a malicious purpose, that then they might suffer some punishment for their faults, though not to the full of that they had deserved. The King, seeming to grant his reasonable desire, yet told him that he must tarry a parliament that such offenders might be punished by judgment of their peers; and so for that time he was dismissed, with great love and signs of fatherly affection.

Thus were the father and the son reconciled, betwixt whom the said pickthanks had sown division, insomuch that the son, upon a vehement conceit of unkindness sprung in the father, was in the way to be worn out of favor. Which was the more likely to come to pass by their informations that privily charged him with riot and other uncivil demeanor unseemly for a prince. Indeed, he was youthfully given, grown to audacity, and had chosen him companions agreeable to his age, with whom he spent the time in such recreations, exercises, and delights as he fancied. But yet (it should seem by the report of some writers) that his behavior was not offensive or at least tending to the damage of anybody, sith he had a care to avoid doing of wrong and to tender his affections within the tract of virtue, whereby he opened unto himself a ready passage of good liking among the prudent sort and was beloved of such as could discern his disposition, which was in no degree so excessive as that he deserved in such vehement manner to be suspected. In whose dispraise I find little but to his praise very much. . . .

SAMUEL DANIEL

From The First Four Books of the
Civil Wars between the Two Houses
of Lancaster and York [1595]

[Bolingbroke, having become Henry IV, has military
difficulties.]

86

And yet new Hydras lo, new heads appear
T'afflict that peace reputed then so sure,
And gave him much to do, and much to fear,
And long and dangerous tumults did procure,
And those even of his chiefest followers were
Of whom he might presume him most secure,
Who whether not so graced or so preferred
As they expected, these new factions stirred.

87

The Percys were the men, men of great might,
Strong in alliance, and in courage strong
That thus conspire, under pretense to right
The crookèd courses they had suffered long:
Whether their conscience urged them or despite,
Or that they saw the part they took was wrong,
Or that ambition hereto did them call,
Or others envied grace, or rather all.

88

What cause soever were, strong was their plot,
Their parties great, means good, th' occasion fit:
Their practice close, their faith suspected not,
Their states far off and they of wary wit:
Who with large promises draw in the Scot
To aid their cause—he likes, and yields to it,
Not for the love of them or for their good,
But glad hereby of means to shed our blood.

89

Then join they with the Welsh, who fitly trained
And all in arms under a mighty head
Great Glendow'r, who long warred, and much attained,
Sharp conflicts made, and many vanquishèd:
With whom was Edmund Earl of March retained
Being first his prisoner, now confederèd,
A man the King much feared, and well he might
Lest he should look whether his crown stood right.

90

For Richard, for the quiet of the state,
Before he took those Irish wars in hand
About succession doth deliberate,
And finding how the certain right did stand,
With full consent this man did ordinate
The heir apparent in the Crown and land:
Then judge if this the King might nearly touch,
Although his might were small, his right being much.

91

With these the Percys them confederate,
And as three heads they league in one intent,
And instituting a triumvirate
Do part the land in triple government:
Dividing thus among themselves the state,
The Percys should rule all the North from Trent
And Glendow'r Wales: the Earl of March should be
Lord of the South from Trent; and thus they 'gree.

92

Then those two helps which still such actors find—
Pretense of common good, the King's disgrace—
Doth fit their course, and draw the vulgar mind
To further them and aid them in this case:
The King they accused for cruel, and unkind
That did the state, and Crown, and all deface;
A perjured man that held all faith in scorn,
Whose trusted oaths had others made forsworn.

93

Besides the odious detestable act
Of that late murdered king they aggravate,
Making it his that so had willed the fact
That he the doers did remunerate:
And then such taxes daily doth exact
That were against the orders of the state,
And with all these or worse they him assailed
Who late of others with the like prevailed.

94

Thus doth contentious proud mortality
Afflict each other and itself torment:
And thus O thou, mind-tort'ring misery,
Restless ambition, born in discontent,
Turn'st and retossest with iniquity
The unconstant courses frailty did invent:
And foul'st fair order and defil'st the earth
Fost'ring up war, father of blood and dearth.

95

Great seemed the cause, and greatly, too, did add
The peoples' love thereto, these crimes rehearsed,
That many gathered to the troops they had
And many more do flock from coasts dispersed:
But when the King had heard these news so bad,
Th' unlookt for dangerous toil more nearly pierced;
For bent t'wards Wales t'appease those tumults there,
H' is forced divert his course, and them forbear.

96

Not to give time unto th' increasing rage
And gathering fury, forth he hastes with speed,
Lest more delay or giving longer age
To th' evil grown, it might the cure exceed:
All his best men at arms, and leaders sage
All he prepared he could, and all did need;
For to a mighty work thou goest O King,
To such a field that power to power shall bring.

97

There shall young Hotspur with a fury led
Meet with thy forward son as fierce as he:
There warlike Worcester long experiencèd
In foreign arms, shall come t' encounter thee:
There Douglas to thy Stafford shall make head:
There Vernon for thy valiant Blunt shall be:
There shalt thou find a doubtful bloody day,
Though sickness keep Northumberland away.

98

Who yet reserved, though after quit for this,
Another tempest on thy head to raise,
As if still-wrong revenging *Nemesis*
Did mean t' afflict all thy continual days:
And yet this field he happily might miss
For thy great good, and therefore well he stays:
What might his force have done being joined thereto
When that already gave so much to do?

99

The swift approach and unexpected speed
The King had made upon this new-raised force
In th' unconfirmèd troops much fear did breed,
Untimely hind'ring their intended course;
The joining with the Welsh they had decreed
Was hereby stopped which made their part the worse,
Northumberland with forces from the North
Expected to be there, was not set forth.

100

And yet undaunted Hotspur seeing the King
So near approached leaving the work in hand
With forward speed his forces marshaling,
Sets forth his father coming to withstand:
And with a cheerful voice encouraging
By his great spirit his well emboldened band,
Brings a strong host of firm resolvèd might,
And placed his troops before the King in sight.

101

This day (saith he) O faithful valiant friends,
Whatever it doth give, shall glory give:
This day with honor frees our state, or ends
Our misery with fame, that still shall live,
And do but think how well this day he spends
That spends his blood his country to relieve:
Our holy cause, our freedom, and our right,
Sufficient are to move good minds to fight.

102

Besides th' assurèd hope of victory
That we may even promise on our side
Against this weak-constrainèd company,
Whom force and fear, not will and love doth guide
Against a prince whose foul impiety
The heavens do hate, the earth cannot abide,
Our number being no less, our courage more,
What need we doubt if we but work therefor.

103

This said, and thus resolved even bent to charge
Upon the King, who well their order viewed
And careful noted all the form at large
Of their proceeding, and their multitude:
And deeming better if he could discharge
The day with safety, and some peace conclude,
Great proffers sends of pardon, and of grace
If they would yield, and quietness embrace.

SAMUEL DANIEL

104

But this refused, the King with wrath incensed
Rage against fury doth with speed prepare:
And O, saith he, though I could have dispensed
With this day's blood, which I have sought to spare
That greater glory might have recompensed
The forward worth of these that so much dare,
That we might honor had by th' overthrown,
That th' wounds we make, might not have been our own.

105

Yet since that other men's iniquity
Calls on the sword of wrath against my will,
And that themselves exact this cruelty,
And I constrainèd am this blood to spill:
Then on my masters, on courageously
True-hearted subjects against traitors ill,
And spare them not who seek to spoil us all,
Whose foul confusèd end soon see you shall.

106

Straight moves with equal motion equal rage
The like incensèd armies unto blood,
One to defend, another side to wage
Foul civil war, both vows their quarrel good:
Ah too much heat to blood doth now enrage
Both who the deed provokes and who withstood,
That valor here is vice, here manhood sin,
The forward'st hands doth O least honor win.

107

But now begin these fury-moving sounds
The notes of wrath that music brought from hell,
The rattling drums which trumpets voice confounds,
The cries, th' encouragements, the shouting shrill;
That all about the beaten air rebounds,
Thund'ring confusèd, murmurs horrible,
To rob all sense except the sense to fight:
Well hands may work, the mind hath lost his sight.

108

O war! begot in pride and luxury,
The child of wrath and of dissension,
Horrible good; mischief necessary,
The foul reformer of confusion,
Unjust-just scourge of our iniquity,
Cruel recurrer of corruption:
O that these sin-sick states in need should stand
To be let blood with such a boist'rous hand!

109

And O how well thou hadst been spared this day
Had not wrong-counseled Percy been perverse,
Whose young undangered hand now rash makes way
Upon the sharpest fronts of the most fierce:
Where now an equal fury thrusts to stay
And rebeat-back that force and his disperse,
Then these assail, then those chase back again,
Till stayed with new-made hills of bodies slain.

110

There lo that new-appearing glorious star
Wonder of Arms, the terror of the field,
Young Henry, laboring where the stoutest are,
And even the stoutest forces back to yield,
There is that hand bold'ned to blood and war
That must the sword in woundrous° actions wield:
But better hadst thou learned with others' blood
A less expense to us, to thee more good.

111

Hadst thou not there lent present speedy aid
To thy endangered father nearly tired,
Whom fierce encountring Douglas overlaid,
That day had there his troublous life expired:
Heroical courageous Blunt arrayed
In habit like as was the King attired

°**woundrous** (Daniel's pun on "wound" and "wondress")

And deemed for him, excused that fate with his,
For he had what his lord did hardly miss.

112

For thought a king he would not now disgrace
The person then supposed, but princelike shows
Glorious effects of worth that fit his place,
And fighting dies, and dying overthrows:
Another of that forward name and race
In that hot work his valiant life bestows,
Who bare the standard of the King that day,
Whose colors overthrown did much dismay.

113

And dear it cost, and O much blood is shed
To purchase thee this losing victory
O travailed King: yet hast thou conquerèd
A doubtful day, a mighty enemy:
But O what wounds, what famous worth lies dead!
That makes the winner look with sorrowing eye,
Magnanimous Stafford lost that much had wrought,
And valiant Shirley who great glory got.

114

Such wreck of others' blood thou didst behold,
O furious Hotspur, ere thou lost thine own!
Which now once lost that heat in thine waxed cold,
And soon became thy army overthrown;
And O that this great spirit, this courage bold,
Had in some good cause been rightly shown!
So had not we thus violently then
Have termed that rage, which valor should have been.

ANONYMOUS

The Famous Victories of Henry the Fifth

[Dramatis Personae

King Henry IV
Prince Henry of Monmouth, his son (later
   King Henry V)
Duke of York   } brothers of Henry IV
Duke of Exeter
Earl of Oxford
Archbishop of Canterbury
The Lord Chief Justice
The Lord Mayor of London
The Sheriff
Ned
Tom   } friends to Prince Henry
Sir John Oldcastle, alias Jockey
English Captain
English Soldier
Two Receivers
Clerk of the King's Bench
The Jailer
The Thief, Cutbert Cutter, alias Gad's Hill
Derick, a poor carrier
John Cobbler
Robin Pewterer   } the Watch
Lawrence Costermonger
The Vintner's Boy, Robin
The Porter
King Charles VI, of France
The Dolphin, his son

Duke of Burgundy
Archbishop of Bourges
The Constable
A Herald
A Messenger
A French Captain
Jack Drummer
French Soldiers
A Frenchman

Princess Katherine, daughter of Charles VI
Mistress Cobbler

Lords, Ladies, Attendants

Scene: England and France]

The Famous Victories of Henry the Fifth
Containing the
Honorable Battle of Agincourt

[*Scene 1*]

Enter the young Prince, Ned, and Tom.

Prince. Come away, Ned and Tom.

Both. Here, my lord.

Prince. Come away, my lads. Tell me, sirs, how much
gold have you got?

Ned. Faith, my lord, I have got five hundred pound. 5

Prince. But tell me, Tom, how much hast thou got?

Tom. Faith, my lord, some four hundred pound.

Prince. For hundred pounds! Bravely spoken, lads! But
tell me, sirs, think you not that it was a villainous part
of me to rob my father's receivers? 10

Ned. Why, no, my lord; it was but a trick of youth.

Prince. Faith, Ned, thou sayest true. But tell me, sirs,
whereabouts are we?

Tom. My lord, we are now about a mile off London.

Prince. But, sirs, I marvel that Sir John Oldcastle comes 15
not away. Zounds, see where he comes.

Enter Jockey [*i.e., John Oldcastle*]*.*

How now, Jockey, what news with thee?

145

John Oldcastle. Faith, my lord, such news as passeth!
For the town of Deptford is risen with hue and cry
20   after your man, which parted from us the last night
and has set upon and hath robbed a poor carrier.

Prince. Zounds, the villain that was wont to spy out our
booties?

John Oldcastle. Ay, my lord, even the very same.

25   *Prince.* Now base-minded rascal to rob a poor carrier!
Well, it skills not; I'll save the base villain's life, ay,
I may. But tell me, Jockey, whereabouts be the re-
ceivers?

John Oldcastle. Faith, my lord, they are hard by; but
30   the best is we are ahorseback and they be afoot, so
we may escape them.

Prince. Well, if the villains come, let me alone with
them! But tell me, Jockey, how much gotst thou from
the knaves? For I am sure I got something, for one
35   of the villains so belammed me about the shoulders
as I shall feel it this month.

John Oldcastle. Faith, my lord, I have got a hundred
pound.

Prince. A hundred pound! Now bravely spoken,
40   Jockey. But come, sirs, lay all your money before
me. Now, by heaven, here is a brave show! But, as
I am true gentleman, I will have the half of this spent
tonight! But, sirs, take up your bags; here comes the
receivers. Let me alone.

Enters two Receivers.°

45   *First Receiver.* Alas, good fellow, what shall we do? I
dare never go home to the court, for I shall be
hanged. But look, here is the young Prince. What
shall we do?

Prince. How now, you villains! What are you?

44 s.d. **Receivers** i.e., of taxes

First Receiver. Speak you to him.   50

Second Receiver. No, I pray, speak you to him.

Prince. Why, how now, you rascals! Why speak you
not?

First Receiver. Forsooth, we be—pray speak you to
him.   55

Prince. Zounds, villains, speak, or I'll cut off your
heads!

Second Receiver. Forsooth, he can tell the tale better
than I.

First Receiver. Forsooth, we be your father's receivers.   60

Prince. Are you my father's receivers? Then I hope ye
have brought me some money.

First Receiver. Money? Alas, sir, we be robbed!

Prince. Robbed! How many were there of them?

First Receiver. Marry, sir, there were four of them;   65
and one of them had Sir John Oldcastle's bay hobby,
and your black nag.

Prince. Gog's wounds! How like you this, Jockey?
Blood, you villains! My father robbed of his money
abroad, and we robbed in our stables! But tell me,   70
how many were of them?

First Receiver. If it please you, there were four of them;
and there was one about the bigness of you—but I
am sure I so belammed him about the shoulders that
he will feel it this month.   75

Prince. Gog's wounds! You lammed them fairly—so
that they have carried away your money. But come,
sirs, what shall we do with the villains?

Both Receivers. I beseech your Grace, be good to us.

Ned. I pray you, my lord, forgive them this once.   80

[*Prince.*] Well, stand up, and get you gone. And look

that you speak not a word of it—for, if there be—
zounds! I'll hang you and all your kin!

Exit [Receivers].

Prince. Now, sirs, how like you this? Was not this
85 bravely done? For now the villains dare not speak a
word of it, I have so feared them with words. Now,
whither shall we go?

All. Why, my lord, you know our old host's at Faversham.

90 *Prince.* Our host's at Faversham! Blood, what shall we
do there? We have a thousand pound about us, and
we shall go to a petty ale-house? No, no! You know
the old tavern in Eastcheap; there is good wine—
besides, there is a pretty wench that can talk well;
95 for I delight as much in their tongues as any part
about them.

All. We are ready to wait upon your Grace.

Prince. Gog's wounds! "Wait"? We will go altogether;
we are all fellows. I tell you, sirs, and the King my
100 father were dead, we would be all kings. Therefore,
come away!

Ned. Gog's wounds, bravely spoken, Harry!

[Exeunt omnes.]

[Scene 2]

Enter John Cobbler, Robin Pewterer,
Lawrence Costermonger.

John. All is well here; all is well, masters.

Lawrence. How say you, neighbor John Cobbler? I
think it best that my neighbor, Robin Pewterer, went
to Pudding Lane End, and we will watch here at
5 Billingsgate Ward. How say you, neighbor Robin?
How like you this?

Robin. Marry, well, neighbors; I care not much if I go to Pudding Lane's End. But, neighbors, if you hear any ado about me, make haste; and if I hear any ado about you, I will come to you.   *Exit Robin.*   10

Lawrence. Neighbor, what news hear you of the young Prince?

John. Marry, neighbor, I hear say he is a toward young prince; for, if he meet any by the highway, he will not let° to—talk with him. I dare not call him thief,   15 but sure he is one of these taking fellows.

Lawrence. Indeed, neighbor, I hear say he is as lively a young prince as ever was.

John. Ay, and I hear say if he use it long, his father will cut him off from the Crown. But, neighbor, say noth-   20 ing of that!

Lawrence. No, no, neighbor, I warrant you!

John. Neighbor, methinks you begin to sleep. If you will, we will sit down; for I think it is about midnight.

Lawrence. Marry, content, neighbor; let us sleep.   25

Enter Derick, roving.

Derick. Who! Who there, who there!   *Exit Derick.*

Enter Robin.

Robin. Oh, neighbors, what mean you to sleep, and such ado in the streets?

Both. How now, neighbor, what's the matter?

Enter Derick again.

Derick. Who there! Who there! Who there!   30

John. Why, what ailst thou? Here is no horses.

Derick. O alas, man, I am robbed! Who there! Who there!

---

15 **let** hesitate (the speaker is about to add "rob," then thinks better of it)

Robin. Hold him, neighbor Cobbler. Why, I see thou
35   art a plain clown.°

Derick. Am I a clown? Zounds, masters, do clowns go
in silk apparel? I am sure all we gentlemen-clowns in
Kent scant go so well. Zounds, you know clowns very
well! Hear you, are you Master Constable? And you
40   be, speak, for I will not take it at his hands.

John. Faith, I am not Master Constable; but I am one
of his bad° officers, for he is not here.

Derick. Is not Master Constable here? Well, it is no matter. I'll have the law at his hands.

45   *John.* Nay, I pray you, do not take the law of us.

Derick. Well, you are one of his beastly officers.

John. I am one of his bad° officers.

Derick. Why, then, I charge thee, look to him!

John. Nay, but hear you, sir; you seem to be an honest
50   fellow, and we are poor men; and now 'tis night, and
we would be loath to have anything ado; therefore,
I pray thee, put it up.

Derick. First, thou sayest true; I am an honest fellow
—and a proper, handsome fellow, too! And you
55   seem to be poor men; therefore I care not greatly.
Nay, I am quickly pacified. But, and you chance to
spy the thief, I pray you lay hold on him.

Robin. Yes, that we will, I warrant you.

Derick. 'Tis a wonderful thing to see how glad the knave
60   is, now I have forgiven him.

John. Neighbors, do you look about you. How now,
who's there?

Enter the Thief.

Thief. Here is a good fellow. I pray you, which is the
way to the old tavern in Eastcheap?

35 **clown** rustic   42, 47 **bad** regularly installed (i.e., "bade")

Derick. Whoop halloo! Now, Gad's Hill, knowest   65
.thou me?

Thief. I know thee for an ass.

Derick. And I know thee for a taking fellow upon
Gad's Hill in Kent. A bots light upon ye.

Thief. The whoreson villain would be knocked.   70

Derick. Masters, villain, and ye be men, stand to him,
and take his weapon from him. Let him not pass you!

John. My friend, what make you abroad now? It is too
late to walk now.

Thief. It is not too late for true men to walk.   75

Lawrence. We know thee not to be a true man.

[They seize the Thief.]

Thief. Why, what do you mean to do with me? Zounds!
I am one of the King's liege people.

Derick. Hear you, sir, are you one of the King's liege   80
people?

Thief. Ay, marry am I, sir! What say you to it?

Derick. Marry, sir, I say you are one of the King's
filching people.

John. Come, come, let's have him away.

Thief. Why, what have I done?   85

Robin. Thou hast robbed a poor fellow, and taken
away his goods from him.

Thief. I never saw him before.

Derick. Masters, who comes here?

Enter the Vintner's Boy.

Boy. How now, goodman Cobbler.   90

John. How now, Robin, what makes thou abroad at
this time of night?

Boy. Marry, I have been at the Counter;° I can tell such news as never you have heard the like!

95 *John.* What is that, Robin? What is the matter?

Boy. Why, this night, about two hours ago, there came the young Prince, and three or four more of his companions, and called for wine good store; and then they sent for a noise of musicians, and were very
100 merry for the space of an hour; then, whether their music liked them not, or whether they had drunk too much wine or no, I cannot tell, but our pots flew against the walls; and then they drew their swords and went into the street and fought, and some took
105 one part and some took another; but for the space of half an hour there was such a bloody fray as passeth! And none could part them until such time as the Mayor and Sheriff were sent for; and then, at the last, with much ado, they took them; and so the
100 young Prince was carried to the Counter; and then, about one hour after, there came a messenger from the Court in all haste from the King for my Lord Mayor and the Sheriff—but for what cause I know not.

115 *John.* Here is news, indeed, Robert!

Lawrence. Marry, neighbor, this news is strange, indeed! I think it best, neighbor, to rid our hands of this fellow first.

Thief. What mean you to do with me?

120 *John.* We mean to carry you to the prison, and there to remain till the sessions day.

Thief. Then, I pray you, let me go to the prison where my master is.

John. Nay, thou must go to the country prison, to New-
125 gate. Therefore, come away.

Thief. [*To Derick*] I prithee, be good to me, honest fellow.

93 **Counter** London prison under jurisdiction of the Lord Mayor

Derick. Ay, marry, will I; I'll be very charitable to thee, for I will never leave thee—till I see thee on the gallows.   130

                              [*Exeunt omnes.*]

                         [*Scene 3*]

          Enter Henry the Fourth [*attended*], *with the
           Earl of Exeter, and the Lord of Oxford.*

Oxford. And please your Majesty, here is my Lord Mayor and the Sheriff of London to speak with your Majesty.

King. Admit them to our presence.

              Enter the Mayor and the Sheriff.

King. Now, my good Lord Mayor of London, the   5
cause of my sending for you at this time is to tell you of a matter which I have learned of my council. Herein I understand that you have committed my son to prison without our leave and license. What! Although he be a rude youth, and likely to give occa-   10
sion, yet you might have considered that he is a prince, and my son, and not to be haled to prison by every subject.

Mayor. May it please your Majesty to give us leave to tell our tale?   15

King. Or else God forbid! Otherwise, you might think me an unequal judge, having more affection to my son than to any rightful judgment.

Mayor. Then I do not doubt but we shall rather de-serve commendations at your Majesty's hands than   20
any anger.

King. Go to, say on.

Mayor. Then, if it please your Majesty, this night be-

twixt two and three of the clock in the morning my
lord the young Prince, with a very disordered company, came to the old tavern in Eastcheap; and
whether it was that their music liked them not, or
whether they were overcome with wine, I know not,
but they drew their swords, and into the street they
went; and some took my lord the young Prince's
part, and some took the other; but betwixt them
there was such a bloody fray for the space of half
an hour that neither watchmen nor any other could
stay them; till my brother, the Sheriff of London,
and I were sent for; and, at the last, with much ado,
we stayed them. But it was long first, which was a
great disquieting to all your loving subjects thereabouts. And then, my good lord, we knew not
whether your Grace had sent them to try us whether
we would do justice, or whether it were of their own
voluntary will or not, we cannot tell. And, therefore,
in such a case, we knew not what to do; but, for our
own safeguard, we sent him to ward; where he
wanteth nothing that is fit for his Grace and your
Majesty's son. And thus, most humbly beseeching
your Majesty to think of our answer—

King. Stand aside until we have further deliberated on
your answer.

Exit Mayor [*with Sheriff*].
Ah, Harry, Harry, now thrice-accursed Harry, that
hath gotten a son which with grief will end his
father's days! Oh, my son, a prince thou art, ay, a
prince indeed—and to deserve imprisonment! And
well have they done, and like faithful subjects. [*To
his Attendants*] Discharge them, and let them go.

Exeter. I beseech your Grace, be good to my lord the
young Prince.

King. Nay, nay, 'tis no matter; let him alone.

Oxford. Perchance the Mayor and the Sheriff have been
too precise in this matter.

King. No, they have done like faithful subjects. I will go   60
myself to discharge them and let them go.

Exit omnes.

[*Scene 4*]

Enter Lord Chief Justice, Clerk of the Office,
Jailer, John Cobbler, Derick, and the Thief.

Judge. Jailer, bring the prisoner to the bar.

Derick. Hear you, my lord; I pray you, bring the bar
to the prisoner.

Judge. Hold thy hand up at the bar.

Thief. Here it is, my lord.   5

Judge. Clerk of the Office, read his indictment.

Clerk. What is thy name?

Thief. My name was known before I came here, and
shall be when I am gone, I warrant you.

Judge. Ay, I think so; but we will know it better be-   10
fore thou go.

Derick. Zounds, and you do but send to the next jail,
we are sure to know his name; for this is not the first
prison he hath been in, I'll warrant you.

Clerk. What is thy name?   15

Thief. What need you to ask, and have it in writing?

Clerk. Is not thy name Cutbert Cutter?

Thief. What the devil need you ask, and know it so
well?

Clerk. Why then, Cutbert Cutter, I indict thee, by the   20
name of Cutbert Cutter, for robbing a poor carrier
the 20th day of May last past, in the fourteenth year

of the reign of our sovereign lord King Henry the
Fourth, for setting upon a poor carrier upon Gad's

25   Hill, in Kent, and having beaten and wounded the
said carrier, and taken his goods from him—

Derick. Oh, masters, stay there! Nay, let's never belie
the man, for he hath not beaten and wounded me
also, but he hath beaten and wounded my pack, and

30   hath taken the great raze° of ginger that Bouncing
Bess with the jolly buttocks should have had. That
grieves me most.

Judge. Well, what sayest thou? Art thou guilty, or not
guilty?

35   *Thief.* Not guilty, my lord.

Judge. By whom wilt thou be tried?

Thief. By my lord the young Prince, or by myself,
whether you will.

        Enter the young Prince, with Ned and Tom.

Prince. Come away, my lads. Gog's wounds, ye villain,

40   what make you here? I must go about my business
myself and you must stand loitering here?

Thief. Why, my lord, they have bound me, and will not
let me go.

Prince. Have they bound thee, villain? Why, how now,

45   my lord?

Judge. I am glad to see your Grace in good health.

Prince. Why, my lord, this is my man. 'Tis marvel you
knew him not long before this. I tell you, he is a
man of his hands.

50   *Thief.* Ay, Gog's wounds, that I am! Try me, who dare.

Judge. Your Grace shall find small credit by acknowl-
edging him to be your man.

Prince. Why, my lord, what hath he done?

30 **raze** root

Judge. And it please your Majesty, he hath robbed a
poor carrier.   55

Derick. Hear you, sir; marry, it was one Derick, goodman Hobling's man, of Kent.

Prince. What! Was't you, buttonbreech? Of my word,
my lord, he did it but in jest.

Derick. Hear you, sir, is it your man's quality to rob   60
folks in jest? In faith, he shall be hanged in earnest.

Prince. Well, my lord, what do you mean to do with
my man?

Judge. And please your Grace, the law must pass on
him according to justice; then he must be executed.   65

Prince. Why, then, belike you mean to hang my man?

Judge. I am sorry that it falls out so.

Prince. Why, my lord, I pray you, who am I?

Judge. And it please your Grace, you are my lord the
young Prince, our king that shall be after the decease   70
of our sovereign lord King Henry the Fourth, whom
God grant long to reign!

Prince. You say true, my lord. And you will hang my
man?

Judge. And it like your Grace, I must needs do justice.   75

Prince. Tell me, my lord, shall I have my man?

Judge. I cannot, my lord.

Prince. But will you not let him go?

Judge. I am sorry that his case is so ill.

Prince. Tush, case me no casings! Shall I have my man?   80

Judge. I cannot, nor I may not, my lord.

Prince. Nay, and "I shall not," say—and then I am
answered?

Judge. No.

85   *Prince.* No! Then I will have him.

                                          He giveth him a box on the ear.

      Ned. Gog's wounds, my lord, shall I cut off his head?

      Prince. No. I charge you, draw not your swords. But
      get you hence. Provide a noise of musicians. Away,
      begone!

                                          Exeunt Ned and Tom.

80   *Judge.* Well, my lord, I am content to take it at your
      hands.

      Prince. Nay, and you be not, you shall have more!

      Judge. Why, I pray you, my lord, who am I?

      Prince. You, who knows not you? Why, man, you are
95   Lord Chief Justice of England.

      Judge. Your Grace hath said truth; therefore, in strik-
      ing me in this place you greatly abuse me; and not
      me only but also your father, whose lively person
      here in this place I do represent. And therefore to
100   teach you what prerogatives mean, I commit you to
      the Fleet until we have spoken with your father.

      Prince. Why, then, belike you mean to send me to the
      Fleet!

      Judge. Ay, indeed; and therefore, carry him away.
                                   Exeunt Harry V with the Officers.
105   Jailer, carry the prisoner to Newgate again until the
      next 'sizes.

      Jailer. At your commandment, my lord, it shall be
      done.
                     [Exeunt all except] Derick and John Cobbler.

                                [Scene 5]

      Derick. Zounds, masters, here's ado when princes must
      go to prison! Why, John, didst ever see the like?

John. O Derick, trust me, I never saw the like!

Derick. Why, John, thou mayst see what princes be in
choler. A judge a box on the ear! I'll tell thee, John,   5
O John, I would not have done it for twenty shillings.

John. No, nor I. There had been no way but one with
us—we should have been hanged.

Derick. Faith, John, I'll tell thee what; thou shalt be
my Lord Chief Justice, and thou shalt sit in the chair;   10
and I'll be the young Prince, and hit thee a box on
the ear; and then thou shalt say, "To teach you what
prerogatives mean, I commit you to the Fleet."

John. Come on; I'll be your judge! But thou shalt not
hit me hard?   15

Derick. No, no.

[*John Cobbler takes the Judge's seat.*]

John. What hath he done?

Derick. Marry, he hath robbed Derick.

John. Why, then, I cannot let him go.

Derick. I must needs have my man.   20

John. You shall not have him!

Derick. Shall I not have my man? Say No, and you
dare! How say you? Shall I not have my man?

John. No, marry, shall you not!

Derick. Shall I not, John?   25

John. No, Derick.

Derick. Why, then, take you that [*boxing his ear*] till
more come! Zounds, shall I not have him?

John. Well, I am content to take this at your hand.
But, I pray you, who am I?   30

Derick. Who art thou? Zounds, dost not know thyself?

John. No.

Derick. Now away, simple fellow. Why, man, thou art John the Cobbler.

35   *John.* No, I am my Lord Chief Justice of England.

Derick. Oh, John, mass, thou sayst true, thou art indeed.

John. Why, then, to teach you what prerogatives mean, I commit you to the Fleet.

40   *Derick.* Well, I will go; but, i'faith, you gray-beard knave, I'll course° you.

                   Exit. And straight enters again.
   Oh, John, come, come out of thy chair. Why, what a clown wert thou to let me hit thee a box on the ear! And now thou seest they will not take me to the Fleet.

45   I think that thou art one of these Worenday° clowns.

John. But I marvel what will become of thee.

Derick. Faith, I'll be no more a carrier.

John. What wilt thou do, then?

Derick. I'll dwell with thee, and be a cobbler.

50   *John.* With me? Alas, I am not able to keep thee. Why, thou wilt eat me out of doors.

Derick. Oh, John! No, John; I am none of these great slouching fellows that devour these great pieces of beef and brews.° Alas, a trifle serves me—a wood-
55   cock, a chicken, or a capon's leg, or any such little thing serves me.

John. A capon! Why, man, I cannot get a capon once a year—except it be at Christmas, at some other man's house; for we cobblers be glad of a dish of
60   roots.

Derick. Roots, why, are you so good at rooting? Nay, cobbler, we'll have you ringed.°

John. But, Derick,

41 **course** keep pace with   45 **Worenday** workaday (?)   54 **brews** beef
broth   62 **ringed** i.e., in the nose, like a pig

> Though we be so poor,
> Yet will we have in store   65
> A crab in the fire,
> With nut-brown ale
> That is full stale,°
> Which will a man quail
> And lay in the mire.   70

Derick. A bots on you! And be but for your ale, I'll
dwell with you. Come, let's away as fast as we can.
                                            Exeunt.

[Scene 6]

Enter the young Prince, with Ned and Tom.

Prince. Come away, sirs. Gog's wounds, Ned, didst
thou not see what a box on the ear I took my Lord
Chief Justice?

Tom. By Gog's blood, it did me good to see it. It made   5
his teeth jar in his head!

Enter Sir John Oldcastle.

Prince. How now, Sir John Oldcastle, what news with
you?

John Oldcastle. I am glad to see your Grace at liberty.
I was come, I, to visit you in prison.

Prince. To visit me! Didst thou not know that I am a   10
prince's son? Why, 'tis enough for me to look into
a prison, though I come not in myself. But here's
such ado nowadays—here's prisoning, here's hanging, whipping, and the devil and all. But I tell you,
sirs, when I am King we will have no such things.   15
But, my lads, if the old King, my father, were dead,
we would be all kings.

68 **stale** strong

John Oldcastle. He is a good old man; God take him to his mercy the sooner!

20 *Prince.* But, Ned, so soon as I am King, the first thing I will do shall be to put my Lord Chief Justice out of office, and thou shalt be my Lord Chief Justice of England.

Ned. Shall I be Lord Chief Justice? By Gog's wounds, 25 I'll be the bravest Lord Chief Justice that ever was in England!

Prince. Then, Ned, I'll turn all these prisons into fence-schools, and I will endue thee with them, with lands to maintain them withal. Then I will have a bout 30 with my Lord Chief Justice. Thou shalt hang none but pick-purses, and horse-stealers, and such base-minded villains; but that fellow that will stand by the highway side courageously with his sword and buckler and take a purse—that fellow, give him 35 commendations! Beside that, send him to me, and I will give him an annual pension out of my exchequer to maintain him all the days of his life.

John Oldcastle. Nobly spoken, Harry! We shall never have a merry world till the old King be dead.

40 *Ned.* But whither are you going now?

Prince. To the court; for I hear say my father lies very sick.

Tom. But I doubt he will not die.

Prince. Yet will I go thither; for the breath shall be no 45 sooner out of his mouth but I will clap the crown on my head.

John Oldcastle. Will you go to the court with that cloak so full of needles?

Prince. Cloak, eyelet-holes, needles, and all was of 50 mine own devising; and therefore I will wear it.

Tom. I pray you, my lord, what may be the meaning thereof?

Prince. Why, man, 'tis a sign that I stand upon thorns
till the crown be on my head.

John Oldcastle. Or that every needle might be a prick   55
to their hearts that repine at your doings?

Prince. Thou sayst true, Jockey. But there's some will
say the young Prince will be "a well toward young
man"—and all this gear,° that I had as leave they
would break my head with a pot as to say any such   60
thing. But we stand prating here too long; I must
needs speak with my father. Therefore, come away!
[*They cross the stage, and rap.*]

[*Enter a Porter.*]

Porter. What a rapping keep you at the King's court-
gate?

Prince. Here's one that must speak with the King.   65

Porter. The King is very sick, and none must speak
with him.

Prince. No? You rascal, do you not know me?

Porter. You are my lord, the young Prince.

Prince. Then go and tell my father that I must, and will,   70
speak with him.

Ned. Shall I cut off his head?

Prince. No, no. Though I would help you in other
places, yet I have nothing to do here. What, you are
in my father's court.   75

Ned. I will write him in my tables; for so soon as I am
made Lord Chief Justice I will put him out of his
office.   *The trumpet sounds.*

Prince. Gog's wounds, sirs, the King comes. Let's all
stand aside.   80
    Enter the King, with the Lord of Exeter.

King. And is it true, my lord, that my son is already
sent to the Fleet? Now, truly, that man is more fitter

59 **gear** nonsense

85 to rule the realm than I; for by no means could I rule my son, and he, by one word, hath caused him to be ruled. Oh, my son, my son, no sooner out of one prison but into another? I had thought once whiles I had lived to have seen this noble realm of England flourish by thee, my son; but now I see it goes to ruin and decay. *He weepeth.*

Enters Lord of Oxford.

90 *Oxford.* And please your Grace, here is my lord your son that cometh to speak with you. He saith he must, and will, speak with you.

King. Who? My son Harry?

Oxford. Ay, and please your Majesty.

95 *King.* I know wherefore he cometh. But look that none come with him.

Oxford. A very disordered company, and such as make very ill rule in your Majesty's house.

King. Well, let him come; but look that none come
100 with him. *He goeth.*

Oxford. And please your Grace, my lord the King sends for you.

Prince. Come away, sirs, let's go all together.

Oxford. And please your Grace, none must go with
105 you.

Prince. Why, I must needs have them with me; otherwise I can do my father no countenance: therefore, come away.

Oxford. The King your father commands there should
110 none come.

Prince. Well, sirs, then be gone—and provide me three noise of musicians. *Exeunt Knights.*

Enters the Prince, with a dagger in his hand,
[to the King, attended].

King. Come, my son; come on, a God's name! I know
wherefore thy coming is. Oh, my son, my son, what
cause hath ever been that thou shouldst forsake me,   *115*
and follow this vile and reprobate company, which
abuseth youth so manifestly? Oh, my son, thou
knowest that these thy doings will end thy father's
days.   *He weeps.*
Ay, so, so, my son, thou fearest not to approach the   *120*
presence of thy sick father in that disguised sort. I
tell thee, my son, that there is never a needle in thy
cloak but it is a prick to my heart, and never an
eyelet-hole but it is a hole to my soul; and wherefore
thou bringest that dagger in thy hand I know not, but-   *125*
by conjecture.   *He weeps.*

Prince. My conscience accuseth me. Most sovereign
lord, and well-beloved father, to answer first to the
last point, that is, whereas you conjecture that this
hand and this dagger shall be armed against your   *130*
life, no! Know, my beloved father, far be the
thoughts of your son—"son," said I? an unworthy
son for so good a father!—but far be the thoughts
of any such pretended mischief. And I most humbly
render it [*giving him the dagger*] to your Majesty's   *135*
hand. And live, my lord and sovereign, forever! And
with your dagger-arm show like vengeance upon the
body of—"that, your son," I was about to say, and
dare not; ah, woe is me therefore!—that, your wild°
slave. 'Tis not the crown that I come for, sweet   *140*
father, because I am unworthy. And those vile and
reprobate companions—I abandon and utterly abol-
ish their company forever! Pardon, sweet father,
pardon, the least thing and most desire. And this
ruffianly cloak I here tear from my back, and sacri-   *145*
fice it to the devil, which is master of all mischief.
Pardon me, sweet father, pardon me! Good my
Lord of Exeter, speak for me. Pardon me, pardon,
good father! Not a word? Ah, he will not speak one
word! Ah, Harry, now thrice-unhappy Harry! But
what shall I do? I will go take me into some solitary   *150*

139 **wild** (the quarto has *wilde*=vilde=vile? cf. the King's previous speech)

place, and there lament my sinful life; and, when I
have done, I will lay me down and die.   *Exit.*

King. Call him again! Call my son again!

[*Enter the Prince.*]

155   *Prince.* And doth my father call me again? Now,
      Harry, happy be the time that thy father calleth thee
      again! [*He kneels.*]

King. Stand up, my son; and do not think thy father
but at the request of thee, my son, I will pardon thee.
160   And God bless thee, and make thee his servant.

Prince. Thanks, good my lord. And no doubt but this
day, even this day, I am born new again.

King. Come, my son and lords, take me by the hands.
                                        Exeunt omnes.

[*Scene 7*]

*Enter Derick [shouting at Mistress Cobbler
within].*

Derick. Thou art a stinking whore, and a whoreson
stinking whore! Dost think I'll take it at thy hands?

Enter John Cobbler, running.

John. Derick, Derick, Derick, hearest 'a? Do, Derick,
never while thou livest use that! Why, what will my
5   neighbors say and thou go away so?

Derick. She's an arrant whore; and I'll have the law on
you, John.

John. Why, what hath she done?

Derick. Marry, mark thou, John. I will prove it, that
10   I will!

John. What wilt thou prove?

Derick. That she called me in to dinner—John, mark
  the tale well, John—and when I was set, she brought
  me a dish of roots and a piece of barrel-butter°
  therein! And she is a very knave, and thou a drab   *15*
  if thou take her part.

John. Hearest 'a, Derick? Is this the matter? Nay, if
  it be no worse we will go home again, and all shall
  be amended.

Derick. Oh, John, hearest 'a, John? Is all well?   *20*

John. Ay, all is well.

Derick. Then I'll go home before, and break all the
  glass windows.   [*Exeunt Derick and John.*]

[*Scene 8*]

Enter the King with his Lords.

King. Come, my lords. I see it boots me not to take
  any physic, for all the physicians in the world cannot cure me; no, not one. But, good my lords, remember my last will and testament concerning my
  son; for truly, my lords, I do not think but he will   *5*
  prove as valiant and victorious a king as ever reigned
  in England.

Both. Let heaven and earth be witness between us if we
  accomplish not thy will to the uttermost.

King. I give you most unfeigned thanks, good my lords.   *10*
  Draw the curtains, and depart my chamber awhile;
  and cause some music to rock me asleep.
                        He sleepeth. Exeunt Lords.

                Enter the Prince.

Prince. Ah, Harry, thrice-unhappy, that hath neglect
  so long from visiting of thy sick father! I will go.

14 **barrel-butter** butter heavily salted (to preserve it)

15   Nay, but why do I not go to the chamber of my sick
      father to comfort the melancholy soul of his body?
      His soul, said I? Here is his body, indeed, but his
      soul is whereas it needs no body. Now, thrice-
      accursed Harry, that hath offended thy father so
20   much! And could not I crave pardon for all? O my
      dying father! Cursed be the day wherein I was born,
      and accursed be the hour wherein I was begotten!
      But what shall I do? If weeping tears, which come
      too late, may suffice the negligence neglected to
25   some,° I will weep day and night until the fountain
      be dry with weeping.   *Exit* [*taking the crown.*]
            Enter Lord[*s*] *of Exeter and Oxford.*

Exeter. Come easily, my lord, for waking of the King.

King. [*Waking*] Now, my lords?

Oxford. How doth your Grace feel yourself?

30   *King.* Somewhat better after my sleep. But, good my
      lords, take off my crown. Remove my chair a little
      back, and set me right.

Both. And please your Grace, the crown is taken away.

King. The crown taken away! Good my Lord of
35   Oxford, go see who hath done this deed.
                                    [*Exit Oxford.*]
      No doubt 'tis some vile traitor that hath done it to
      deprive my son. They that would do it now would
      seek to scrape and scrawl for it after my death.
            Enter Lord of Oxford with the Prince.

Oxford. Here, and please your Grace, is my lord the
40   young Prince with the crown.

King. Why, how now, my son? I had thought the last
      time I had you in schooling I had given you a lesson
      for all; and do you now begin again? Why, tell me,
      my son, dost thou think the time so long that thou

24–25 **suffice ... some** atone for my neglect toward some (but "too
some" may be an error for "too soon," intended to match "too late" in
line 24)

wouldst have it before the breath be out of my   45
mouth?

Prince. Most sovereign lord and well-beloved father, I
came into your chamber to comfort the melancholy
soul of your body; and finding you at that time past
all recovery, and dead, to my thinking—God is my   50
witness—and what should I do, but with weeping
tears lament the death of you, my father? And after
that, seeing the crown, I took it. And tell me, my
father, who might better take it than I, after your
death? But, seeing you live, I most humbly render   55
it into your Majesty's hands; and the happiest man
alive that my father live. And live, my lord and
father, forever!

King. Stand up, my son. Thine answer hath sounded
well in mine ears; for I must need confess that I was   60
in a very sound sleep, and altogether unmindful of
thy coming. But come near, my son, and let me put
thee in possession whilst I live, that none deprive
thee of it after my death.

Prince. Well may I take it at your Majesty's hands; but   65
it shall never touch my head so long as my father
lives.   *He taketh the crown.*

King. God give thee joy, my son. God bless thee, and
make thee his servant, and send thee a prosperous
reign! For God knows, my son, how hardly I came   70
by it, and how hardly I have maintained it.

Prince. Howsoever you came by it I know not; but now
I have it from you, and from you I will keep it. And
he that seeks to take the crown from my head, let
him look that his armor be thicker than mine, or I   75
will pierce him to the heart, were it harder than brass
or bullion.

King. Nobly spoken, and like a king! Now trust me, my
lords, I fear not but my son will be as warlike and
victorious a prince as ever reigned in England.   80

Both Lords. His former life shows no less.

King. Well, my lords, I know not whether it be for
sleep, or drawing near of drowsy summer of death,
but I am very much given to sleep. Therefore, good
85   my lords, and my son, draw the curtains; depart my
chamber; and cause some music to rock me asleep.
                      Exeunt omnes. The King dieth.

[*Scene 9*]

Enter the Thief.

Thief. Ah, God, I am now much like to a bird which
hath escaped out of the cage; for so soon as my Lord
Chief Justice heard that the old King was dead he
was glad to let me go for fear of my lord the young
5   Prince. But here come some of his companions. I
will see if I can get anything of them for old acquaintance.

Enter Knights, ranging.

Tom. Gog's wounds, the King is dead!

John Oldcastle. Dead! Then, Gog's blood, we shall be
10   all kings!

Ned. Gog's wounds, I shall be Lord Chief Justice of
England.

Tom. [*To the Thief*] Why, how! Are you broken out
of prison?

15   *Ned.* Gog's wounds, how the villain stinks!

John Oldcastle. Why, what will become of thee now?
Fie upon him, how the rascal stinks!

Thief. Marry, I will go and serve my master again.

Tom. Gog's blood, dost think that he will have any
20   such scabbed knave as thou art? What, man, he is
a king now.

Ned. [*Giving him money*] Hold thee. Here's a couple of angels for thee. And get thee gone, for the King will not be long before he come this way. And hereafter I will tell the King of thee.   *Exit Thief.*   25

John Oldcastle. Oh, how it did me good to see the King when he was crowned! Methought his seat was like the figure of heaven, and his person was like unto a god.

Ned. But who would have thought that the King would   30
have changed his countenance so?

John Oldcastle. Did you not see with what grace he sent his embassage into France to tell the French King that Harry of England hath sent for the crown, and Harry of England will have it?   35

Tom. But 'twas but a little to make the people believe that he was sorry for his father's death.
                    The trumpet sounds.

Ned. Gog's wounds, the King comes! Let's all stand aside.

> *Enter the King with the Archbishop* [*of Canterbury*], *and the Lord of Oxford.*

John Oldcastle. How do you, my lord?   40

Ned. How now, Harry? Tut, my lord, put away these dumps. You are a king, and all the realm is yours. What, man, do you not remember the old sayings? You know I must be Lord Chief Justice of England. Trust me, my lord, methinks you are very much   45
changed. And 'tis but with a little sorrowing, to make folks believe the death of your father grieves you—and 'tis nothing so.

King. I prithee, Ned, mend thy manners, and be more modester in thy terms; for my unfeigned grief is not   50
to be ruled by thy flattering and dissembling talk. Thou sayst I am changed; so I am, indeed; and so must thou be, and that quickly, or else I must cause thee to be changed.

55 *John Oldcastle.* Gog's wounds, how like you this?
    Zounds, 'tis not so sweet as music.

    Tom. I trust we have not offended your Grace no way.

    King. Ah, Tom, your former life grieves me, and makes
    me to abandon and abolish your company forever.
60 And therefore, not upon pain of death to approach
    my presence by ten miles space. Then, if I hear well
    of you, it may be I will do somewhat for you; other-
    wise, look for no more favor at my hands than at
    any other man's. And, therefore, begone! We have
65 other matters to talk on.   *Exeunt Knights.*

    Now, my good Lord Archbishop of Canterbury,
    what say you to our embassage into France?

    Archbishop. Your right to the French crown of France
    came by your great grandmother Isabel, wife to King
70 Edward the Third, and sister to Charles, the French
    king. Now, if the French king deny it, as likely
    enough he will, then must you take your sword in
    hand and conquer the right. Let the usurped French-
    man know, although your predecessors have let it
75 pass, you will not; for your countrymen are willing
    with purse and men to aid you. Then, my good lord,
    as it hath been always known that Scotland hath been
    in league with France by a sort of pensions which
    yearly come from thence, I think it therefore best to
80 conquer Scotland; and then I think that you may go
    more easily into France. And this is all that I can
    say, my good lord.

    King. I thank you, my good Lord Archbishop of Can-
    terbury. What say you, my good Lord of Oxford?

85 *Oxford.* And please your Majesty, I agree to my Lord
    Archbishop, saving in this: "He that will Scotland
    win must first with France begin," according to the
    old saying. Therefore, my good lord, I think it best
    first to invade France; for in conquering Scotland
90 you conquer but one; and conquer France and con-
    quer both.

Exeter. And please your Majesty, my Lord Ambassador is come out of France.

King. Now trust me, my lord, he was the last man that we talked of. I am glad that he is come to resolve us of our answer. Commit him to our presence. 95

Enter Duke of York.

York. God save the life of my sovereign lord the King!

King. Now, my good lord the Duke of York, what news from our brother, the French king?

York. And please your Majesty, I delivered him my 100 embassage, whereof I took some deliberation. But for the answer, he hath sent my Lord Ambassador of Bourges, the Duke of Burgundy, Monsieur le Cole, with two hundred and fifty horsemen to bring the embassage. 105

King. Commit my Lord Archbishop of Bourges into our presence.

Enter Archbishop of Bourges.

King. Now, my Lord Archbishop of Bourges, we do learn by our Lord Ambassador that you have our message to do from our brother, the French king. 110 Here, my good lord, according to our accustomed order, we give you free liberty and license to speak with good audience.

Archbishop. God save the mighty King of England! My lord and master, the most Christian king, Charles 115 the Seventh, the great and mighty King of France, as a most noble and Christian king not minding to shed innocent blood, is rather content to yield somewhat to your unreasonable demands—that, if fifty thousand crowns a year, with his daughter, the said 120 Lady Katherine, in marriage; and some crowns which he may well spare not hurting of his kingdom, he is content to yield so far to your unreasonable desire.

125 *King.* Why, then, belike your lord and master thinks to puff me up with fifty thousands crowns a year? No! Tell thy lord and master that all the crowns in France shall not serve me, except the crown and kingdom itself! And perchance hereafter I will have his daugh-
130 ter.

Archbishop. If it please your Majesty, my Lord Prince Dolphin greets you well with this present.
                    He delivereth a tun of tennis balls.

King. What, a gilded tun! I pray you, my Lord of York, look what is in it.

135 *York.* And it please your Grace, here is a carpet, and a tun of tennis balls.

King. A tun of tennis balls! I pray you, good my Lord Archbishop, what might the meaning thereof be?

Archbishop. And it please you, my lord, a messenger,
140 you know, ought to keep close his message—and specially an ambassador.

King. But I know that you may declare your message to a king; the Law of Arms allows no less.

Archbishop. My lord, hearing of your wildness before
145 your father's death, sent you this, my good lord, meaning that you are more fitter for a tennis court than a field, and more fitter for a carpet than the camp.

King. My Lord Prince Dolphin is very pleasant with
150 me! But tell him that instead of balls of leather we will toss him balls of brass and iron—yea, such balls as never were tossed in France. The proudest tennis court shall rue it! Ay, and thou, Prince of Bourges, shalt rue it! Therefore, get thee hence; and tell him
155 thy message quickly, lest I be there before thee. Away, priest! Begone!

Archbishop. I beseech your Grace to deliver me your safe conduct under your broad seal manual.°

King. Priest of Bourges, know that the hand and seal of a king, and his word, is all one. And instead of my hand and seal I will bring him my hand and sword. And tell thy lord and master that I, Harry of England, said it; and I, Harry of England, will perform it! My Lord of York, deliver him our safe conduct under our broad seal manual.   *165*

Exeunt Archbishop and the Duke of York.

Now, my lords, to arms, to arms! For I vow by heaven and earth that the proudest Frenchman in all France shall rue the time that ever these tennis balls were sent into England. My lord, I will that there be provided a great navy of ships with all speed   *170* at Southampton, for there I mean to ship my men; for I would be there before him, if it were possible. Therefore come—but stay! I had almost forgot the chiefest thing of all with chafing with this French ambassador. Call in my Lord Chief Justice of England.   *175*

Enters Lord Chief Justice of England.

Exeter. Here is the King, my lord.

Justice. God preserve your Majesty!

King. Why, how now, my lord, what is the matter?

Justice. I would it were unknown to your Majesty.

King. Why, what ail you?   *180*

Justice. Your Majesty knoweth my grief well.

King. Oh, my lord, you remember you sent me to the Fleet, did you not?

Justice. I trust your Grace have forgotten that.   *185*

King. Ay, truly, my lord; and for revengement I have chosen you to be my Protector over my realm, until

158 **manual** inscribed by hand

it shall please God to give me speedy return out of
France.

190   *Justice.* And if it please your Majesty, I am far unworthy of so high dignity.

King. Tut, my lord, you are not unworthy, because I
think you worthy; for you that would not spare me,
I think, will not spare another. It must needs be so.
195   And therefore, come, let us be gone, and get our
men in a readiness.   *Exeunt omnes.*

[*Scene 10*]

Enter a Captain, John Cobbler, and his Wife.

Captain. Come, come; there's no remedy. Thou must
needs serve the King.

John. Good master Captain, let me go. I am not able
to go so far.

5   *Wife.* I pray you, good master Captain, be good to my
husband.

Captain. Why, I am sure he is not too good to serve the
King.

John. Alas, no—but a great deal too bad; therefore, I
10   pray you, let me go.

Captain. No, no; thou shalt go.

John. Oh, sir, I have a great many shoes at home to
cobble.

Wife. I pray you, let him go home again.

15   *Captain.* Tush, I care not. Thou shalt go.

John. Oh, wife, and you had been a loving wife to me
this had not been; for I have said many times that I

would go away, and now I must go—against my will.
He weepeth.

Enter Derick [with a pot-lid for a shield].

Derick. How now, ho! *Basillus manus,*° for an old cod-
piece! Master Captain, shall we away? Zounds, how   20
now, John? What, a-crying? What make you and
my dame there? [*To the Wife*] I marvel whose head
you will throw the stools at now we are gone.

Wife. I'll tell you! Come, ye cloghead! What do you
with my pot-lid? Here you, will you have it rapped   25
about your pate?   *She beateth him with her pot-lid.*

Derick. Oh good dame!   *Here he shakes her.*
And I had my dagger here I would worry you all to
pieces—that I would!

Wife. Would you so? I'll try that.   *She beateth him.*   30

Derick. Master Captain, will you suffer her? Go to,
dame! I will go back as far as I can; but, and you
come again—I'll clap the law on your back, that's
flat! I'll tell you, Master Captain, what you shall do:
press her for a soldier! I warrant you she will do as   35
much good as her husband and I too.

Enters the Thief.

Zounds, who comes yonder?

Captain. How now, good fellow; dost thou want a master?

Thief. Ay, truly, sir.   40

Captain. Hold thee, then. I press thee for a soldier to
serve the King in France.

Derick. How now, Gads! What, dost know us, thinkest?

Thief. Ay, I knew thee long ago.   45

Derick. Hear you, Master Captain.

19 **Basillus manus** (corruption of *besa las manos* = kiss the hands, say
good-bye)

Captain. What sayst thou?

Derick. I pray you, let me go home again.

Captain. Why, what wouldst thou do at home?

Derick. Marry, I have brought two shirts with me, and
50   I would carry one of them home again; for I am sure
      he'll steal it from me, he is such a filching fellow.

Captain. I warrant thee he will not steal it from thee.
      Come, let's away.

Derick. Come, Master Captain, let's away. Come, fol-
55   low me.

John. Come, wife, let's part lovingly.

Wife. Farewell, good husband.

Derick. Fie, what a kissing and crying is here! Zounds,
      do you think he will never come again? Why, John,
60   come away! Dost think that we are so base-minded
      to die among Frenchmen? Zounds, we know not
      whether they will lay us in their church or no. Come,
      Master Captain, let's away.

Captain. I cannot stay no longer; therefore, come away.
                                        Exeunt omnes.

                          [*Scene 11*]

          Enter the [French] King, Prince Dolphin, and
                Lord High Constable of France.

King. Now, my Lord High Constable, what say you to
      our embassage into England?

Constable. And it please your Majesty, I can say noth-
      ing until my lords ambassadors be come home. But
5   yet methinks your Grace hath done well to get your
      men in so good a readiness for fear of the worst.

King. Ay, my lord, we have some in a readiness; but if
      the King of England make against us we must have
      thrice so many more.

Dolphin. Tut, my lord; although the King of England   10
be young and wild-headed, yet never think he will be
so unwise to make battle against the mighty King of
France.

King. Oh, my son, although the King of England be
young and wild-headed, yet never think but he is   15
ruled by his wise councillors.

Enter Archbishop of Bourges.

Archbishop. God save the life of my sovereign lord the
King!

King. Now, my good Lord Archbishop of Bourges,
what news from our brother, the English king?   20

Archbishop. And please your Majesty, he is so far from
your expectation that nothing will serve him but the
crown and kingdom itself. Besides, he bade me haste
quickly lest he be there before me. And, so far as I
hear, he hath kept promise; for they say he is already   25
landed at Kidocks in Normandy upon the River
Seine, and laid his siege to the garrison-town of Harfleur.

King. You have made great haste in the meantime, have
you not?   30

Dolphin. I pray you, my lord, how did the King of England take my presents?

Archbishop. Truly, my lord, in very ill part. For these
your balls of leather he will toss you balls of brass
and iron. Trust me, my lord, I was very afraid of him,   35
he is such a haughty and high-minded prince. He is
as fierce as a lion.

Constable. Tush, we will make him as tame as a lamb,
I warrant you.

Enters a Messenger.

Messenger. God save the mighty King of France!   40

King. Now, messenger, what news?

Messenger. And it please your Majesty, I come from
your poor distressed town of Harfleur, which is so
beset on every side, if your Majesty do not send pres-
45   ent aid the town will be yielded to the English king.

King. Come, my lords, come! Shall we stand still till
our country be spoiled under our noses? My lords,
let the Normans, Brabanters, Picards, and Danes be
sent for with all speed. And you, my Lord High Con-
50   stable, I make General over all my whole army;
Monsieur le Colle, Master of the Bows, Seigneur
Devens, and all the rest, at your appointment.

Dolphin. I trust your Majesty will bestow some part of
the battle on me. I hope not to present any otherwise
55   than well.

King. I tell thee, my son, although I should get the victory, and thou lose thy life, I should think myself
quite conquered, and the Englishmen to have the victory.

60   *Dolphin.* Why, my lord and father, I would have the
petty king of England to know that I dare encounter
him in any ground of the world.

King. I know well, my son; but at this time I will have
it thus. Therefore, come away.   *Exeunt omnes.*

[*Scene 12*]

Enters Henry the Fifth, with his Lords.

King. Come, my lords of England. No doubt this good
luck of winning this town is a sign of an honorable
victory to come! But, good my lord, go and speak
to the captains with all speed, to number the host of
5   the Frenchmen, and by that means we may the better know how to appoint the battle.

York. And it please your Majesty, there are many of
your men sick and diseased, and many of them die
for want of victuals.

King. And why did you not tell me of it before? If we   *10*
   cannot have it for money we will have it by dint of
   sword; the Law of Arms allows no less.

Oxford. I beseech your Grace to grant me a boon.

King. What is that, my good lord?

Oxford. That your Grace would give me the vanguard   *15*
   in the battle.

King. Trust me, my Lord of Oxford, I cannot; for I
   have already given it to my uncle, the Duke of York.
   Yet I thank you for your good will.

                                    A trumpet sounds.
   How now, what is that?   *20*

York. I think it be some herald of arms.

                  Enters a Herald.

Herald. King of England, my Lord High Constable and
   others of the noblemen of France sends me to defy
   thee as open enemy to God, our country, and us;
   and hereupon they presently bid thee battle.   *25*

King. Herald, tell them that I defy them as open enemies to God, my country, and me, and as wrongful
   usurpers of my right. And whereas thou sayst they
   presently bid me battle, tell them, that I think they
   know how to please me. But, I pray thee, what place   *30*
   hath my lord Prince Dolphin here in battle?

Herald. And it please your Grace, my Lord and King,
   his father, will not let him come into the field.

King. Why, then, he doth me great injury. I thought
   that he and I should have played at tennis together;   *35*
   therefore I have brought tennis balls for him—but
   other manner of ones than he sent me. And, Herald,
   tell my Lord Prince Dolphin that I have inured my
   hands with other kind of weapons than tennis balls
   ere this time of day, and that he shall find it, ere it   *40*
   be long. And so, adieu, my friend. And tell my
   lord that I am ready when he will.   *Exit Herald.*

Come, my lords. I care not and I go to our captains;
and I'll see the number of the French army myself.
45   Strike up the drum!   *Exeunt omnes.*

[*Scene 13*]

Enter French Soldiers.

First Soldier. Come away, Jack Drummer! Come away
all, and me will tell you what me will do. Me will tro
one chance on the dice who shall have the King of
England and his lords.

5   *Second Soldier.* Come away, Jack Drummer, and tro
your chance; and lay down your drum.

Enter Drummer.

Drummer. Oh, the brave apparel that the English-mans
hay broth° over! I will tell you what me ha done. Me
ha provided a hundreth trunks, and all to put the
10   fine 'parel of the English-mans in.

First Soldier. What do thou mean by "trunks"?

Second Soldier: A shest, man, a hundred shests.

First Soldier. Awee, awee, awee. Me will tell you what:
me ha put five shildren out of my house, and all too
15   little to put the fine apparel of the English-mans in.

Drummer. Oh, the brave, the brave apparel that we
shall have anon! But come, and you shall see what
me will tro at the king's drummer and fife. Ha, me
ha no good luck. Tro you.

20   *Third Soldier.* Faith, me will tro at the Earl of Northumberland, and my Lord o' Willoughby, with his
great horse, snorting, farting—oh brave horse!

First Soldier. Ha! By'r Lady, you ha reasonable good
luck. Now I will tro at the King himself. Ha! Me
25   have no good luck.

8 **hay broth** i.e., have brought

Enters a Captain.

Captain. How now, what make you here so far from the camp?

Second Soldier. Shall me tell our captain what we have done here?

Drummer. Awee, awee.   30
              Exeunt Drummer and one Soldier.

Second Soldier. I will tell you what we have done. We have been troing our chance on the dice; but none can win the King.

Captain. I think so. Why, he is left behind for me! And I have set three or four chair-makers a-work to make   35 a new disguised chair to set that womanly King of England in, that all the people may laugh and scoff at him.

Second Soldier. Oh brave captain!

Captain. I am glad, and yet with a kind of pity, to see   40 the poor King—why, who ever saw a more flourishing army in France in one day than here is? Are not here all the peers of France? Are not here the Normans, with their fiery handguns and flaunching° curtleaxes?'° Are not here the barbarians, with their   45 bard° horses and launching spears? Are not here the Picards, with their cross-bows and piercing darts? The Henneys° with their cutting glaives° and sharp carbuncles?° Are not here the lance-knights of Burgundy? And, on the other side, a sight of poor Eng-   50 lish scabs! Why, take an English-man out of his warm bed and his stale drink but one month, and, alas, what will become of him? But give the Frenchman a

---

44 **flaunching** (a word of uncertain origin and meaning, which is perhaps here intended to mean "flaming," but has been confused or conflated with the armorial and heraldic term "flaunch" = any subdevice borne on an escutcheon)   44–45 **curtleaxes** cutlasses   46 **bard** barded, armed with metal plates   48 **Henneys** men of Hainault   48 **glaives** broadswords 49 **carbuncles** eight-rayed blazon (escarbucle) on the French shields, which often had a spike at its center

55   radish root, and he will live with it all the days of his
        life.   *Exit.*

        Second Soldier. Oh, the brave apparel that we shall
        have of the English-mans.   *Exit.*

                              [Scene 14]

                Enters the King of England and his Lords.

        King. Come, my lords and fellows of arms. What com-
        pany is there of the Frenchmen?

        Oxford. If it please your Majesty, our captains have
        numbered them, and, so near they can judge, they
5   are about threescore thousand horsemen and forty
        thousand footmen.

        King. They threescore thousand horsemen, and we but
        two thousand! They forty thousand footmen, and we
        twelve thousand! They are a hundred thousand, and
10   we forty thousand! Ten to one! My lords and loving
        countrymen, though we be few, and they many, fear
        not. Your quarrel is good, and God will defend you.
        Pluck up your hearts, for this day we shall either
        have a valiant victory, or a honorable death! Now,
15   my lords, I will that my uncle, the Duke of York,
        have the vanguard in the battle; the Earl of Derby,
        the Earl of Oxford, the Earl of Kent, the Earl of
        Nottingham, the Earl of Huntingdon I will have be-
        side the army, that they may come fresh upon them;
20   and I myself, with the Duke of Bedford, the Duke of
        Clarence, and the Duke of Gloucester will be in the
        midst of the battle. Furthermore, I will that my Lord
        of Willoughby and the Earl of Northumberland, with
        their troops of horsemen, be continually running like
25   wings on both sides of the army—my Lord of North-
        umberland on the left wing. Then I will that every
        archer provide him a stake of a tree, and sharp it at
        both ends; and, at the first encounter of the horse-

men, to pitch their stakes down into the ground before them, that they may gore themselves upon them;   30
and then, to recoil back, and shoot wholly altogether,
and so discomfit them.

Oxford. And it please your Majesty, I will take that in
charge, if your Grace be therewith content.

King. With all my heart, my good Lord of Oxford. And   35
go and provide quickly.

Oxford. I thank your Highness.   *Exit.*

King. Well, my lords, our battles are ordained, and the
French making of bonfires, and at their banquets.
But let them look, for I mean to set upon them.   40
                    The trumpet sounds.
Soft, here comes some other French message.

                    Enters Herald.

Herald. King of England, my Lord High Constable and
other of my lords, considering the poor estate of thee
and thy poor countrymen, sends me to know what
thou wilt give for thy ransom. Perhaps thou mayst   45
agree better cheap° now than when thou art conquered.

King. Why then, belike, your High Constable sends to
know what I will give for my ransom? Now trust me,
Herald, not so much as a tun of tennis balls—no,
not so much as one poor tennis ball! Rather shall   50
my body lie dead in the field to feed crows than ever
England shall pay one penny ransom for my body.

Herald. A kingly resolution!

King. No, Herald; 'tis a kingly resolution and the resolution of a king. Here, take this for thy pains.   55
                    Exit Herald.

King. But stay, my lords; what times is it?

All. Prime, my lord.

46 **agree better cheap** make a better bargain

King. Then is it good time, no doubt, for all England
60   prayeth for us. What, my lords! Methinks you look
cheerfully upon me. Why, then, with one voice, and
like true English hearts, with me throw up your caps,
and for England cry, "Saint George!" And God and
Saint George help us!

Strike Drummer. Exeunt omnes.

[*Scene 15*]

*The Frenchmen cry within, "Saint Denis! Saint Denis!
Mount Joy! Saint Denis!"*

The battle.
Enters King of England and his Lords.

King. Come, my lords, come! By this time our swords
are almost drunk with French blood. But, my lords,
which of you can tell me how many of our army be
slain in the battle?

5   *Oxford.* And it please your Majesty, there are of the
French army slain above ten thousand twenty-six
hundred, whereof are princes and nobles bearing
banners; besides, all the nobility of France are taken
prisoners. Of your Majesty's army are slain none but
10   the good Duke of York, and not above five or six
and twenty common soldiers.

King. For the good Duke of York, my uncle, I am
heartily sorry, and greatly lament his misfortune.
Yet the honorable victory which the Lord hath given
15   us doth make me much rejoice. But, stay! Here
comes another French message.   *Sound trumpet.*

Enters a Herald, and kneeleth.

Herald. God save the life of the most mighty conqueror,
the honorable King of England!

King. Now, Herald, methinks the world is changed with

you now. What! I am sure it is a great disgrace for   20
a herald to kneel to the King of England! What is
thy message?

Herald. My lord and master, the conquered King of
France, sends thee long health, with hearty greeting.

King. Herald, his greetings are welcome; but I thank   25
God for my health. Well, Herald, say on.

Herald. He hath sent me to desire your Majesty to give
him leave to go into the field to view his poor count-
trymen, that they may all be honorably buried.

King. Why, Herald, doth thy lord and master send to   30
me to bury the dead? Let him bury them, a God's
name! But, I pray thee, Herald, where is my Lord
High Constable, and those that would have had my
ransom?

Herald. And it please your Majesty, he was slain in the   35
battle.

King. Why, you may see—you will make yourselves
sure before the victory be won. But, Herald, what
castle is this so near adjoining to our camp?

Herald. And it please your Majesty, 'tis called the   40
Castle of Agincourt.

King. Well then, my lords of England, for the more
honor of our Englishmen, I will that this be forever
called The Battle of Agincourt.

Herald. And it please your Majesty, I have a further   45
message to deliver to your Majesty.

King. What is that, Herald? Say on.

Herald. And it please your Majesty, my lord and master
craves to parley with your Majesty.

King. With a good will—so some of my nobles view the   50
place for fear of treachery and treason.

Herald. Your Grace needs not to doubt that.

King. Well, tell him, then, I will come.   *Exit Herald.*
Now, my lords, I will go into the field myself to view
55   my countrymen, and to have them honorably buried;
for the French king shall never surpass me in courtesy whiles I am Harry, King of England. Come on,
my lords.   *Exeunt omnes.*

[*Scene 16*]

Enters John Cobbler and Robin Pewterer.

Robin. Now, John Cobbler, didst thou see how the King
did behave himself?

John. But, Robin, didst thou see what a policy the King
had? To see how the Frenchmen were killed with
5   the stakes of the trees!

Robin. Ay, John, there was a brave policy!

Enters an English Soldier, roaming.

Soldier. What are you, my masters?

Both. Why, we be Englishmen.

Soldier. Are you Englishmen? Then change your lan-
10   guage, for the King's tents are set afire, and all they
speak English will be killed.   [*Exit.*]

John. What shall we do, Robin? Faith, I'll shift, for I
can speak broken French.

Robin. Faith, so can I. Let's hear how thou canst speak.

15   *John.* Commodevales,° Monsieur?

Robin. That's well. Come, let's be gone.   [*Exeunt.*]

15 **Commodevales** *Comment allez* [*-vous*]? How are you?

[*Scene 17*]

Drum and trumpet sounds.

Enters Derick, roaming. After him a Frenchman,
and takes him prisoner.

Derick. Oh, good *Mounser!*°

Frenchman. Come, come, you *villeaco.*°

Derick. Oh, I will, sir, I will.

Frenchman. Come quickly, you peasant!

Derick. I will, sir. What shall I give you?   5

Frenchman. Marry, thou shalt give me one, two, tre,
  four hundred crowns.

Derick. Nay, sir, I will give you more; I will give you
  as many crowns as will lie on your sword.

Frenchman. Wilt thou give me as many crowns as will   10
  lie on my sword?

Derick. Ay, marry, will I. Ay, but you must lay down
  your sword, or else they will not lie on your sword.

Here the Frenchman lays down his sword, and the
Clown [Derick] takes it up, and hurls him down.

Derick. Thou villain! darest thou look up?

Frenchman. Oh, good *Monsieur, comparteve!*° *Mon-*   15
  sieur, pardon me!

Derick. O you villain! Now you lie at my mercy. Dost
  thou remember since thou lammedst me in thy short
  ell?° O villain! Now I will strike off thy head.

Here, whiles he turns his back, the Frenchman
runs his ways.   20

Derick. What, is he gone? Mass, I am glad of it. For, if
  he had stayed, I was afraid he would have stirred

1 *Mounser Monsieur*   2 *villeaco villanaccio* (?) = rustic   15 *com-*
parteve compat[iss]ez vous (?) = have pity   18–19 **lammedst ... ell**
gave me a short measure

again, and then I should have been spilt. But I will
away to kill more Frenchmen.   [*Exit.*]

[*Scene 18*]

Enters King of France, King of England, and
Attendants.

King of England. Now, my good brother of France, my
coming into this land was not to shed blood, but for
the right of my country; which, if you can deny, I
am content peaceably to leave my siege and to depart
5   out of your land.

King of France. What is it you demand, my loving
brother of England?

King of England. My secretary hath it written. Read it.

Secretary. Item, that immediately Henry of England be
10   crowned King of France.

King of France. A very hard sentence, my good brother
of England.

King of England. No more but right, my good brother
of France!

15 *King of France.* Well, read on.

Secretary. Item, that after the death of the said Henry
the crown remain to him and his heirs forever.

King of France. Why then, you do not only mean to
dispossess me, but also my son!

20 *King of England.* Why, my good brother of France, you
have had it long enough. And as for Prince Dolphin,
it skills not though he sit beside the saddle. Thus I
have set it down, and thus it shall be!

King of France. You are very peremptory, my good
25   brother of England.

King of England. And you as perverse, my good brother
of France.

King of France. Why then, belike all that I have here
is yours!

King of England. Ay, even as far as the kingdom of   30
France reaches.

King of France. Ay, for by this hot beginning we shall
scarce bring it to a calm ending.

King of England. It is as you please. Here is my resolution.   35

King of France. Well, my brother of England, if you
will give me a copy we will meet you again tomorrow.

King of England. With a good will, my good brother of
France. Secretary, deliver him a copy.

       Exit King of France and all their Attendants.

King of England. My lords of England, go before, and   40
I will follow you.   *Exeunt Lords.*
Speaks to himself. Ah, Harry, thrice-unhappy Harry!
Hast thou now conquered the French king, and begins a fresh supply with his daughter? But with what
face canst thou seek to gain her love which hath   45
sought to win her father's crown? Her father's crown,
said I? No, it is mine own.

    Ay, but I love her, and must crave her—
    Nay, I love her, and will have her!

    Enters Lady Katherine and her Ladies.

King of England. But here she comes. How now, fair   50
Lady Katherine of France, what news?

Katherine. And it please your Majesty, my father sent
me to know if you will debate any of these unreasonable demands which you require.

King of England. Now trust me, Kate, I commend thy   55
father's wit greatly in this; for none in the world
could sooner have made me debate it, if it were possible. But tell me, sweet Kate, canst thou tell how to
love?

60 *Katherine.* I cannot hate, my good lord; therefore, far
    unfit were it for me to love.

    King of England. Tush, Kate! but tell me in plain terms,
    canst thou love the King of England? I cannot do as
    these countries do that spend half their time in woo-
65 ing. Tush, wench, I am none such. But, wilt thou go
    over to England?

    Katherine. I would to God that I had your Majesty as
    fast in love as you have my father in wars! I would
    not vouchsafe so much as one look until you had
70 abated all these unreasonable demands.

    King of England. Tush, Kate! I know thou wouldst not
    use me so hardly. But tell me, canst thou love the
    King of England?

    Katherine. How should I love him that hath dealt so
75 hardly with my father?

    King of England. But I'll deal as easily with thee as thy
    heart can imagine, or tongue can require. How sayst
    thou? What! will it be?

    Katherine. If I were of my own direction I could give
80 you answer; but seeing I stand at my father's direc-
    tion, I must first know his will.

    King of England. But shall I have thy good will in the
    mean season?

    Katherine. Whereas I can put your Grace in no assur-
85 ance, I would be loath to put you in any despair.

    King of England. Now, before God, it is a sweet wench!

    She goes aside, and speaks as followeth.

    Katherine. I may think myself the happiest in the world
    that is beloved of the mighty King of England!

    King of England. Well, Kate, are you at host° with me?
90 Sweet Kate, tell thy father from me that none in the

    89 **at host** in accord

world could sooner have persuaded me to it than
thou; and so tell thy father from me.

Katherine. God keep your Majesty in good health.
                                        Exit Katherine.

King of England. Farewell, sweet Kate. In faith, it is a
sweet wench! But if I knew I could not have her   95
father's good will, I would so rouse the towers over
his ears that I would make him be glad to bring her
me upon his hands and knees.   *Exit King.*

[*Scene 19*]

Enters Derick with his girdle full of shoes.

Derick. How, now! Zounds, it did me good to see how
I did triumph over the Frenchmen!

*Enters John Cobbler, roving, with a pack
full of apparel.*

John. Whoop, Derick! How dost thou?

Derick. What, John! *Comedevales?* Alive yet?

John. I promise thee, Derick, I scaped hardly; for I was   5
within half a mile when one was killed!

Derick. Were you so?

John. Ay, trust me. I had like been slain.

Derick. But, once killed—why it—'tis nothing. I was
four or five times slain.   10

John. Four or five times slain. Why, how couldst thou
have been alive now?

Derick. O John, never say so! For I was called "the
bloody soldier" amongst them all.

John. Why, what didst thou?   15

Derick. Why, I will tell thee, John. Every day when I
went into the field I would take a straw and thrust

it into my nose and make my nose bleed; and then
I would go into the field. And when the captain saw
20   me, he would say, "Peace, a bloody soldier!" and
bid me stand aside. Whereof I was glad. But mark
the chance, John: I went and stood behind a tree—
but mark, then, John—I thought I had been safe;
but on a sudden there steps to me a lusty, tall
25   Frenchman; now he drew, and I drew; now I lay
here, and he lay there; now I set this leg before, and
turned this backward—and skipped quite over a
hedge; and he saw me no more there that day! And
was not this well done, John?

30   *John.* Mass, Derick, thou hast a witty head.

Derick. Ay, John, thou mayst see, if thou hadst taken
my counsel. But what hast thou there? I think thou
hast been robbing the Frenchmen.

John. In faith, Derick, I have gotten some reparel to
35   carry home to my wife.

Derick. And I have got some shoes; for I'll tell thee
what I did: when they were dead, I would go take
off all their shoes.

John. Ay, but Derick, how shall we get home?

40   *Derick.* Nay, zounds, and they take thee they will hang
thee. O, John, never do so! If it be thy fortune to be
hanged, be hanged in thy own language, whatsoever
thou dost!

John. Why, Derick, the wars is done; we may go home
45   now.

Derick. Ay, but you may not go before you ask the
King leave. But I know a way to go home and ask
the King no leave.

John. How is that, Derick?

50   *Derick.* Why, John, thou knowest the Duke of York's
funeral must be carried into England, dost thou not?

John. Ay, that I do.

Derick. Why, then, thou knowest we'll go with it.

John. Ay, but Derick, how shall we do for to meet
them?   55

Derick. Zounds, if I make not shift to meet them, hang
me! Sirrah, thou knowest that in every town there
will be ringing, and there will be cakes and drink.
Now I will go to the clerk and sexton, and keep
a-talking and say, "Oh, this fellow rings well!" And   60
thou shalt go and take a piece of cake. Then I'll ring,
and thou shalt say, "Oh, this fellow keeps a good
stint!" And then I will go drink to thee all the way.
But I marvel what my dame will say when we come
home, because we have not a French word to cast   65
at a dog by the way.

John. Why, what shall we do, Derick?

Derick. Why, John, I'll go before and call my dame
whore; and thou shalt come after and set fire on the
house. We may do it, John, for I'll prove it—because   70
we be soldiers.   *The trumpets sound.*

John. Derick, help me to carry my shoes and boots.
                              [*Exeunt Derick and John.*]

[*Scene 20*]

*Enters King of England, Lord of Oxford and
Exeter, then the King of France, Prince Dolphin,
and the Duke of Burgundy, [Princess Katherine]
and Attendants.*

King of England. Now, my good brother of France,
I hope by this time you have deliberated of your
answer.

King of France. Ay, my well-beloved brother of England. We have viewed it over with our learned coun-   5
cil, but cannot find that you should be crowned
King of France.

King of England. What, not King of France? Then
nothing. I must be King. But, my loving brother of
France, I can hardly forget the late injuries offered
me when I came last to parley; the Frenchmen had
better 'a raked the bowels out of their fathers' carcasses than to have fired my tents. And if I knew thy
son Prince Dolphin, for one, I would so rouse him
as he was never so roused!

King of France. I dare swear for my son's innocency in
this matter. But if this please you, that immediately
you be proclaimed the crowned Heir and Regent
of France, not King, because I myself was once
crowned king—

King of England. Heir and Regent of France? That is
well. But that is not all that I must have.

King of France. The rest my secretary hath in writing.

Secretary. [*Reads*] Item, that Henry, King of England,
be crowned Heir and Regent of France during the
life of King Charles; and after his death the crown
with all rights to remain to King Henry of England,
and to his heirs forever.

King of England. Well, my good brother of France,
there is one thing I must needs desire.

King of France. What is that, my good brother of
England?

King of England. That all your nobles must be sworn
to be true to me.

King of France. Whereas they have not stuck with
greater matters, I know they will not stick with such
a trifle. Begin you, my Lord Duke of Burgundy.

King of England. Come, my Lord of Burgundy; take
your oath upon my sword.

Burgundy. I, Philip, Duke of Burgundy, swear to
Henry, King of England, to be true to him, and to
become his liege man; and that if I, Philip, hear of

any foreign power coming to invade the said Henry,
or his heirs, then I, the said Philip, to send him word,
and aid him with all the power I can make. And   *45*
thereunto I take my oath.   *He kisseth the sword.*

King of England. Come, Prince Dolphin, you must
swear, too.   *He kisseth the sword.*
Well, my brother of France, there is one thing more
I must needs require of you.   *50*

King of France. Wherein is it that we may satisfy your
Majesty?

King of England. A trifle, my good brother of France;
I mean to make your daughter Queen of England, if
she be willing, and you therewith content. How sayst   *55*
thou, Kate? Canst thou love the King of England?

Katherine. How should I love thee, which is my father's
enemy?

King of England. Tut, stand not upon these points. 'Tis
you must make us friends. I know, Kate, thou art   *60*
not a little proud that I love thee. What, wench, the
King of England?

King of France. Daughter, let nothing stand betwixt
the King of England and thee. Agree to it.

Katherine. [*Aside*] I had best whilst he is willing, lest   *65*
when I would he will not—I rest at your Majesty's
command.

King of England. Welcome, sweet Kate! But, my
brother of France, what say you to it?

King of France. With all my heart I like it. But when   *70*
shall be your wedding day?

King of England. The first Sunday of the next month,
God willing.   *Sound trumpets. Exeunt omnes.*

FINIS

Commentaries

SAMUEL JOHNSON

From The Plays of William Shakespeare

None of Shakespeare's plays are more read than the *First and Second Parts of Henry the Fourth*. Perhaps no author has ever in two plays afforded so much delight. The great events are interesting, for the fate of kingdoms depends upon them; the slighter occurrences are diverting and, except one or two, sufficiently probable; the incidents are multiplied with wonderful fertility of invention, and the characters diversified with the utmost nicety of discernment and the profoundest skill in the nature of man.

The Prince, who is the hero both of the comic and tragic part, is a young man of great abilities and violent passions, whose sentiments are right, though his actions are wrong; whose virtues are obscured by negligence, and whose understanding is dissipated by levity. In his idle hours he is rather loose than wicked; and when the occasion forces out his latent qualities, he is great without effort and brave without tumult. The trifler is roused into a hero, and the hero again reposes in the trifler. This character is great, original, and just.

Percy is a rugged soldier, choleric, and quarrelsome, and has only the soldier's virtues, generosity and courage.

But Falstaff, unimitated, unimitable Falstaff, how shall I describe thee? Thou compound of sense and vice; of sense which may be admired but not esteemed, of vice which may be despised but hardly detested. Falstaff is a character loaded with faults, and with those faults which naturally produce contempt. He is a thief and a glutton, a coward and a boaster, always ready to cheat the weak and prey upon the poor; to terrify the timorous and insult the defenseless. At once obsequious and malignant, he satirizes in their absence those whom he lives by flattering. He is familiar with the Prince only as an agent of vice, but of this familiarity he is so proud as not only to be supercilious and haughty with common men but to think his interest of importance to the Duke of Lancaster. Yet the man thus corrupt, thus despicable, makes himself necessary to the Prince that despises him, by the most pleasing of all qualities, perpetual gaiety, by an unfailing power of exciting laughter, which is the more freely indulged as his wit is not of the splendid or ambitious kind but consists in easy escapes and sallies of levity, which make sport but raise no envy. It must be observed that he is stained with no enormous or sanguinary crimes, so that his licentiousness is not so offensive but that it may be borne for his mirth.

The moral to be drawn from this representation is that no man is more dangerous than he that, with a will to corrupt, hath the power to please; and that neither wit nor honesty ought to think themselves safe with such a companion when they see Henry seduced by Falstaff. [1765]

From H. C. Robinson's Memoranda

Falstaff Coleridge also considered as an instance of the predominance of intellectual power. He is content to be thought both a liar and a coward in order to obtain influence over the minds of his associates. His aggravated lies about the robbery are conscious and purposed, not inadvertent untruths. On my observing that this account seemed to justify [George Frederick] Cooke's representation, according to which a foreigner imperfectly understanding the character would fancy Falstaff to be the designing knave who actually does outwit the Prince, Coleridge answered that in his *own* estimation Falstaff is the superior who cannot easily be convinced that the Prince has escaped him; but that as in other instances Shakespeare has shown us the defeat of mere intellect by a noble feeling, the Prince being the superior moral character who rises above his insidious companion.

From Seven Lectures

Falstaff was no coward, but pretended to be one merely for the sake of trying experiments on the credulity of mankind: he was a liar with the same object, and not because he loved falsehood for itself. He was a man of such preeminent abilities, as to give him a profound contempt for all those by whom he was usually surrounded, and to lead to

Both selections by Coleridge come from *Shakespearean Criticism* by Samuel Taylor Coleridge, 2nd ed., ed. Thomas Middleton Raysor. 2 vols. (New York: E. P. Dutton and Company, Inc., 1960; London: J. M. Dent & Sons, Ltd., 1961). The first passage is Robinson's memorandum of one of Coleridge's conversations of 1810; the second passage is J. P. Collier's memorandum of a conversation of 1811. In the first, abbreviations have been expanded.

a determination on his part, in spite of their fancied superiority, to make them his tools and dupes. He knew, however low he descended, that his own talents would raise him and extricate him from any difficulty. While he was thought to be the greatest rogue, thief, and liar, he still had that about him which could render him not only respectable, but absolutely necessary to his companions. It was in characters of complete moral depravity, but of first-rate wit and talents, that Shakespeare delighted; and Coleridge instanced Richard the Third, Falstaff, and Iago.

From The Fortunes of Falstaff

Falstaff may be the most conspicuous, he is certainly the most fascinating, character in *Henry IV*, but all critics are agreed, I believe, that the technical center of the play is not the fat knight but the lean prince. Hal links the low life with the high life, the scenes at Eastcheap with those at Westminster, the tavern with the battlefield; his doings provide most of the material for both Parts, and with him too lies the future, since he is to become Henry V, the ideal king, in the play that bears his name; finally, the mainspring of the dramatic action is the choice I have already spoken of, the choice he is called upon to make between Vanity and Government, taking the latter in its accepted Tudor meaning, which includes Chivalry or prowess in the field, the theme of Part I, and Justice, which is the theme of Part II. Shakespeare, moreover, breathes life into these abstractions by embodying them, or aspects of them, in prominent characters, who stand, as it were, about the Prince, like attendant spirits: Falstaff typifying Vanity in every sense of the word, Hotspur Chivalry, of the old anarchic kind, and the Lord Chief Justice the Rule of Law or the new ideal of service to the state.

Thus considered, Shakespeare's *Henry IV* is a Tudor version of a time-honored theme, already familiar for decades, if not centuries, upon the English stage. Before its final secularization in the first half of the sixteenth century, our drama was concerned with one topic, and one only: human salvation. It was a topic that could be represented in either of two ways: (i) historically, by means of miracle plays,

From *The Fortunes of Falstaff* by John Dover Wilson (Cambridge: Cambridge University Press, 1943), pp. 17–21.

which in the Corpus Christi cycles unrolled before spectators' eyes the whole scheme of salvation from the Creation
to the Last Judgment; or (ii) allegorically, by means of
morality plays, which exhibited the process of salvation in
the individual soul on its road between birth and death, beset with the snares of the World or the wiles of the Evil One.
In both kinds the forces of iniquity were allowed full play
upon the stage, including a good deal of horseplay, provided
they were brought to nought, or safely locked up in Hell, at
the end. Salvation remains the supreme interest, however
many capers the Devil and his Vice may cut on Everyman's
way thither, and always the powers of darkness are withstood, and finally overcome, by the agents of light. But as
time went on the religious drama tended to grow longer and
more elaborate, after the encyclopedia fashion of the Middle
Ages, and such development invited its inevitable reaction.
With the advent of humanism and the early Tudor court,
morality plays became tedious and gave place to lighter and
much shorter moral interludes dealing, not with human life
as a whole, but with youth and its besetting sins.

An early specimen, entitled *Youth* and composed about
1520, may be taken as typical of the rest. The plot, if plot it
can be called, is simplicity itself. The little play opens with
a dialogue between Youth and Charity. The young man,
heir to his father's land, gives insolent expression to his
self-confidence, lustihood, and contempt for spiritual things.
Whereupon Charity leaves him, and he is joined by Riot,
that is to say wantonness, who presently introduces him to
Pride and Lechery. The dialogue then becomes boisterous,
and continues in that vein for some time, much no doubt to
the enjoyment of the audience. Yet, in the end, Charity reappears with Humility; Youth repents; and the interlude
terminates in the most seemly fashion imaginable.

No one, I think, reading this lively playlet, no one certainly who has seen it performed, as I have seen it at the
Malvern Festival, can have missed the resemblance between
Riot and Falstaff. The words he utters, as he bounces onto
the stage at his first entry, give us the very note of Falstaff's
gaiety:

> Huffa! huffa! who calleth after me?
> I am Riot full of jollity.
> My heart is as light as the wind,
> And all on riot is my mind,
> Wheresoever I go.

And the parallel is even more striking in other respects. Riot, like Falstaff, escapes from tight corners with a quick dexterity; like Falstaff, commits robbery on the highway; like Falstaff, jests immediately afterward with his young friend on the subject of hanging; and like Falstaff, invites him to spend the stolen money at a tavern, where, he promises, "We will drink diuers wine" and "Thou shalt haue a wench to kysse Whansoeuer thou wilte"; allurements which prefigure the Boar's Head and Mistress Doll Tearsheet.

But Youth at the door of opportunity, with Age or Experience, Charity or Good Counsel, offering him the yoke of responsibility, while the World, the Flesh, and the Devil beckon him to follow them on the primrose way to the everlasting bonfire, is older than even the medieval religious play. It is a theme to which every generation gives fresh form, while retaining its eternal substance. Young men are the heroes of the Plautine and Terentian comedy which delighted the Roman world; and these young men, generally under the direction of a clever slave or parasite, disport themselves, and often hoodwink their old fathers, for most of the play, until they too settle down in the end. The same theme appears in a very different story, the parable of the Prodigal Son. And the similarity of the two struck humanist teachers of the early sixteenth century with such force that, finding Terence insufficiently edifying for their pupils to act, they developed a "Christian Terence" by turning the parable into Latin plays, of which many examples by different authors have come down to us. In these plot and structure are much the same. The opening scene shows us Acolastus, the prodigal, demanding his portion, receiving good counsel from his father, and going off into a far country. Then follow three or four acts of entertainment almost purely Terentian in atmosphere, in which he wastes his substance in riotous living and falls at length to feeding with the pigs. Finally, in the last act he returns home, penniless and repentant, to receive his pardon. This ingenious blend of classical comedy and humanistic morality preserves, it will be noted, the traditional ratio between edification and amusement, and distributes them in the traditional manner. So long as the serious note is duly emphasized at the beginning and end of the play, almost any quantity of fun, often of the most unseemly nature, was allowed and expected during the intervening scenes.

All this, and much more of a like character, gave the pattern for Shakespeare's *Henry IV*. Hal associates Falstaff in turn with the Devil of the miracle play, the Vice of the morality, and the Riot of the interlude, when he calls him "that villainous abominable misleader of Youth, that old white-bearded Satan," "that reverend Vice, that gray Iniquity, that father Ruffian, that Vanity in years," and "the tutor and the feeder of my riots." "Riot," again, is the word that comes most readily to King Henry's lips when speaking of his prodigal son's misconduct. And, as heir to the Vice, Falstaff inherits by reversion the functions and attributes of the Lord of Misrule, the Fool, the Buffoon, and the Jester, antic figures the origins of which are lost in the dark backward and abysm of folk custom. We shall find that Falstaff possesses a strain, and more than a strain, of the classical *miles gloriosus* as well. In short, the Falstaff-Hal plot embodies a composite myth which had been centuries amaking, and was for the Elizabethans full of meaning that has largely disappeared since then: which is one reason why we have come so seriously to misunderstand the play.

Nor was Shakespeare the first to see Hal as the prodigal. The legend of Harry of Monmouth began to grow soon after his death in 1422; and practically all the chroniclers, even those writing in the fifteenth century, agree on his wildness in youth and on the sudden change that came upon him at his accession to the throne. The essence of Shakespeare's plot is, indeed, already to be found in the following passage about King Henry V taken from Fabyans' *Chronicle* of 1516:

This man, before the death of his fader, applyed him unto all
vyce and insolency, and drewe unto hym all ryottours and
wylde disposed persones; but after he was admytted to the rule
of the lande, anone and suddenly he became a newe man, and
tourned al that rage into sobernesse and wyse sadnesse, and the
vyce into constant vertue. And for he wolde contynewe that
vertue, and not to be reduced thereunto by the familiarytie of
his olde nyse company, he therefore, after rewardes to them
gyuen, charged theym upon payne of theyr lyues, that none of
them were so hardy to come within x. myle of such place as he
were lodgyd, after a day by him assigned.

There appears to be no historical basis for any of this, and
Kingsford has plausibly suggested that its origin may be
"contemporary scandal which attached to Henry through his
youthful association with the unpopular Lollard leader" Sir
John Oldcastle. "It is noteworthy," he points out, "that
Henry's political opponents were Oldcastle's religious per-
secutors; and also that those writers who charge Henry with
wildness as Prince find his peculiar merit as King in the
maintaining of Holy Church and destroying of heretics. A
supposed change in his attitude on questions of religion may
possibly furnish a partial solution for his alleged 'change
suddenly into a new man.' " The theory is the more attractive that it would account not only for Hal's conversion but
also for Oldcastle's degradation from a Protestant martyr
and distinguished soldier to what Ainger calls "a broken-
down Lollard, a fat old sensualist, retaining just sufficient
recollection of the studies of his more serious days to be
able to point his jokes with them."

Yet when all is said, the main truth seems to be that the
fifteenth and early sixteenth centuries, the age of allegory in
poetry and morality in drama, needed a Prodigal Prince,
whose miraculous conversion might be held up as an example by those concerned (as what contemporary political
writer was not?) with the education of young noblemen and
princes. And could any more alluring fruits of repentance be
offered such pupils than the prowess and statesmanship of
Henry V, the hero of Agincourt, the mirror of English king-

ship for a hundred years? In his miracle play, *Richard II*, Shakespeare had celebrated the traditional royal martyr; in his morality play, *Henry IV*, he does the like with the traditional royal prodigal.

ROBERT ORNSTEIN

From A Kingdom for a Stage

I do not think that it is "sentimental" to enjoy Hotspur's openness and good humor, so long as we recognize the conceit and infatuation with risk that sully his noblest impulse. Hungering for reputation in the way other men hunger for power, he will let another sit on the throne, but he must wear the dignities of great renown "without corrival." Generous in spirit, he would open his veins in a "good cause," but he will not think of the misery of the thousands of other men who will unwillingly bleed because of the rebellion. Too narrow in his devotion to family and too trusting of his kin, he cannot admit the egotism of his motives or realize the contradictions of his outrage. On the one hand, he would see his family as innocent dupes of the vile politician Bolingbroke, who deceived them by pledging that he came back only for his ducal rights. On the other hand, he fumes at the ingratitude of Henry, who reneged on his promises and now orders the Percies about as if he owed them nothing. Thus, Hotspur would be innocent of the "crime" of having aided Henry to the throne even as he is furious that his family was not sufficiently rewarded for their aid to Bolingbroke. In Hotspur's view, the Percies acted as Henry's hangman but did not receive the hangman's perquisite. They helped to kill a king but did not receive the king's clothes, for it is the cankered Bolingbroke who wears the robes of majesty and denies their present suit for Mortimer.

The richness and delight of Hotspur's personality makes one wonder at the desire of some critics to treat him as a clown or as the sullen ground on which Hal's princely bril-

From *A Kingdom for a Stage: The Achievement of Shakespeare's History Plays* by Robert Ornstein (Cambridge, Mass.: Harvard University Press, 1972), pp. 134–39.

liance glitters. The actors who play Hotspur will not demean him in this way. They make us aware of his warmth, exuberance, and poetry, qualities somewhat lacking in Hal; and they almost convince us that the rebel is more attractive than the prince. For if Hal's poise accentuates Hotspur's recklessness, Hotspur's frankness calls attention to what is calculating and disingenuous in Hal's relations with others. When Hotspur teases his adoring wife, the humor is tender and intimate; when Hal, slightly bored and drunk, teases Francis, the joke smacks of contempt and casual cruelty.

We can say that Hotspur is the better companion, Hal the better prince. The one is more engaging as a man, the other far better suited to great responsibility. To grant Hal the fullest measure of his princely talents is not, however, to agree that he is Shakespeare's ideal of rule—a character whose personal defects are a part of his princely perfection, whose coldness and calculation are seen by Shakespeare as necessary virtues in a leader. If Shakespeare gave us the Hal of the folk legend, a youth who loved the low company which he ultimately turned away, we might speak of his aloofness in the tavern scenes as a schooling of self for the impersonal demands of office. But what shall we say of the Prince who in his first appearance speaks contemptuously of his tavern companions, whom he intends to use to line his princely enterprise? Just as Falstaff keeps his eye on the main chance and expects to profit in times to come from his friendship with Hal, Hal confesses in soliloquy that he intends to turn a small investment in seeming prodigality into a handsome profit of reputation. Although he obviously enjoys Falstaff's company, Hal tells us that he plays at comradeship as well as at prodigality and not only plans to discard his cronies but even now considers them the base contagion that momentarily obscures his princely radiance.

To be sure, Hal is not, as some have pictured him, a Machiavellian prince who craftily deceives his tavern cronies even as he will later "dupe" his English subjects into supporting his claim to the throne of France. He never pretends deep feeling for Falstaff and Poins, and, if anything, he is more ingenious in his self-justifications than cunning in his dissimulations. He is more candid in his conversations

with other men than in his colloquies with himself in which
he labors to rationalize his behavior. When Hotspur embroi-
ders the truth about Mortimer's soldiership, his artificiality
of manner betrays him; when he tries to argue before
Shrewsbury that rashness is caution, his illogic is transparent. More conscious of, and subtle in, his casuistries, Hal is
more difficult to "see through." Though we know him better
than does Falstaff, who claims to know him "like the Lord
that made ye," we cannot say that we fully understand the
prince who plays a limited engagement as tavern roisterer
and who explains his tavern holiday as a clever public relations stunt. This is a man whose reasons and rationalizations
so finely commingle that they cannot be sorted out, but
whose bent of mind is consistent in conversation and soliloquy. Shrewd in his appraisals and thoroughly pragmatic, he
studies other men so that he may learn to master them; and
because his moral attitudes are attuned to those of the practical world, he sees no reason to justify his manipulation of
others, though he feels compelled to justify his seeming dis-
sipation. It would not occur to him that drinking sack and
sugar may be less of a fault than falsifying men's hopes, and
he could not imagine that his tavern holiday might seem to
others more attractive than his utilitarian justification of it.[1]

Although we cannot allow one soliloquy to determine our
view of a character as fully developed as Hal is in dialogue
and dramatic action, neither can we ignore the fact that in
each play in which Hal appears, he is allowed only one soliloquy, and in each instance that soliloquy is a crucial reve-
lation of character and motive.[2] The alternative to viewing
Hal's soliloquy in 1.2 as a disclosure of self is to regard it,
as many critics have done, as a choric device by which

---

[1] John Palmer shrewdly notes that if Hal "is merely looking for a reason to
be merry with his friends, surely he might have found a better one. To plead
that he is permitting their base contagious clouds to smother up his beauty in
order that he may shine all the more brightly when they have served his turn is
not the sort of excuse which would have suggested itself to a really good companion" (*Political Characters*, p. 185).

[2] Compare the soliloquy at the end of the first tavern scene with the one soliloquy which Hal speaks in *Henry IV Part II*, when he takes the crown from
his father's pillow (4.5.21–47); and with his one soliloquy in *Henry V*, which
occurs after his encounter with his soldiers about the campfire on the eve of
Agincourt (4.1.247–301).

Shakespeare communicates essential narrative information to his audience, assuring them that Hal "will exhibit all the proper regal virtues" when the time comes.[3] One must wonder, however, why an Elizabethan audience needed reassurance about the princely character or destiny of the greatest of England's heroic kings, whose exploits at Agincourt were celebrated in poems and ballads, in the Chronicles, and in the source play *The Famous Victories*. If, as Professor Tillyard argues, Shakespeare was compelled to make Hal a "copybook paragon" in *Henry V* because his audience knew the legend of Harry's perfection by heart,[4] surely there was no need to dispel any doubts about Hal's future greatness in scene 2 of *Henry IV Part I*, especially when, as Tillyard notes, there is not the slightest intimation that Hal can be seduced by Falstaff. Describing Hal as "aloof and Olympian from the start," Tillyard remarks that he "never treats Falstaff any better than his dog, with whom he condescends once in a way to have a game."[5]

Even if we grant that Shakespeare may have thought his audience too gross to see what Tillyard and others do in the Hal of the first tavern scene, we must still wonder why he did not just allow the groundlings to enjoy their superficial view of Hal as the prodigal of the legend. Unless Shakespeare's audience was made up of prigs and Puritans, they could not really have trembled for Hal's future because, like thousands of theatergoers, he enjoyed Falstaff. After all, we never see Hal in the throes of debauchery and we find his capacity for holiday reassuring; we like and trust a man who can drink and joke, unbend and stoop to the level of our own tastes. To have our confidence and good will, a youthful profligate need not apologize for his casual "vices." If he appears generous, frank in his affections, and fundamentally innocent in spirit, we are perfectly ready to grant that having sowed his wild oats, he deserves—as do all the youthful

---

[3] Tillyard, *History Plays*, p. 300. J. Dover Wilson also insists that the soliloquy has a conventional function of conveying "information to the audience about the general drift of the play" (*The Fortunes of Falstaff* [Cambridge: Cambridge Univ. Press, 1964], p. 41).

[4] *History Plays*, p. 305.

[5] *History Plays*, pp. 271–72.

profligates of seventeenth-century comedy—a good wife, a handsome fortune, and a noble future.[6] In other words, Hal needs no choric soliloquy to warn us that he is the Cinderella prince of the legend. He needs the soliloquy to underline the fact that he is not prodigal in temperament at all, and certainly not a happy-go-lucky youth indifferent to his royal future. Rather than a Huck Finn who prefers the freedom of the tavern to the restrictions imposed by his noble destiny, he is a Tom Sawyer who enjoys his moment of raffishness but by inclination is one of the respectable and perhaps even one of the Elect. Very conscious of the way that men respond to the image of royalty, and no less instinctive a politician than his father, Hal is the creator as well as the creature of political mythology, the author as well as the hero of his legend.

It seems to me preferable to interpret the soliloquy as soliloquy rather than to turn Shakespeare into a blunderer who did not realize the chilling effect of Hal's contemptuous lines about his comrades and who failed to see how Hal's diction and metaphors associate his calculated redemption with the crassness of commodity and sharp business practices:

> So, when this loose behavior I throw off
> And pay the debt I never promised,
> By how much better than my word I am,
> By so much shall I falsify men's hopes;
> And, like bright metal on a sullen ground,
> My reformation, glitt'ring o'er my fault,
> Shall show more goodly and attract more eyes
> Than that which hath no foil to set it off.
> I'll so offend to make offense a skill,
> Redeeming time when men think least I will.

>   (1.2.212–21)

Like a clever Elizabethan shopkeeper, Hal knows how to display the merchandise of his behavior in such a light that

---

[6] The generous rake enjoys a happy career also in Restoration comedy. Indeed, his type can be seen in any number of Hollywood movies in which a slightly ribald, reckless, and warmhearted young hero wins the heroine away from the proper, respectable young banker whom the parents prefer.

it appears richer than it is. He knows, too, how to play the princely bankrupt—how to conceal his princely assets until they bring a double profit. We may not like this element of calculation in him, but it is one of his fundamental traits. The Hal who will "use" his tavern companions is the same Hal who will make Percy his factor and who promises to tear the reckoning of honor out of Hotspur's heart. He is also the same Hal who in soliloquy in *Part II* will promise to "pay plenteously" with tears for the crown he takes from his father's pillow, and who in soliloquy in *Henry V* will ask what are the "rents" and "comings-in" of Ceremony and promise God to pay more fully the debt of conscience.

Far from being a neutral choric announcement, Hal's soliloquy in the tavern strikes the keynote of his characterization in succeeding plays. For just as he explains to the audience why he wastes his time with low companions in *Part I*, he will explain to Poins in *Part II* why he cannot weep for his dying father, and to the traitors in *Henry V* why he cannot be merciful to them.[7] We can take Hal's part in Hal's casuistic way and explain that it is Francis's fault that Hal plays nasty jokes on him—because the "subhuman" deserve subhuman treatment. Or we can accept Hal for what he is: fascinating but not endearing; not quite the paragon some would have him nor the heartless prig others see. Although quick-witted, he is rarely a match for Falstaff because he cannot anticipate the sudden dazzling reversals and agile leaps of Falstaff's thought and mood. Thus, even though he holds the trump cards after Gadshill, he does not win the game of wits, because Falstaff makes the very questions of cowardice and truth seem ridiculous. In these encounters Hal has a grave disadvantage in that he cannot, like Falstaff, ridicule everything. Although he jokes coarsely about cheapening maidenheads, he will not cheapen courage or princeliness; he will not pretend to be a good fellow at the price of his royal dignity.

The time will come when Henry V will look back with shame on the "riots" of his tavern days. Even now there is a

<hr>

[7]Palmer writes very penetratingly of the need for self-justification which characterizes Harry in each play in which he appears (*Political Characters*, pp. 185–87).

faint tinge of disgust in his reference to the base contagion that smothers up his beauty from the world. He can take Falstaff's bulk as a subject for his wit, but he does not share Falstaff's pleasure in the flesh. When Sir John plays at being king, corpulence is rhapsodized as well as licensed. When Hal becomes the kingly homilist, Falstaff's great belly becomes an emblem of surfeited appetite as well as of festive indulgence:

> Why dost thou converse with that trunk of humors, that bolting-hutch of beastliness, that swoll'n parcel of dropsies, that huge bombard of sack, that stuffed cloakbag of guts, that roasted Manningtree ox with the pudding in his belly, that reverend vice, that gray iniquity, that father ruffian, that vanity in years?
> (2.4.448–54)

For Falstaff the urge to repentance is a fleeting impulse or a comic pose. For Hal the thought of redemption is no laughing matter. Earnest even in holiday, he scrupulously examines his conduct and finds it good; he explains to us and to himself that he labors in the tavern in his vocation as a prince just as Falstaff explains that he labors in his vocation as a highway robber. Knowing how men merchandize their reputations and hope for bargain redemptions, Falstaff jokes about finding a commodity of good names. Hal, on the other hand, seriously intends to gain that commodity even as he seriously intends to reject Falstaff as the "tutor and feeder" of his "riots." After all, it is not Shakespeare who casts Hal as the hero of a Morality drama of temptation and redemption. It is Hal who casts himself in the role even as he casts Falstaff in the role of reverend Vice and gray iniquity. I do not mean to suggest that beneath the loose behavior of the pseudo-libertine is the tight-lipped manner of the Precisian to be. I do suggest that Shakespeare's conception of Harry, as it unfolds in the second tetralogy, is all of one piece, a marvelously unified and sustained study of a personality that develops in Aristotelian fashion from potentiality to essence—from seeming roisterer to devout conqueror. The more we see of Hal in the tavern, the less we fear that he will grow too attached to Falstaff. We wonder, however, whether this poised, ironic, self-absorbed prince will ever be capable of intimacy or of emotional attachment to another person. We sense, even in *Part I*, that Hal needs Falstaff even as he needs ultimately to banish him.

MICHAEL GOLDMAN

From Shakespeare and the Energies of Drama

   Falstaff is always at Hal's mercy, and we love him for the
way he stretches the limits of his situation and gets away
with it; it is an aspect of his fatness. At the end of the Boar's
Head Tavern scene, when it is learned that the Sheriff and
his watch are at the door hunting Falstaff, he hides behind
the arras while the Prince persuades the Sheriff to leave.
The curtain is then drawn back, and Falstaff is revealed,
asleep and "snorting like a horse." The Prince goes through
his pockets. Falstaff sleeps on for twenty lines as the
scene concludes. The episode is memorable, funny, famous
even among familiar quotations ("O monstrous! but one
half-pennyworth of bread to this intolerable deal of sack!"),
and—perhaps because Falstaff cannot speak—suggests
with a fascinating strength the intensity and complexity of
our attachment to him. Falstaff asleep is the man we have
seen wildly and ingeniously awake moments before, and we
look forward to the moment he will rise again. His belches
and snorts undoubtedly have more life in them than an army
of tapsters. Francis's actions belong to the comedy of mech-
anism; he has responded to the Prince's commands like an
automaton. Falstaff's, even asleep, belong to the comedy of
irrepressibility; he is doing what he wants in the most unlikely of circumstances. And yet perhaps because he is
asleep, certain other strands of our feeling toward him are
allowed to take on new prominence. The contrast with the
long, energetic, increasingly fantastic comic scene that has
been interrupted, the relative stillness, our new awareness

   From *Shakespeare and the Energies of Drama* by Michael Goldman
(Princeton, N.J.: Princeton University Press, 1972), pp. 55–57.

that it is late at night, our growing certainty that a decisive return to the great world of politics and combat is imminent, all these tend to heighten whatever is protective and elegiac in our response. It is a good scene to meditate on.

Falstaff at this moment seems not only grandly self-indulgent and indifferent to crisis but particularly vulnerable. The Prince stands over him; Falstaff's life is in his hands in more ways than one. He has promised the Sheriff that the fat knight will make good his thefts. He makes Peto read aloud the ludicrous facts of Falstaff's internal economy. Falstaff's utter relaxation is enviable, his snorting and belching delightfully irreverent, but the guard that has been up so splendidly throughout the long tavern scene is down and the soft belly is exposed. We feel drawn to him and we see how easily we can hurt him; we know now that the wars have begun, that he won't do as he is. Falstaff must suffer. He must submit to the indignities of realism, of number and measure. Today his appetites are converted into arithmetic ("Item, Sack, two gallons . . . 5s. 8d."); to-morrow he must lead a charge of foot. ("I know his death will be a march of twelve-score. The money shall be paid back again with advantage.") We know that Falstaff will respond resourcefully; he is far from finished. But we have always known that finished he eventually must be.

Falstaff is not only endlessly inventive and delightful, audacious and dangerous, but vulnerable. This is also true about the things for which he comes to stand—our sensuality and our impulse to anarchy. The tenderness, broad humor, and absurdity that are mixed in this tableau come close to the mystery of Falstaff—or more correctly the mystery of the play, for our emotion here includes Hal, whose stance is the already familiar one of authority and detachment, and whose heroic career is plainly about to begin. The Prince of our reason stands over the attractive, grotesque, audacious, pathetically vulnerable body of our sensuality—an image for one of the many selves inside us, indeed for more than one—a sleeping child that we will have to punish, the silly, dying father we are destined to displace.

COPPÉLIA KAHN

From Man's Estate: Masculine Identity in Shakespeare

In the course of the two *Henry IV* plays, Shakespeare presents a conception of the father-son bond and its part in the formation of a masculine identity vastly different from that in the first tetralogy. In place of the emphasis on repetition and the past there, with its taut emulation of the father and inflexible vendettas, Shakespeare conceives of a relationship with some give to it, literally some free play, some space for departure from paternal priority and for experiences fundamentally opposed to it. In place of the failures in transition from sonship to fatherhood represented by Henry VI, John Talbot, Young Clifford, and Richard III, he tries to portray a successful passage negotiated, paradoxically, as lawful rebellion and responsible play. He makes Hal the stage manager of his own growing up, the embodiment of a wish to let go—but to let go only so far, without real risks. In the end, Falstaff's regressive appeal is so dangerously strong for Shakespeare that he cannot afford to integrate it into Hal's character, and must, to Hal's loss, exclude it totally. From the sonnets to *The Winter's Tale*, the idea of remaining "boy eternal" exerts a powerful pull on Shakespeare's imagination that he strenuously resists. At the same time, however, he discovers new dimensions in the lifelong process of becoming a man; he begins to see how the father's identity is shaped by his son, as well as the son's by his father. In Henry and Hal he uses the renewal of the principle of succession as a way to validate Henry's king-

From *Man's Estate: Masculine Identity in Shakespeare* by Coppélia Kahn (Berkeley, Calif.: University of California Press, 1981), pp. 70-74.

ship as much as Hal's; identity becomes a reciprocal process
between father and son.

The relationship between the two men has three focal
points of overdetermined needs and signals at which crises
are defined or resolved. The first is the Boar's Head and
Hal's reign there as madcap prince under the tutelage of
Falstaff, who is usually seen as anti-king and anti-father,
standing for misrule as opposed to rule. But he is also the
opposite of the king in the sense of being his predecessor
psychologically, the king of childhood and omnipotent
wishes, as Henry is king in the adult world of rivalry and
care. Franz Alexander describes Falstaff as the personifica-
tion of "the primary self-centered narcissistic libido of the
child," commenting that

> the child in us applauds, the child who knows only one princi-
> ple and that is to live. . . . Since the child cannot actually over-
> come any external interferences, it takes refuge in fantastic,
> megalomaniac self-deception.[1]

"Banish plump Jack, and banish all the world!" Falstaff
cries. Because of his sophisticated adult wit, however, he
makes social capital out of his megalomania; men love his
gloriously ingenious lies better than their own truth. Falstaff is a world unto himself, shaped like the globe and containing multitudes of contradictions as the world itself
does; fat and aging in body, but ever young in spirit and
nimble in wit; a shape-shifter in poses and roles, yet always
inimitably himself; a man with a curiously feminine sen-
sual abundance.

A fat man can look like a pregnant woman, and Falstaff's
fatness is fecund; it spawns symbols. In the context of Hal's
growing up, its feminine meaning has particular importance.[2] As W. H. Auden says, it is "the expression of a psy-
chological wish to withdraw from sexual competition and

---

[1] Franz Alexander, "A Note on Falstaff," *Psychoanalytic Quarterly* 2
(1933): 392-406.
[2] W. H. Auden, "The Prince's Dog," in his *The Dyer's Hand* (New York:
Random House), p. 196.

by combining mother and child in his own person, to become emotionally self-sufficient." Falstaff is said to be fond of hot wenches and leaping-houses, but he is no Don Juan even in Part 2 when his sexual relations with Doll Tearsheet and Mistress Quickly are made more explicit. They are fond of him rather than erotically drawn to him. It is not only tactful regard for Hal's legendary dignity as the perfect king that keeps Shakespeare from compromising him by making Falstaff a lecher. Rather, Falstaff represents the wish to bypass women; he has grown old, but remains young, and yet in terms of women has "detoured manhood," as Harold Goddard says.[3] In the first tetralogy Shakespeare avoided treating the woman's part in male development by making women witches or helpless victims. In the second tetralogy he again treats the feminine obliquely, through its absence, as Falstaff's avoidance of sexual maturity. The fat knight desires food and drink more than he desires women. And though women are devoted to him, he cheats and deceives them, giving his own deepest affections to a boy. No wonder that, for Hal, Falstaff incarnates his own rebellion against growing up into a problematic adult identity.

Hal himself is unaware that his affinity for the fat knight constitutes rebellion; he conceives it, rather, as part of his long-term strategy for assuming a proper identity as king. That strategy reveals his likeness to his father, his ability to think and act in the same terms of political image-building as his father, his fitness for the very role he seems to be rejecting. Many parallels between Hal's first soliloquy (1.2) and the king's long admonitory speech to him (3.2) reveal the essential similarities between father and son. Both speeches dwell on the proper management of one's political visibility and the importance of avoiding overexposure. Hal pictures himself as the sun obscured by clouds and therefore more "wonder'd at" when he reappears, while Henry compares himself to a comet "wonder'd at" because it is "seldom seen." He implies that his is that "sun-like majesty"

[3]Harold C. Goddard, *"Henry IV,"* in his *The Meaning of Shakespeare*, 2 vols. (Chicago: University of Chicago Press, 1951), vol. 1, p. 184.

that, when it "shines seldom," wins an "extraordinary gaze," and Hal says that his reformation "shall show more goodly, and attract more eyes" because of his fault. Both use clothing imagery to denote a kingliness they put on or off at will; Hal says he can "throw off this loose behaviour," and Henry says that he too dressed himself in humility, then donned his "presence like a robe pontifical." Hal's soliloquy implies that the Hal we have just seen with Falstaff is no more genuine and spontaneous than the self he will assume as king, and it is immediately followed by Henry addressing the Percys in equally ambiguous terms:

> I will from henceforth rather be myself,
> Mighty and to be feared, than my condition.[4]
>
> (1.3. 5–6)

Neither man can freely express his true self, whatever that is, because each has something to hide . . . Hal hides his sympathy with his father, while Henry hides his guilt over the deposition and murder of Richard. Nonetheless, that guilt is revealed in the way he splits his son into two contending images: the bad son, Hal the wastrel; and the good son, Hotspur the king of honor. For Hal to become his father's son personally (to be loved) and politically (to be trusted as fit to succeed his father), he must restore his reputation as heir apparent, triumph over Hotspur, and assume Hotspur's identity as the model of chivalric manhood in England. This he obediently promises and economically does, in the sum-zero terms of heroic combat:

> Percy is but my factor, good my lord,
> To engross up glorious deeds on my behalf
> And I will call him to so strict account
> That he shall render every glory up,
> Yea, even the slightest worship of his time,
> Or I will tear the reckoning from his heart.
>
> (3.2. 147–52)

[4] A. R. Humphreys, editor of the new Arden text, glosses *condition* as "natural disposition."

Thus Shrewsbury is the second focal point of the father-son relationship, and constitutes Hal's and Henry's first mutual reaffirmation of identity.

Interpreting *1 Henry IV*: Four Productions

[*Editor's note*: Wharton discusses three productions by the Royal Shakespeare Company (1964, directed by Peter Hall, John Barton, and Clifford Williams; 1975, directed by Terry Hands; 1982, directed by Trevor Nunn) and also the BBC television production (1979).]

Henry and Hal

The traditional portrayal of Henry IV has been in terms of anguished guilt. John Gielgud's performance in the Orson Welles film *Chimes at Midnight* (1966) might be called the classic example. Here the king seemed at once ennobled and soured by his burden of conscience. The voice was majestic, but the face betrayed the dyspeptic sufferings of a man for whom life had turned bitter.

In the 1964 Royal Shakespeare Company production (directed jointly by Peter Hall, John Barton, and Clifford Williams), Henry was played by Eric Porter. In his interpretation, the king was less bilious than stricken. Dignified—even graceful—in movement and voice, his eyes were haunted by the past. At times, with a characteristic gesture of raising his hands, he seemed to be trying to ward off his ghosts.

Yet in the vital matter of his relationship with Hal there seemed not even the contact of pity between father and son. Their meeting in Part 1 was played with great physical and emotional distance between the two men. When the time came for Hal (Ian Holm) to declare his loyalty, he first went over and closed the door: a telling gesture with its

From T. F. Wharton, *Henry the Fourth Parts I and II: Text and Performance Series* (Macmillan, 1983). We reprint here, with the permission of Macmillan, an abridgement of pages 45–80.

suggestion of guarded secrecy. He remained inaccessible to his father.

Other directors have taken widely differing approaches. The most innovative was certainly Terry Hands's 1975 RSC production at Stratford, with Emrys James cast as Henry.

In this revolutionary interpretation, Henry was presented as being far from inert. This was an abrasive self-made man: contemptuous, possessive, domineering. He was a man who courted aggression. In his first brush with the Northern lords, over the issue of Mortimer's ransom [1.3], he followed Hotspur across the stage to stab a blunt finger at his face on "he never did encounter with Glendower." Openly laughing at Hotspur, he turned to give Blunt his cue to join in the laugh, which he dutifully did. Returning to the throne, Henry peremptorily beckoned Northumberland across to him, only to dismiss him with another stab of the finger: "We license your departure with your son."

A particularly striking detail in this scene—one which reinforced the impression of Henry as a ruthless businessman—involved the use of a coin. Arguing that Mortimer would have to be ransomed from Wales at the Percy family's own cost, with not "one penny" of the crown's money spent on rescuing a "traitor," Henry flung down a coin at Hotspur's feet. Yet as if to reinforce the idea of "not one penny," he checked his exit at the end of the interview and came back to retrieve the coin from the stage.

With such a man as this, one could well understand the hatred the Percy faction bore him. He was insufferable; his aggression made friendship, even compromise, impossible.

Interestingly, Emrys James's Henry clearly alienated his own son, played by Alan Howard. Here, of course, the king wished to inspire love rather than hate. His affection, however, was just as aggressive as his hatred. He seemed to need to possess Hal: seizing him, dragging him down into his lap, kissing him resoundingly, even on the lips. It was small wonder that Hal recoiled with some revulsion. When, before the battle of Shrewsbury, the prince stepped forward to give defiance to Worcester, his father brusquely pulled him back, and took over.

The problem with the 1975 RSC interpretation of Henry

is that the father's unattractiveness explains all too easily the son's antipathy. The question of a punishment for Henry's sins in the past becomes irrelevant in the face of his behavior in the present. Nevertheless, the 1975 production enjoyed the considerable advantage of signaling very clearly the idea of Hal's "two fathers." As Hal recoiled from his natural father, his adopted home was in Eastcheap, with Falstaff. There he seemed completely at ease.

In Patrick Stewart's interpretation of the role [in the Royal Shakespeare Company production at the Barbican Theatre in London in 1982], the king emerged almost as a nobody. Neither as sick as Eric Porter's Henry IV nor as aggressive as Emrys James's, he is a man in whom almost everything is clamped down under control and neutralized. His costume is the plainest imaginable: a simple white tunic, buttoned high at the neck; black trousers, just visible, tucked into black knee-boots. It indicated cleanliness and fastidiousness—an impression reinforced by his short-cut hair, his extreme economy of movement, and the characteristic habit of taking a refined sip of cordial from a goblet that was always at hand for him when he entered and sat.

In the first reconciliation scene with Hal [3.2], the same tightly inhibited Henry was evident. There was the same almost prim fastidiousness about the set. The king sat in a sparsely furnished room, with only a table, a chair, and a ewer for washing his hands. The table and the ewer-stand were covered with purple cloths, each with a small gold emblem of the crown. Henry kept his son standing. He yielded nothing. Rather, he actually produced, from a drawer in the table, the bags which had been stolen at Gadshill, slamming them down on the table. Crossing to Hal and carrying a cushion, he perched it on his son's head, making him both feel and look a fool, wearing his mock-crown as he had done in the earlier tavern scene. Returning to his seat, as Hal began his apology in earnest, the king hardly looked at him. He wore, in fact, his most characteristic facial expression: eyes screwed up tight, mouth twisted into an ambiguous ironic smile. Only at the very end of the prince's speech did Henry's expression seem less sardonic, and the son was permitted, for a few seconds, an expression of genuine pleasure on "A hundred thousand rebels die in this." Then, immediately, he tidied the bags back into the drawer of his table and bent back to his paperwork, hardly raising his eyes to his son again.

In all three of the interpretations we have been discussing, one common factor is detectable in regard to the relationship of father and son, among widely differing emphases. It is that, however Hal responds to his father, the king emerges as a figure who is tightly bound up in his own obsessions. He need not be exactly withdrawn. Emrys James's extrovert King Henry in Terry Hands's production shows this. Yet he gives very little to his son. If understanding can be achieved between them, it falls to Hal to penetrate the barriers, not only in himself, but also in his father.

In this respect, the production of the *Henry IV* plays in the BBC's televised "complete Shakespeare" series ran entirely true to form. Directed by David Giles and first broadcast in December 1979, it presented the king, again, as a figure of harsh remoteness. In the end, whatever contact was established between him and his son was made to seem both odd and unsatisfactory.

The director had evidently intended that this scene between father and son should be played very "dead." Jon Finch delivered his complaints moving forward to the camera to ³/₄-shot, leaving David Gwillim's Hal in long-shot behind him. Hal watched his father with a face absolutely neutral and lifeless. Whenever his father turned to look at him, Hal looked down, avoiding his eyes, raising his own again only when his father had turned away. He seemed locked in a kind of numbness, until stirred by the king's wilder allegations (that Hal was as much his father's enemy as Hotspur) into self-defense. Yet even here, the scene avoided any sense of real contact. Hal's promises of reform were delivered with a smug half-smile, conveying a sense of secrecy and private knowledge. He remained as immobile as before, giving nothing to his father.

Hal and Falstaff and Hotspur

The interpretation of the play which has been most committed to the idea of a "cold-blooded" Hal was the RSC 1964 version. Hal was played by Ian Holm, a physically ideal choice. Small, tidy, economical in his acting, everything about him contrasted with Hugh Griffith's Falstaff. Our first view of the two men was of them emerging from sleep from under the straw in a wagon. They went across to a pump, to douse each other with water. Falstaff was in a nightshirt the size of a bell-tent. Hal wore a neat dark doublet and hose. His physical appearance suggested Hamlet rather than a prodigal son.

Holm played the part neither primly nor censoriously. There were moments when his Hal seemed entirely at ease in the world of Eastcheap: the moments when he would lay an arm on Falstaff's shoulder, or allow himself to be picked up and hugged by the fat knight. Yet the impression was always of self-containment. In the great tavern scene of Part 1 [2.4], there was a good deal of laughter, but the joke was clearly on Falstaff rather than shared with him. One remembers Hal's turning his back on Falstaff's gouty tirade on cowardice, to shake with silent giggles; his assuming an expression of mock wonderment at Falstaff's Gadshill exploits; his bending over the fat knight in the chair, eyebrows raised, gleefully openmouthed, his head giving little sharp nods, as he issued his challenge for Falstaff to wriggle out of the truth. It was all good fun, but the overwhelming impression of Hal's brand of humor was its stress on the ironic and the preposterous in what he saw around him. When Falstaff claimed, "I knew ye," Hal turned away in disgust. When he "deposed" Falstaff in the role of King Henry, in the "mock reprimand," his expression became much tighter, and with Falstaff groping for comfort—"banish not him thy Harry's company"—looked at him pitilessly as he said, "I do, I will."

The point was made all the clearer by the carefully contrasted figure of Hotspur, lovingly portrayed by Roy Dotrice. This was a kilted, wild Hotspur, yet everything about him was full of warmth and exuberance.

The major scene with his wife, Lady Percy, is often played as knockabout [2.3]. In the Roy Dotrice/Janet Suzman version, it was still rough, but also very intimate, with a good deal of the scene played on the floor—husband and

wife pushing over, kissing, tumbling, wrapping-up, kneeling astride or lying on top. Although Roy Dotrice is not
physically large, everything about him seemed impressive.
His accent was notably thicker than that of his kinsmen.
Where every other warrior was content with a normal
sword, Hotspur's was a huge two-handed cleaver.

In war, he was in his element. In anticipation of it, he had
"ridden" his saddle, which his servant brought in on a saddle-
stand. When the event arrived, he seemed on fire. All his
restless energy, so evident from the very beginning, found
its fulfillment as he leaped to do battle with Hal, laughing
aloud as he swung the huge sword clanging against Hal's
crossed sword and dagger, or forcing him to draw in his
stomach like a hoop to escape it. And when finally, as they
fought around a long horse-trough, and Hotspur's great
sword thudded into the side of it, allowing Hal to get in and
stab him under the ribs and lower him, dying, into the
trough, there was what can only be described as a collective
sigh from the audience. He had won the audience's love by
his joy in life. Now he was dead; and curiously, the man
who remained alive seemed to have no zest for life at all.

Not too far away from Ian Holm's interpretation was
the 1979 television version, with David Gwillim as Hal. In
the tavern scene of Part 1 [2.4], Hal was the one man among
Falstaff's audience who was not won over by his performance. As [Anthony] Quayle's Falstaff prepared for the
play of reprimand, Hal goaded him on the subject of his
cowardly "instinct." His comments raised a laugh, trading
as they did on Falstaff's own jokes and phrases, but Hal
himself did not smile. When, during the reprimand-play, the
roles were reversed, Hal as King Henry described Falstaff in
a list of insults which were also delivered straight-faced.
The company began by laughing at these, willingly enough,
still buoyed up by Falstaff's own performance as King
Henry. Gradually, however, the laughter petered out. The
scene became very still, and the only sound was of Hal's
voice. The camera, moving in $1/2$-shot between the two men,
registered the intentness in Hal, and the injured feelings in
Falstaff. For Falstaff to keep up the pretence of good humor
("I would your grace would take me with you. Whom

means your grace?") required a distinct effort. In his speech of self-defense, his habitual anxiety assumed the proportion of near-desperation. With the bustle of Bardolph noisily running in, and drawing everyone's attention, Hal's words "I do, I will" were spoken quietly and meaningfully, and heard by Falstaff alone. He opened his mouth to speak, but no words came, as Hal still stared him down.

By far the subtlest treatment of the role of Hal, however, was in the 1982 RSC production [at the Barbican]. Gerard Murphy's Hal was a creature of impulse rather than of calculation. His version of "I know you all" seemed surprisingly bitter. He appeared to snarl out the words, as he sat hunched on a barrel, loutishly picking his feet. The tone of the speech seemed to be, "I'll show you," as if what he had in mind was scoring a point against his enemies. In the "mock-reprimand," his dissatisfaction with a life of waste and pointlessness was evident. What began as a convincing impersonation of his father's stiff manner, complete with sips of cordial, became personally vituperative and savage as he spoke of Falstaff's vices.

In this production, however, Joss Ackland's Falstaff remained uncrushed. His, "I would your grace would take me with you. Whom means your grace?" got a laugh that deflated Hal's urgency and irritated him still more. Falstaff's subsequent defense of tavern life was done with confidence, winning growls of approval from the stage-audience of drinkers. This too added to Hal's ill-temper, and when the promised rejection was spoken, it was thrown at Falstaff in the tone of a childish "Yah," and with a nasty coarse laugh.

Yet the same man was capable of great spontaneous affection for his fat friend. Immediately after the promise of rejection he gave Falstaff an ardent hug around the neck. When in Part 1 [4.2], Falstaff with his cannon-fodder recruits met Hal on the road—or when, rather, Hal almost fell over him, since Falstaff was stretched out for a nap—the director altered the text so that Westmoreland's entry was not with Hal but delayed. By the time he did arrive, Hal and Falstaff were not only enjoying a good laugh together, but actually rolling on the ground, in tavern rough-and-tumble. They both scrambled guiltily to their feet when he entered.

Again, the figure of Hotspur helped to form our response to Hal. Here, most unusually, he emerged (in Timothy Dalton's interpretation) not as a contrast but as a parallel. The warmhearted side of him was played down, and replaced by moodiness. Many of his more "poetic" lines were cut. His impulsiveness was much like Hal's own. In the first scene with his wife [2.3], he knelt, reading, as his wife came creeping downstairs. Played by Harriet Walter as a very submissive lady, she crouched beside him. The two figures became, suddenly, two people talking about their marriage. They looked grim and lugubrious. Hotspur jumped up, to call for his horse. Lady Percy followed, attempting playfully to wheedle his secrets out of him. Quite suddenly he turned on her. The line, "Away, you trifler" was delivered with ferocious force. When he said, "I care not for thee, Kate," there was no doubt that he meant it. If at the end he relented, holding out a hand to her, which eventually she took, the patching-up of their marriage was only temporary. In their only other scene together [3.1]—a scene which is usually nothing more than a piece of pleasant domestic nonsense, with the Welsh lady's song—Hotspur's declared fancy for the Welsh lady's bed looked all too probably true. When his wife took offense and refused to sing as requested, he seemed deliberately to pick a quarrel on this trivial matter in order to break away and leave her. Like Hal, he was a difficult man. They were alike; and this made much more sense than usual of their rivalry.

The chosen nature of Hal in any given production will necessarily condition and entail much else. If Hal is shallow (as in the TV production) or cold and withdrawn (as in 1964), the corollary is automatically that Hotspur or Falstaff will and must emerge as "warm." If Hal is, on the other hand, played as impulsive or immature (as in 1982 and 1975), then the Hotspur contrast tends to be obliterated entirely. Far more significantly, so does the contrast with Eastcheap.

Both approaches have support in the text, and the 1964 and 1982 versions particularly vividly represent the possibilities of each. Notably, in both versions, Hal is trapped between court and tavern; though in one case nothing at all touches the prince, while in the other he is racked with conflicting emotions toward both worlds. The second interpretation is more humanly comprehensible. The first makes more sense of the idea of a man awaiting a national destiny. Fortunately the play is big enough to accommodate both interpretations.

SYLVAN BARNET

Henry IV, Part One on Stage and Screen

> This is a play which all men admire, and which most women
> dislike. Many revolting expressions in the comic parts, much
> boisterous courage in some of the graver scenes, together with
> Falstaff's unwieldy person, offend every female auditor.
>
> Elizabeth Inchbald, writing in 1808

Henry IV, Part One has for most of its history been im-
mensely popular on the stage, not only in England but also in
the United States, probably because at least until recently
men rather than women paid for most of the tickets. Perhaps
because of Shakespeare's prestige and because Falstaff is
usually seen as an evocation of Merrie England, the play is
considered a safe choice for opening a new theater: it was the
first play staged when the Shakespeare Memorial Theatre
(which had been destroyed by fire in 1926) reopened in 1932,
the first play staged when the Royal Shakespeare Company
moved into its new quarters at the Barbican Theatre in 1982,
and the first play staged by the American National Theater, in
1985, at the Kennedy Center in Washington, D.C.

This essay cannot hope to touch on all of the major productions, but it will very briefly survey the early centuries
and then will look a bit more closely at a few productions
since World War II.[1]

[1]For a concise survey of performances up to 1935, consult *A New Variorum
Edition of Shakespeare: Henry the Fourth, Part 1*, ed. Samuel Burdett Hemingway, and for some corrections to Hemingway, *Supplement to Henry IV, Part 1*,
ed. G. Blakemore Evans, also published in *Shakespeare Quarterly* 7 (1956):
104-05. For a general yet erudite survey, see Arthur Colby Sprague, *Shakespeare's Histories: Plays for the Stage*, and for relatively full discussions of
three stage performances in England (1964, 1975, 1982) as well as the BBC
television version (1979), see T. F. Wharton, *Henry the Fourth, Parts 1 and 2:
Text and Performance*, selections of which appear as the preceding essay here..

We have a few records of early performances—for instance, we know that it was staged as part of the entertainment offered to the Flemish ambassador in 1600—but the best evidence that *1 Henry IV* was popular in Shakespeare's day is the fact that it was published five times between 1598 and 1613. Another bit of evidence of its popularity in the theater is a line by Leonard Digges, written about 1623:

> let but Falstaff come,
> Hal, Poins, the rest—you scarce shall have a room.

About 1622 *1 Henry IV* and *2 Henry IV* were combined into one play, for a private performance. More precisely, Part 1 was slightly abridged (the only scenes completely omitted were 2.1 and 4.4, both of which are short); three-fourths of the composite play comes from Part 1, and one-fourth from Part 2. (The taste for combining the two plays into one play persists. In 1964 Joan Littlewood directed *1 Henry IV*, with rearrangements and with additions from *2 Henry IV*, at the Edinburgh Festival, and, as we shall see, Orson Welles combined elements from several of Shakespeare's plays in a film.) But *1 Henry IV* continued to hold the stage in its original form until the Civil War broke out in 1642, when Parliament closed the London theaters and dramatic activity in England nearly ceased. Yet even under these severely adverse conditions *1 Henry IV* lived on the stage, in a highly abbreviated form called a *droll*. The drolls were comic extracts from plays, for instance the scenes of the grave diggers in *Hamlet* and Bottom the Weaver in *A Midsummer Night's Dream*. These brief plays were surreptitiously acted not only in London but in the provinces at fairs, in halls, and in taverns. In 1662 a droll from *1 Henry IV* was published, entitled *The Bouncing Knight, or, The Robbers Robbed,*[2] in a collection of drolls entitled *The Wits, or, Sport upon Sport*, with a preface by one Henry Marsh. In 1662 the book was reissued, this time by a bookseller named Francis Kirkman. It is not known who edited the individual drolls, but one can

---

[2]For the record, *The Bouncing Knight* essentially consists of these parts of *1 Henry IV*: 2.4.113–284, 328–33, 376–485; 3.3.1–73, 84–157; 4.2.12–49, 62–68; 5.1.125–41; 5.4.101–28, 130–63.

read them in J. J. Elson's excellent scholarly edition of *The
Wits*. A second droll, *The Boaster*, was published in 1704 in
a collection called *The Theatre of Ingenuity*. It is based
chiefly on Falstaff's description in 2.4 of his fight with the
men in buckram, with lots of cuts and rewordings.

The Commonwealth prohibition of theatrical performances ended in 1660, when Charles II was restored to the
throne, and *1 Henry IV* was regularly performed during the
rest of the seventeenth century. In 1682 Thomas Betterton
played Hotspur (a role that since has been played by such
eminent actors as Laurence Olivier and Michael Redgrave),
but when Betterton revived the play in 1700 he took the role
of Falstaff, establishing the tradition of putting the company's leading actor in this role. Judging from the acting
edition of this production, published in 1700, Betterton did
not heighten his part by making extensive cuts in the historical portions of the play, though later Falstaffs have done so
when they controlled the company. His cuts were chiefly
matters of decorum, though he also reduced Lady Percy's
role and (because the end of 3.1 is cut) deleted the small part
of Lady Mortimer, which is odd when one considers that ac-
tresses (having replaced boy actors in female roles) were
now making an important contribution to the popularity of
the theater. The Welsh scene with Lady Mortimer was
abridged in most productions of the early eighteenth century, and omitted in the late eighteenth century, but it was
restored in the middle of the nineteenth.

In the first half of the eighteenth century *1 Henry IV*
seems (like *Hamlet*) to have been acted in London at least
once every year, and the evidence suggests that for the entire eighteenth century *1 Henry IV* was more popular than
any of Shakespeare's comedies. In the early nineteenth it
somewhat declined in popularity, possibly because it has so
few female roles, and possibly because taste was moving in
the direction of Mrs. Inchbald, quoted at the start of this essay, though there were still some important performances:
praise was given to John Philip Kemble and William
Charles Macready as Hotspur, and to Barry Sullivan and
Samuel Phelps as Falstaff. In the second half of the nineteenth century the play was rarely performed in England,

perhaps for the reasons just given, or perhaps because Victorian taste preferred a nobler view of English history than Shakespeare offered. What is especially puzzling is that from the end of the eighteenth century to the last quarter of the nineteenth, the "play extempore" of 2.4.380-481, in which Falstaff at first impersonates the king and then (when Hal takes over the role of the king) impersonates Hal, was usually omitted. Abraham Lincoln was as puzzled as we are. When he spent the evening of December 13, 1863, with the actor James Henry Hackett (Hackett was the first American to appear as a star in London, playing Falstaff in 1833), Lincoln asked why this scene was omitted. Hackett replied that it reads well but is not effective on the stage, a judgment that can only puzzle us further.

In 1905 Frank Benson, probably for the first time since Shakespeare's day, staged *1 Henry IV* along with Shakespeare's three other plays related to the reign of Henry IV, that is, with *Richard II*, *2 Henry IV*, and *Henry V*, and in 1921 the Birmingham Repertory Company, under Barry Jackson, staged the two parts of *Henry IV* in one day, a practice occasionally repeated in recent years. Jackson's production was given on April 23, supposedly Shakespeare's birthday, and we can detect here an implication that *Henry IV*, far from being immoral or unpatriotic, is quintessentially Shakespearean and by the same token quintessentially English. In the following year Nugent Monck's Norwich Players staged an Elizabethan-style *1 Henry IV* on a stage without a drop curtain, reflecting the belief (championed especially by William Poel) that Shakespeare's plays can best be performed on a stage that resembles the stage for which they were written.

Reluctantly passing over the 1935 production that cast George Robey as Falstaff (an especially interesting choice, since Robey was a music-hall performer, and the choice thus resembled casting W. C. Fields as Micawber in the film *David Copperfield*, or Bert Lahr as Estragon in *Waiting for Godot*), and even more reluctantly passing over the 1945 production with Ralph Richardson as Falstaff and Laurence Olivier as Hotspur, we can for a moment pursue the idea of performing the play on a more or less Elizabethan stage. In

1951 the four Henry plays were produced at Stratford-upon-
Avon. A single setting was used for all four, which were
viewed (partly under the influence of E. M. W. Tillyard's
writings on the history plays) as a tetralogy. Tanya Moisei-
witsch constructed in the Shakespeare Memorial Theatre a
bulky scaffolding that served as a sort of Elizabethan stage
with three chief acting areas: an upper stage or gallery, an
inner stage (sometimes concealed by two doors) below it,
and a main stage. Stairs curving down on each side connected the upper playing area with the main stage. The tim-
ber set, looking somewhat like the popular idea of Tudor
architecture, was enlivened, when appropriate, with colorful
banners.[3]

In this production Anthony Quayle (who with John Kidd
directed Part 1) played Falstaff, Michael Redgrave played
Hotspur, and Richard Burton played Hal. Reviewers
pointed out that Quayle's Falstaff was both a courtier and a
brute. A toady with his superiors, he was ruthless with his
inferiors, especially with the recruits in Part 2. If we take a
broad view of the stage history of the play, we can see that
there are two kinds of Falstaffs: 1) the convivial boozer, the
lovable reprobate, a "huge bombard of sack" irresistibly
drawn toward the "sweet wag" Hal, and 2) the shrewd—
even depraved—contriver who plays the role of the genial
lush but who is much more than mere physical appetite, or,
to put it a bit differently, whose appetite is for power as well
as for sack and capon and women. This second kind of Falstaff, uncertain of his control over Hal but eager for advancement at court, must continually keep an uneasy eye on
the prince. Thus, where the first kind of Falstaff (secure in
the knowledge that he has Hal's love) can be convulsed
with laughter when Hal in 2.4.224-67 denounces Falstaff's
lies about fighting men in buckram, the second kind—and
Quayle was of this sort—by no means enjoys the exposure.
Quayle seemed pressed, almost distraught, until he hit upon
a way out. Indeed, throughout, Falstaff's increasing exag-

[3]For illustrations of the set, see *Shakespeare Quarterly* 2 (1951), plate facing page 328; *Shakespeare Survey* 6, Plate 5; and all of the plates in J. Dover
Wilson and T. C. Worsley, *Shakespeare's Histories at Stratford, 1951.*

gerations seemed somewhat desperate attempts to win a smile from an unsmiling Hal. George Robey apparently had been a Falstaff of the first sort. Something of the difference in the relationship between Hal and Falstaff, between Robey's Falstaff and Quayle's, can be seen even in the first scene between the two characters, 2.2. Burton's Hal first appeared on the upper stage, stretched, washed himself from a bucket, and then descended, violently awakening Quayle's Falstaff (asleep in the inner stage) by throwing a boot at the door; Robey's Falstaff woke up Hal, and then listened to Hal's rebukes while laughing and looking at the audience. Similarly, when we last see Falstaff in *1 Henry IV*, carrying off the body of Hotspur, he can (like Robey) seem comic— or he can (like Quayle) seem disgusting and evil. It should be added, however, that because in 1951 Part 1 was followed by the much darker Part 2, there was (for the sake of consistency) an inducement to darken even the early Falstaff, thus making the rejection of Falstaff in Part 2 thoroughly acceptable.

And Hal's rejection of Falstaff—though the final rejection of course comes only in Part 2—was evident in Part 1. Burton's Hal was never the madcap prince. For instance, in the "play extempore," in 2.4.378-481, when Hal takes over from Falstaff the role of king, Burton did not play the role comically. It *can* be played comically, for instance with Hal continuing to use as a crown the cushion that Falstaff used. Burton's Hal, however, soon dropped the jesting; his indictment of the "old fat man," "that bolting-hutch of beastliness, that swoll'n parcel of dropsies," was an earnest denunciation. His Hal, in short, always kept Falstaff at a distance. (Quayle plays Falstaff also in the BBC television version, released in 1979, interpreting the role pretty much in the vein of the stage production. Hal, played by David Gwillim, is unamused by Falstaff's performance as the king, and, a little later in the scene, when he himself takes over the impersonation of the king, he delivers his insults with a straight face. As Hal ceases playing and becomes earnest, the on-stage audience ceases laughing; the camera focuses on Hal's unsmiling face and on Falstaff's hurt expression. After Hal's "I do, I will," Falstaff opens his mouth to speak, but no words come out.)

The tetralogy (to use an imprecise but convenient expression) was again presented at Stratford-upon-Avon in 1964, this time directed by Peter Hall, John Barton, and Clifford Williams, along with the three parts of *Henry VI* (though these three were combined into two plays). The set was in marked contrast to the "Elizabethan" set of the 1951 production, for now it was highly mobile (four tall structures that could be moved about separately), perhaps adding welcome variety to the eyes of those who witnessed the entire sequence of six plays. This Falstaff (Hugh Griffith) was chiefly in the tradition of the lovable rogue, full of Rabelaisian vitality. If that sounds a trifle too simple, it should be said that the play was complicated in other ways. Reviewers commented especially on the violence of the combats (for instance, Hotspur with a two-handed sword against Hal with sword and buckler), and on the influence of the Theater of Cruelty, especially at the end, when Vernon was hanged, cut down, and Worcester ascended the scaffold to take Vernon's place.

The Royal Shakespeare Company's production at the Barbican Theatre in 1982 allows us to make a neat comparison with Griffith's Falstaff. Joss Ackland's Falstaff was conceived somewhat in Quayle's shifty manner. He was not a Rabelaisian comic figure, and indeed was not especially funny in any way. Rather he was by turns moody, manic, and savage. Ackland said he modeled his Falstaff on Orson Welles, a man whom he regarded as one who wasted his great talents. Hal, too, played by Gerard Murphy, was relatively joyless, something of a petulant hippie (long blond hair), irritable but also capable of giving affection. In the "play extempore," he put little weight on the banishment of Falstaff ("I do, I will," in 2.4.481); rather, after speaking these words, he gave Falstaff an affectionate hug, thus making the whole episode contrast strongly with those productions (such as at Stratford in 1964) that make this scene a key to the entire play.

Something has been said about interpretations of Falstaff and of Hal; it is time to say a word about Hotspur. After Falstaff's, the chief part has usually been regarded as Hotspur's; few actors of importance have wanted to play Hal. In the late seventeenth century Thomas Betterton was praised for those "wild, impatient starts, that fierce and flashing fire, which he threw into Hotspur," and in the early nineteenth century Macready was praised for his "impetuous declamation." A curious stage tradition has developed, giving Hotspur a stammer or some comparable speech impediment. The idea apparently is rooted in Lady Percy's comment, in *2 Henry IV*, 2.3.24, that her late husband was known for "speaking thick, which nature made his blemish." "Thick" here means "fast," as in "thick and fast"; that is, Hotspur crowded his words, but a misinterpretation of "thick" has given rise to the idea that his speech was impaired, or that he spoke with a northern burr or brogue. The earliest record of a stuttering Hotspur is in nineteenth-century Germany; Schlegel translated "thick" as *stottern*, and so German Hotspurs stuttered. In 1914 the English actor-manager Beerbohm Tree told his Hotspur (Matheson Lang) to stammer, and the impediment took root in England. Most effective of all was Olivier's Hotspur at the Old Vic in 1945. This Hotspur could pronounce his *w*'s only after a slight hesitation. His dying speech, in the last lines of which he addresses himself, was thus given an added poignancy:

> O, I could prophesy,
> But that the earthy and cold hand of death
> Lies on my tongue. No, Percy, thou art dust,
> And food for—

Prince. For worms, brave Percy.   (5.4.82-86)

In 1951 Michael Redgrave's Hotspur spoke with thick *r*'s, suggesting northern speech, and in 1955 John Neville, at the Old Vic, stammered on his *m*'s. There still plenty of letters left in the alphabet for actors to find fresh ways of speaking "thick."

It has already been mentioned that *1 Henry IV* was the premier production of the American National Theater, at the Kennedy Center in Washington, D.C., in 1985. The production was a failure (it was withdrawn after only five previews and five performances), largely, it seems, because it was a rather sophomoric and highly inconsistent exercise in assimilating the play to Brechtian drama. Thus, the travelers who are robbed by Falstaff and his companions were represented by dummies on a wagon (shades of Mother Courage's wagon); stagehands sometimes (but not always) visibly hauled props; pieces of the set were sometimes left on the stage; some battle scenes were done in slow motion; a priest walked about on the battlefield at Shrewsbury, providing the smoke of battle from his censer (although in Shakespeare's play only in the brief scene between York and Michael—4.4—is there anything about the relation of politics to religion); and at the end of the play, Hal and King Henry rode on carousel horses. One other bit of mischief: the actor John McMartin doubled as Falstaff and King Henry, thus needlessly emphasizing the idea that Hal has two father figures, and (worse) needlessly slowing down the play, since time had to be allotted for McMartin's costume changes, and (still worse) needlessly irritating the audience by using a double, his back to the audience, in scenes where both characters appear. It was all pretty silly. Less silly, but even more offensive, was Hal's conquest of Hotspur. He threw a knife into Hotspur, at a distance of some 20 feet.

A much more interesting American production, directed by Michael Edwards, was given at Santa Cruz in 1984.[4] The set in this Santa Cruz production was a mock-up of the Globe Theatre, but with a military helicopter crashed into the roof (stage right). The production was in modern dress: Hal (long hair, made-up eyebrows, bright red lips, tight shiny blue trousers) was something of a Boy George, and Falstaff, in leather and chains, was something of an aging member of Hell's Angels. In Hal's interview with his father, however, the makeup was gone, and so was the flamboyant costume—though now, since he wore a kimono and was barefoot, there was still a suggestion of the rebellious youth.

[4]This production is discussed in some detail by Mary Judith Dunbar in *Shakespeare Quarterly* 35 (1984): 475-78, and also by Alan C. Dessen in *Shakespeare Quarterly* 36 (1985): 75-79. Since I have not seen this production my comments are based on these two sources.

Henry IV was dressed at first in a three-piece dark suit, and later in the uniform of a five-star general. In the battle scenes Hal, too, wore the dress of a soldier (combat fatigues), and his hair was short. The king's opening speech was treated as a press conference for reporters, who were equipped with television cameras and tape recorders. Westmoreland was in attendance as a five-star general, and Sir Walter Blunt, in a dark suit, as a cabinet officer. The last four lines of the play were yet another press conference. Staging of this sort usually leads to great liberties with the text, but in this production the text was scarcely tinkered with, though there were of course bits of business not specified in the text. For instance, at the end of the play Falstaff, cigar in mouth, held his fingers up in a V sign.

The reviews indicate that the production was imaginative, intelligently conceived, and well acted. There is space here to illustrate only one example of its freshness. If we look at the text of 5.2.48–55, we find that when Hal asks Falstaff for his sword, Falstaff offers instead his pistol case; Hal opens the case and finds it contains not a pistol but a bottle of wine, and then, according to the quarto stage direction, Hal "throws the bottle at him." That is, Hal rejects the world of revelry and of escape from combat. In this production the case held a can of beer. Hal started to throw it, thought better, and carried it off. A little later, alone on the stage, he paused to drink some of the beer, and then found, to his surprise, that Hotspur was pointing a gun at him. Hal took a second drink and tossed the can to Hotspur, who also took a drink, and then cooled himself off by pouring the remainder of the beer over his head. Hotspur then tossed aside his own pistol, in order to fight Hal in equal combat. Dessen summarizes his impression of the business:

A clear sense was conveyed here, albeit without the trappings of chivalry, of something shared between the two warriors, an unspoken code that, in modern as well as in Elizabethan terms, may be archaic and unrealistic (especially in the presence of high-powered automatic weapons and with a kingdom at stake), but is nonetheless appealing and moving. On the one hand, I missed the throwing of the bottle-can at Falstaff (one of

Shakespeare's summary images), but I would not have wished
to lose this moment where the imagery set up by the actors and
the director clarified and developed something very important
in the script that can easily be blurred in any production.

Finally, something should be said about two films that
draw on *1 Henry IV*, one by Orson Welles and the other by
Gus Van Sant. Welles's film, made in Spain in 1964, was
released in 1966 under the title of *Chimes at Midnight*, and
was retitled *Falstaff*, with Welles as Falstaff. As a school-
boy Welles had assembled parts of Shakespeare's history
plays into a single play, and the idea remained with him
throughout his career. In 1960 he staged a work called *Five
Kings*, made out of pieces of *Richard II*, *1 Henry IV*, *2
Henry IV*, and *Henry V*, and clarified by a narrator who read
passages from Holinshed's *Chronicles*. (In the film, Ralph
Richardson narrates these passages.) Welles made the film
under difficult circumstances; to be specific, he could raise
very little money, and he could get certain actors for only
brief periods—and not always for the same periods as others who shared scenes with them. Jeanne Moreau (Doll
Tearsheet) was available for only five days (perhaps it
would have been better had she not been available at all),
and Gielgud for only ten. This means that Welles sometimes
had to use doubles, and his attempt to disguise this sub-
terfuge by using long shots is transparent. Moreover, the
soundtrack is very bad—when the voices are not inaudible,
they are often out of sync. One often cannot tell who is
speaking, sometimes because Welles dubbed in his own
voice for other roles. Moreover, because he feared that his
American accent would disturb the other actors, he recorded
his own dialogue separately. Worst of all, however, is the
basic idea of using pieces of several plays, and of distorting
them. Hal, for example, is presented early as an effeminate
bisexual, probably the lover of Poins. Still, there are some
marvelous performances, especially John Gielgud as King
Henry, and sometimes (when he is not a coy and mumbling
Santa Claus) Welles as Falstaff. Almost all Shakespeare
specialists detest the film, understandably and rightly; almost all cinema specialists admire at least portions of the

film, especially the battle. No matter that the battlefield is
hard and dry when we see cavalry, and muddy when we see
foot soldiers. The scene, utterly unheroic, is visually beautiful and worthy of Eisenstein, Welles's inspiration here.
Still, it must be said that the film is a mess, and is utterly un-
faithful to Shakespeare, though Welles didn't see it that
way. In a long interview, published both in *Cahiers du cinema in English,* #11, and in *Sight and Sound,* Autumn 1966
(the language differs slightly, but is obvious that the interview is the same), Welles explains that the film is an elegy
for a vanished Merrie England. It is about death—the death
of Hal's youth, the death of Falstaff's friendship with Hal,
and the death of joy. (Much of Shakespeare's comedy dis-
appears in this film.) "Falstaff," Welles says, "represents a
positive spirit, in many respects courageous. . . . He wages a
struggle lost in advance. I don't believe he is seeking anything. He represents a value; he is goodness. . . . The film
speaks too of the terrible price that the Prince must pay in
exchange for power."[5]

What is especially missing from Welles's *Falstaff* is comedy, a quality Welles said he did not greatly want in this
film. "Comedy can't really dominate a film made to tell this
story, which is all in dark colors." Dark interpretations of
1 Henry IV are now the rule, partly because of our experience with war in the twentieth century, and partly because of
academic criticism that has linked the play closely with the
much darker *2 Henry IV.* The insights of our century should
not (and cannot) be put aside; we cannot go back to Falstaff
who is merely a lovable jester. But perhaps it is time to remember that *1 Henry IV* is, among other things, a richly
comic play. Even Mrs. Inchbald knew this truth almost two
centuries ago, though (as we have seen) she found much in
the comedy that would "offend every female auditor."

Welles's *Chimes at Midnight,* though a highly personal
reworking of Shakespeare's text, is close to Shakespeare
when compared to *My Own Private Idaho* (1991), a film
made by Gus Van Sant, who was already famous for *Drug-*

---

[5]See *Chimes at Midnight,* ed. Bridget Gellert (1988), for the script, interviews, and comments.

store Cowboy (1989), a cult hit starring Matt Dillon. *My Own Private Idaho*—the title comes from a song by a rock group, the B-52s—is set chiefly in the Pacific Northwest, especially in Portland, where Scott (played by Keanu Reeves), the son of the wealthy mayor, is a street hustler. Another young hustler, Mike (River Phoenix), is in love with Scott, and both are associated with an older thief and ex-hustler, Bob Pigeon (William Richert). These three—modernized versions of Hal, Poins, and Falstaff—sometimes engage in activities derived from Shakespeare's plays. For instance, the rogues ambush a rock band (cf. the Gadshill robbery in *1 Henry IV*, 2.2), and then Scott and Mike, disguised in hooded robes, rob Bob Pigeon. Pigeon duly exaggerates the number of his assailants, and when he is exposed as a liar, he says that "instinct" prevented him from harming the heir apparent (cf. 2.4.272–74).

Some of the dialogue in *My Own Private Idaho* derives from Shakespeare's play. Thus, part of the first speech that Shakespeare gives to Hal, in 1.2 ("Unless hours were cups of sack, . . . dials the signs of leaping houses, and the blessed sun himself a fair hot wench in flame-colored taffeta"), is transformed into "Unless hours were lines of coke, dials looked like the signs of gay bars, or time itself was a fair hustler in black leather. . . ." Although the film is set in the present, it evokes Shakespeare's play not only by such dialogue, and by parallel episodes (including the rejection of Pigeon, derived from *2 Henry IV* and a report of Pigeon's death, derived from *Henry V*), but also by vaguely Elizabethan garb for some of the street people, by Elizabethan-sounding music in the background, and by glimpses of ads for Falstaff beer. On the other hand, it includes much material unrelated to Shakespeare's plays, since it is as much concerned with Mike's search for his mother—a motif that takes Scott and Mike to Rome, where Scott takes an Italian bride—as it is with Scott's relationship to his rich, political, bourgeois father. Is the film thematically related to *1 Henry IV*? In Falstaff's words (2.4.409), "A question not to be asked." *My Own Private Idaho* is what it is, but it does derive partly from the relatively new, darker interpretations of the Henry plays. In the older view, the plays showed the schooling of a prince;

a young man for a while lived an engaging yet irresponsible life, but he matured and fulfilled his political responsibilities. The darker view sees Hal as betraying life itself, heartlessly dwindling into a vile, cold-blooded politician, and it is this vision of the plays that has shaped *My Own Private Idaho.* Scott, back in Portland with his Italian bride, gets out of a limousine, where Mike and Bob Pigeon see him enter a posh restaurant. Bob follows him into the restaurant, accosts him, and (as in *2 Henry IV*) is brutally rejected. In the context of the film, Scott has sold out to the repressive bourgeois world of his father, rejecting all the values of the Outsider (the life of poverty, hustling, drugs), the values of street life, the values—we are to believe—of the world of the free. In short, the movie is simple and sentimental, nothing that one can say (whatever one's interpretation) of *Henry IV.*

Bibliographic Note: For material concerning the stage history of *1 Henry IV*, in addition to the items cited in footnotes in this essay, consult material listed below in Suggested References, Section 4 (Shakespeare on Stage and Screen), page 250. See also Scott McMillan, *"Henry IV, Part One": Shakespeare in Performance* (1991); Arthur Colby Sprague, *Shakespeare's Histories: Plays for the Stage* (1966); T. F. Wharton, *Henry the Fourth Parts I and II: Text and Performance Series* (1983). Wharton analyzes three productions (1964, 1975, 1982) by the Royal Shakespeare Company, as well as the BBC television version (1979). Part of Wharton's book is reprinted above, pages 223–31.

Suggested References

The number of possible references is vast and grows alarmingly. (The *Shakespeare Quarterly* devotes one issue each year to a list of the previous year's work, and *Shakespeare Survey*—an annual publication—includes a substantial review of biographical, critical, and textual studies, as well as a survey of performances.) The vast bibliography is best approached through James Harner, *The World Shakespeare Bibliography on CD-Rom: 1900–Present.* The first release, in 1996, included more than 12,000 annotated items from 1990–93, plus references to several thousand book reviews, productions, films, and audio recordings. The plan is to update the publication annually, moving forward one year and backward three years. Thus, the second issue (1997), with 24,700 entries, and another 35,000 or so references to reviews, newspaper pieces, and so on, covered 1987–94.

Though no works are indispensable, those listed below have been found especially helpful. The arrangement is as follows:

1. Shakespeare's Times
2. Shakespeare's Life
3. Shakespeare's Theater
4. Shakespeare on Stage and Screen
5. Miscellaneous Reference Works
6. Shakespeare's Plays: General Studies
7. The Comedies
8. The Romances
9. The Tragedies
10. The Histories
11. *The History of Henry IV [Part One]*

The titles in the first five sections are accompanied by brief explanatory annotations.

1. Shakespeare's Times

Andrews, John F., ed. *William Shakespeare: His World, His Work, His Influence,* 3 vols. (1985). Sixty articles, dealing not only with such subjects as "The State," "The Church," "Law," "Science, Magic, and Folklore," but also with the plays and poems themselves and Shakespeare's influence (e.g., translations, films, reputation)

Byrne, Muriel St. Clare. *Elizabethan Life in Town and Country* (8th ed., 1970). Chapters on manners, beliefs, education, etc., with illustrations.

Dollimore, John, and Alan Sinfield, eds. *Political Shakespeare: New Essays in Cultural Materialism* (1985). Essays on such topics as the subordination of women and colonialism, presented in connection with some of Shakespeare's plays.

Greenblatt, Stephen. *Representing the English Renaissance* (1988). New Historicist essays, especially on connections between political and aesthetic matters, statecraft and stagecraft.

Joseph, B. L. *Shakespeare's Eden: the Commonwealth of England 1558–1629* (1971). An account of the social, political, economic, and cultural life of England.

Kernan, Alvin. *Shakespeare, the King's Playwright: Theater in the Stuart Court 1603–1613* (1995). The social setting and the politics of the court of James I, in relation to *Hamlet, Measure for Measure, Macbeth, King Lear, Antony and Cleopatra, Coriolanus,* and *The Tempest.*

Montrose, Louis. *The Purpose of Playing: Shakespeare and the Cultural Politics of the Elizabethan Theatre* (1996). A poststructuralist view, discussing the professional theater "within the ideological and material frameworks of Elizabethan culture and society," with an extended analysis of *A Midsummer Night's Dream.*

Mullaney, Steven. *The Place of the Stage: License, Play, and Power in Renaissance England* (1988). New Historicist analysis, arguing that popular drama became a cultural institution "only by . . . taking up a place on the margins of society."

Schoenbaum, S. *Shakespeare: The Globe and the World*

(1979). A readable, abundantly illustrated introductory book on the world of the Elizabethans.

Shakespeare's England, 2 vols. (1916). A large collection of scholarly essays on a wide variety of topics, e.g., astrology, costume, gardening, horsemanship, with special attention to Shakespeare's references to these topics.

2. Shakespeare's Life

Andrews, John F., ed. *William Shakespeare: His World, His Work, His Influence,* 3 vols. (1985). See the description above.

Bentley, Gerald E. *Shakespeare: A Biographical Handbook* (1961). The facts about Shakespeare, with virtually no conjecture intermingled.

Chambers, E. K. *William Shakespeare: A Study of Facts and Problems,* 2 vols. (1930). The fullest collection of data.

Fraser, Russell. *Young Shakespeare* (1988). A highly readable account that simultaneously considers Shakespeare's life and Shakespeare's art.

———. *Shakespeare: The Later Years* (1992).

Schoenbaum, S. *Shakespeare's Lives* (1970). A review of the evidence and an examination of many biographies, including those of Baconians and other heretics.

———. *William Shakespeare: A Compact Documentary Life* (1977). An abbreviated version, in a smaller format, of the next title. The compact version reproduces some fifty documents in reduced form. A readable presentation of all that the documents tell us about Shakespeare.

———. *William Shakespeare: A Documentary Life* (1975). A large-format book setting forth the biography with facsimiles of more than two hundred documents, and with transcriptions and commentaries.

3. Shakespeare's Theater

Astington, John H., ed. *The Development of Shakespeare's Theater* (1992). Eight specialized essays on theatrical companies, playing spaces, and performance.

Beckerman, Bernard. *Shakespeare at the Globe, 1599–1609* (1962). On the playhouse and on Elizabethan dramaturgy, acting, and staging.

Bentley, Gerald E. *The Profession of Dramatist in Shakespeare's Time* (1971). An account of the dramatist's status in the Elizabethan period.

———. *The Profession of Player in Shakespeare's Time, 1590–1642* (1984). An account of the status of members of London companies (sharers, hired men, apprentices, managers) and a discussion of conditions when they toured.

Berry, Herbert. *Shakespeare's Playhouses* (1987). Usefully emphasizes how little we know about the construction of Elizabethan theaters.

Brown, John Russell. *Shakespeare's Plays in Performance* (1966). A speculative and practical analysis relevant to all of the plays, but with emphasis on *The Merchant of Venice, Richard II, Hamlet, Romeo and Juliet*, and *Twelfth Night*.

———. *William Shakespeare: Writing for Performance* (1996). A discussion aimed at helping readers to develop theatrically conscious habits of reading.

Chambers, E. K. *The Elizabethan Stage*, 4 vols. (1945). A major reference work on theaters, theatrical companies, and staging at court.

Cook, Ann Jennalie. *The Privileged Playgoers of Shakespeare's London, 1576–1642* (1981). Sees Shakespeare's audience as wealthier, more middle-class, and more intellectual than Harbage (below) does.

Dessen, Alan C. *Elizabethan Drama and the Viewer's Eye* (1977). On how certain scenes may have looked to spectators in an Elizabethan theater.

Gurr, Andrew. *Playgoing in Shakespeare's London* (1987). Something of a middle ground between Cook (above) and Harbage (below).

———. *The Shakespearean Stage, 1579–1642* (2nd ed., 1980). On the acting companies, the actors, the playhouses, the stages, and the audiences.

Harbage, Alfred. *Shakespeare's Audience* (1941). A study of the size and nature of the theatrical public, emphasizing the representativeness of its working class and middle-class audience.

Hodges, C. Walter. *The Globe Restored* (1968). A conjectural restoration, with lucid drawings.

Hosley, Richard. "The Playhouses," in *The Revels History of Drama in English*, vol. 3, general editors Clifford Leech and T. W. Craik (1975). An essay of a hundred pages on the physical aspects of the playhouses.

Howard, Jane E. "Crossdressing, the Theatre, and Gender Struggle in Early Modern England," *Shakespeare Quarterly* 39 (1988): 418–40. Judicious comments on the effects of boys playing female roles.

Orrell, John. *The Human Stage: English Theatre Design, 1567–1640* (1988). Argues that the public, private, and court playhouses are less indebted to popular structures (e.g., innyards and bear-baiting pits) than to banqueting halls and to Renaissance conceptions of Roman amphitheaters.

Slater, Ann Pasternak. *Shakespeare the Director* (1982). An analysis of theatrical effects (e.g., kissing, kneeling) in stage directions and dialogue.

Styan, J. L. *Shakespeare's Stagecraft* (1967). An introduction to Shakespeare's visual and aural stagecraft, with chapters on such topics as acting conventions, stage groupings, and speech.

Thompson, Peter. *Shakespeare's Professional Career* (1992). An examination of patronage and related theatrical conditions.

———. *Shakespeare's Theatre* (1983). A discussion of how plays were staged in Shakespeare's time.

4. Shakespeare on Stage and Screen

Bate, Jonathan, and Russell Jackson, eds. *Shakespeare: An Illustrated Stage History* (1996). Highly readable essays on stage productions from the Renaissance to the present.

Berry, Ralph. *Changing Styles in Shakespeare* (1981). Discusses productions of six plays (*Coriolanus*, *Hamlet*, *Henry V*, *Measure for Measure*, *The Tempest*, and *Twelfth Night*) on the English stage, chiefly 1950–1980.

————. *On Directing Shakespeare: Interviews with Contemporary Directors* (1989). An enlarged edition of a book first published in 1977, this version includes the seven interviews from the early 1970s and adds five interviews conducted in 1988.

Brockbank, Philip, ed. *Players of Shakespeare: Essays in Shakespearean Performance* (1985). Comments by twelve actors, reporting their experiences with roles. See also the entry for Russell Jackson (below).

Bulman, J. C., and H. R. Coursen, eds. *Shakespeare on Television* (1988). An anthology of general and theoretical essays, essays on individual productions, and shorter reviews, with a bibliography and a videography listing cassettes that may be rented.

Coursen, H. P. *Watching Shakespeare on Television* (1993). Analyses not only of TV versions but also of films and videotapes of stage presentations that are shown on television.

Davies, Anthony, and Stanley Wells, eds. *Shakespeare and the Moving Image: The Plays on Film and Television* (1994). General essays (e.g., on the comedies) as well as essays devoted entirely to *Hamlet, King Lear,* and *Macbeth.*

Dawson, Anthony B. *Watching Shakespeare: A Playgoer's Guide* (1988). About half of the plays are discussed, chiefly in terms of decisions that actors and directors make in putting the works onto the stage.

Dessen, Alan. *Elizabethan Stage Conventions and Modern Interpretations* (1984). On interpreting conventions such as the representation of light and darkness and stage violence (duels, battles).

Donaldson, Peter. *Shakespearean Films/Shakespearean Directors* (1990). Postmodernist analyses, drawing on Freudianism, Feminism, Deconstruction, and Queer Theory.

Jackson, Russell, and Robert Smallwood, eds. *Players of Shakespeare 2: Further Essays in Shakespearean Performance by Players with the Royal Shakespeare Company* (1988). Fourteen actors discuss their roles in productions between 1982 and 1987.

————. *Players of Shakespeare 3: Further Essays in Shake-

spearean Performance by Players with the Royal Shakespeare Company (1993). Comments by thirteen performers.

Jorgens, Jack. *Shakespeare on Film* (1977). Fairly detailed studies of eighteen films, preceded by an introductory chapter addressing such issues as music, and whether to "open" the play by including scenes of landscape.

Kennedy, Dennis. *Looking at Shakespeare: A Visual History of Twentieth-Century Performance* (1993). Lucid descriptions (with 170 photographs) of European, British, and American performances.

Leiter, Samuel L. *Shakespeare Around the Globe: A Guide to Notable Postwar Revivals* (1986). For each play there are about two pages of introductory comments, then discussions (about five hundred words per production) of ten or so productions, and finally bibliographic references.

McMurty, Jo. *Shakespeare Films in the Classroom* (1994). Useful evaluations of the chief films most likely to be shown in undergraduate courses.

Rothwell, Kenneth, and Annabelle Henkin Melzer. *Shakespeare on Screen: An International Filmography and Videography* (1990). A reference guide to several hundred films and videos produced between 1899 and 1989, including spinoffs such as musicals and dance versions.

Sprague, Arthur Colby. *Shakespeare and the Actors* (1944). Detailed discussions of stage business (gestures, etc.) over the years.

Willis, Susan. *The BBC Shakespeare Plays: Making the Televised Canon* (1991). A history of the series, with interviews and production diaries for some plays.

5. Miscellaneous Reference Works

Abbott, E. A. *A Shakespearean Grammar* (new edition, 1877). An examination of differences between Elizabethan and modern grammar.

Allen, Michael J. B., and Kenneth Muir, eds. *Shakespeare's Plays in Quarto* (1981). One volume containing facsimiles of the plays issued in small format before they were collected in the First Folio of 1623.

Bevington, David. *Shakespeare* (1978). A short guide to hundreds of important writings on the subject.

Blake, Norman. *Shakespeare's Language: An Introduction* (1983). On vocabulary, parts of speech, and word order.

Bullough, Geoffrey. *Narrative and Dramatic Sources of Shakespeare*, 8 vols. (1957–75). A collection of many of the books Shakespeare drew on, with judicious comments.

Campbell, Oscar James, and Edward G. Quinn, eds. *The Reader's Encyclopedia of Shakespeare* (1966). Old, but still the most useful single reference work on Shakespeare.

Cercignani, Fausto. *Shakespeare's Works and Elizabethan Pronunciation* (1981). Considered the best work on the topic, but remains controversial.

Dent, R. W. *Shakespeare's Proverbial Language: An Index* (1981). An index of proverbs, with an introduction concerning a form Shakespeare frequently drew on.

Greg, W. W. *The Shakespeare First Folio* (1955). A detailed yet readable history of the first collection (1623) of Shakespeare's plays.

Harner, James. *The World Shakespeare Bibliography*. See headnote to Suggested References.

Hosley, Richard. *Shakespeare's Holinshed* (1968). Valuable presentation of one of Shakespeare's major sources.

Kökeritz, Helge. *Shakespeare's Names* (1959). A guide to pronouncing some 1,800 names appearing in Shakespeare.

———. *Shakespeare's Pronunciation* (1953). Contains much information about puns and rhymes, but see Cercignani (above).

Muir, Kenneth. *The Sources of Shakespeare's Plays* (1978). An account of Shakespeare's use of his reading. It covers all the plays, in chronological order.

Miriam Joseph, Sister. *Shakespeare's Use of the Arts of Language* (1947). A study of Shakespeare's use of rhetorical devices, reprinted in part as *Rhetoric in Shakespeare's Time* (1962).

The Norton Facsimile: The First Folio of Shakespeare's Plays (1968). A handsome and accurate facsimile of the first collection (1623) of Shakespeare's plays, with a valuable introduction by Charlton Hinman.

Onions, C. T. *A Shakespeare Glossary*, rev. and enlarged by

R. D. Eagleson (1986). Definitions of words (or senses of words) now obsolete.

Partridge, Eric. *Shakespeare's Bawdy*, rev. ed. (1955). Relatively brief dictionary of bawdy words; useful, but see Williams, below.

Shakespeare Quarterly. See headnote to Suggested References.

Shakespeare Survey. See headnote to Suggested References.

Spevack, Marvin. *The Harvard Concordance to Shakespeare* (1973). An index to Shakespeare's words.

Vickers, Brian. *Appropriating Shakespeare: Contemporary Critical Quarrels* (1993). A survey—chiefly hostile—of recent schools of criticism.

Wells, Stanley, ed. *Shakespeare: A Bibliographical Guide* (new edition, 1990). Nineteen chapters (some devoted to single plays, others devoted to groups of related plays) on recent scholarship on the life and all of the works.

Williams, Gordon. *A Dictionary of Sexual Language and Imagery in Shakespearean and Stuart Literature*, 3 vols. (1994). Extended discussions of words and passages; much fuller than Partridge, cited above.

6. Shakespeare's Plays: General Studies

Bamber, Linda. *Comic Women, Tragic Men: A Study of Gender and Genre in Shakespeare* (1982).

Barnet, Sylvan. *A Short Guide to Shakespeare* (1974).

Callaghan, Dympna, Lorraine Helms, and Jyotsna Singh. *The Weyward Sisters: Shakespeare and Feminist Politics* (1994).

Clemen, Wolfgang H. *The Development of Shakespeare's Imagery* (1951).

Cook, Ann Jennalie. *Making a Match: Courtship in Shakespeare and His Society* (1991).

Dollimore, Jonathan, and Alan Sinfield. *Political Shakespeare: New Essays in Cultural Materialism* (1985).

Dusinberre, Juliet. *Shakespeare and the Nature of Women* (1975).

Granville-Barker, Harley. *Prefaces to Shakespeare*, 2 vols. (1946–47; volume 1 contains essays on *Hamlet, King*

Lear, Merchant of Venice, Antony and Cleopatra, and *Cymbeline*; volume 2 contains essays on *Othello, Coriolanus, Julius Caesar, Romeo and Juliet, Love's Labor's Lost*).

————. *More Prefaces to Shakespeare* (1974; essays on *Twelfth Night, A Midsummer Night's Dream, The Winter's Tale, Macbeth*).

Harbage, Alfred. *William Shakespeare: A Reader's Guide* (1963).

Howard, Jean E. *Shakespeare's Art of Orchestration: Stage Technique and Audience Response* (1984).

Jones, Emrys. *Scenic Form in Shakespeare* (1971).

Lenz, Carolyn Ruth Swift, Gayle Greene, and Carol Thomas Neely, eds. *The Woman's Part: Feminist Criticism of Shakespeare* (1980).

Novy, Marianne. *Love's Argument: Gender Relations in Shakespeare* (1984).

Rose, Mark. *Shakespearean Design* (1972).

Scragg, Leah. *Discovering Shakespeare's Meaning* (1994).

————. *Shakespeare's "Mouldy Tales": Recurrent Plot Motifs in Shakespearean Drama* (1992).

Traub, Valerie. *Desire and Anxiety: Circulations of Sexuality in Shakespearean Drama* (1992).

Traversi, D. A. *An Approach to Shakespeare,* 2 vols. (3rd rev. ed, 1968–69).

Vickers, Brian. *The Artistry of Shakespeare's Prose* (1968).

Wells, Stanley. *Shakespeare: A Dramatic Life* (1994).

Wright, George T. *Shakespeare's Metrical Art* (1988).

7. The Comedies

Barber, C. L. *Shakespeare's Festive Comedy* (1959; discusses *Love's Labor's Lost, A Midsummer Night's Dream, The Merchant of Venice, As You Like It, Twelfth Night*).

Barton, Anne. *The Names of Comedy* (1990).

Berry, Ralph. *Shakespeare's Comedy: Explorations in Form* (1972).

Bradbury, Malcolm, and David Palmer, eds. *Shakespearean Comedy* (1972).

Bryant, J. A., Jr. *Shakespeare and the Uses of Comedy* (1986).

Carroll, William. *The Metamorphoses of Shakespearean Comedy* (1985).

Champion, Larry S. *The Evolution of Shakespeare's Comedy* (1970).

Evans, Bertrand. *Shakespeare's Comedies* (1960).

Frye, Northrop. *Shakespearean Comedy and Romance* (1965).

Leggatt, Alexander. *Shakespeare's Comedy of Love* (1974).

Miola, Robert S. *Shakespeare and Classical Comedy: The Influence of Plautus and Terence* (1994).

Nevo, Ruth. *Comic Transformations in Shakespeare* (1980).

Ornstein, Robert. *Shakespeare's Comedies: From Roman Farce to Romantic Mystery* (1986).

Richman, David. *Laughter, Pain, and Wonder: Shakespeare's Comedies and the Audience in the Theater* (1990).

Salingar, Leo. *Shakespeare and the Traditions of Comedy* (1974).

Slights, Camille Wells. *Shakespeare's Comic Commonwealths* (1993).

Waller, Gary, ed. *Shakespeare's Comedies* (1991).

Westlund, Joseph. *Shakespeare's Reparative Comedies: A Psychoanalytic View of the Middle Plays* (1984).

Williamson, Marilyn. *The Patriarchy of Shakespeare's Comedies* (1986).

8. The Romances (*Pericles, Cymbeline, The Winter's Tale, The Tempest, The Two Noble Kinsmen*)

Adams, Robert M. *Shakespeare: The Four Romances* (1989).

Felperin, Howard. *Shakespearean Romance* (1972).

Frye, Northrop. *A Natural Perspective: The Development of Shakespearean Comedy and Romance* (1965).

Mowat, Barbara. *The Dramaturgy of Shakespeare's Romances* (1976).

Warren, Roger. *Staging Shakespeare's Late Plays* (1990).

Young, David. *The Heart's Forest: A Study of Shakespeare's Pastoral Plays* (1972).

9. The Tragedies

Bradley, A. C. *Shakespearean Tragedy* (1904).

Brooke, Nicholas. *Shakespeare's Early Tragedies* (1968).

Champion, Larry. *Shakespeare's Tragic Perspective* (1976).

Drakakis, John, ed. *Shakespearean Tragedy* (1992).

Evans, Bertrand. *Shakespeare's Tragic Practice* (1979).

Everett, Barbara. *Young Hamlet: Essays on Shakespeare's Tragedies* (1989).

Foakes, R. A. *Hamlet versus Lear: Cultural Politics and Shakespeare's Art* (1993).

Frye, Northrop. *Fools of Time: Studies in Shakespearean Tragedy* (1967).

Harbage, Alfred, ed. *Shakespeare: The Tragedies* (1964).

Mack, Maynard. *Everybody's Shakespeare: Reflections Chiefly on the Tragedies* (1993).

McAlindon, T. *Shakespeare's Tragic Cosmos* (1991).

Miola, Robert S. *Shakespeare and Classical Tragedy: The Influence of Seneca* (1992).

——. *Shakespeare's Rome* (1983).

Nevo, Ruth. *Tragic Form in Shakespeare* (1972).

Rackin, Phyllis. *Shakespeare's Tragedies* (1978).

Rose, Mark, ed. *Shakespeare's Early Tragedies: A Collection of Critical Essays* (1995).

Rosen, William. *Shakespeare and the Craft of Tragedy* (1960).

Snyder, Susan. *The Comic Matrix of Shakespeare's Tragedies* (1979).

Wofford, Susanne. *Shakespeare's Late Tragedies: A Collection of Critical Essays* (1996).

Young, David. *The Action to the Word: Structure and Style in Shakespearean Tragedy* (1990).

——. *Shakespeare's Middle Tragedies: A Collection of Critical Essays* (1993).

10. The Histories

Blanpied, John W. *Time and the Artist in Shakespeare's English Histories* (1983).

Campbell, Lily B. *Shakespeare's "Histories": Mirrors of Elizabethan Policy* (1947).

Champion, Larry S. *Perspective in Shakespeare's English Histories* (1980).

Hodgdon, Barbara. *The End Crowns All: Closure and Contradiction in Shakespeare's History* (1991).

Holderness, Graham. *Shakespeare Recycled: The Making of Historical Drama* (1992).

———, ed. *Shakespeare's History Plays: "Richard II" to "Henry V"* (1992).

Leggatt, Alexander. *Shakespeare's Political Drama: The History Plays and the Roman Plays* (1988).

Ornstein, Robert. *A Kingdom for a Stage: The Achievement of Shakespeare's History Plays* (1972).

Rackin, Phyllis. *Stages of History: Shakespeare's English Chronicles* (1990).

Saccio, Peter. *Shakespeare's English Kings: History, Chronicle, and Drama* (1977).

Tillyard, E. M. W. *Shakespeare's History Plays* (1944).

Velz, John W., ed. *Shakespeare's English Histories: A Quest for Form and Genre* (1996).

11. *Henry IV, Part One*

In addition to the works on stage history cited in the essay on pages 232–45, and the works listed above in Section 10, The Histories, the following are recommended.

Auden, W. H. *The Dyer's Hand and Other Essays* (1962).

Bamber, Linda. *Comic Women, Tragic Men: A Study of Gender and Genre in Shakespeare* (1982).

Barber, C. L. *Shakespeare's Festive Comedy* (1959).

Bradley, A. C. *Oxford Lectures on Poetry* (1909).

Brooks, Cleanth, and Robert B. Heilman. *Understanding Drama* (1945).

Burckhardt, Sigurd. *Shakespearean Meanings* (1968).

Charlton, H. B. *Shakespearian Comedy* (1938).

Council, Norman. "Prince Hal: Mirror of Success." *Shakespeare Studies* 9 (1974): 125–46.

Dickinson, Hugh. "The Reformation of Prince Hal." *Shakespeare Quarterly* 12 (1961): 33–46.

Evans, Gareth Lloyd. "The Comical-tragical-historical Method—*Henry IV*." In *Stratford-upon-Avon Studies 3: Early Shakespeare*. Ed. J. R. Brown and B. Harris (1961), pp. 145–63.

Greenblatt, Stephen. *Shakespearean Negotiations: The Circulation of Social Energy in Renaissance England* (1988).

Hawkins, Sherman. "*Henry IV*: The Structural Problem Revisited." *Shakespeare Quarterly* 33 (1982): 278–301.

Howard, Jean, and Phyllis Rackin. *Engendering a Nation: a Feminist Account of Shakespeare's English Histories* (1997).

Hunter, G. K. "Shakespeare's Politics and the Rejection of Falstaff." *Critical Quarterly* 1 (1959): 229–36.

Hunter, Robert G. "Shakespeare's Comic Sense As It Strikes Us Today: Falstaff and the Protestant Ethic." In *Shakespeare, Pattern of Excelling Nature*. Ed. David Bevington and Jay L. Halio (1978), pp. 125–32.

Jenkins, Harold. *The Structural Problem in "Henry the Fourth"* (1956).

Kris, Ernest. "Prince Hal's Conflict." *Psychoanalytic Quarterly* 17 (1948): 487–505.

Kernan, Alvin B. "*The Henriad*: Shakespeare's Major History Plays." *Yale Review* 59 (Autumn 1969): 3–32.

MacDonald, Ronald R. "Uneasy Lies: Language and History in Shakespeare's Lancastrian Tetralogy." *Shakespeare Quarterly* 35 (1984): 22–39.

McLaverty, J. "No Abuse: The Prince and Falstaff in the Tavern Scenes of *Henry IV*." *Shakespeare Survey* 34 (1982): 105–10.

Palmer, D. J. "Casting Off the Old Man: History and St. Paul in *Henry IV*." *Critical Quarterly* 12 (1970): 267–83.

Seltzer, Daniel. "Prince Hal and Tragic Style." *Shakespeare Survey* 30 (1977): 13–27.

Spivack, Bernard. "Falstaff and the Psychomachia." *Shakespeare Quarterly* 8 (1957): 449–59.

Sprague, Arthur Colby. "Gadshill Revisited" *Shakespeare Quarterly* 4 (1953): 1125–37.

Traversi, D. A. *Shakespeare: From "Richard II" to "Henry V"* (1957).

Watson, R. N. *Shakespeare and Ambition* (1984).

Wilson, J. Dover. *The Fortunes of Falstaff* (1943, partly reprinted in the present edition).